LOVING WORK

To my daughter Angela and all the other strong women who do the world's work while men talk about it – or write about it.

LOVING WORK

Frank Price

Gower

Published by
Gower Publishing Limited
Gower House
Croft Road
Aldershot
Hampshire GU11 3HR
England

Gower
Old Post Road
Brookfield
Vermount 05036
USA

Frank Price has asserted his right under the Copyright, Designs and Patents Act 1988 to be identified as the author of this work.

British Library Cataloguing in Publication Data

Price, Frank
  Loving Work
  I. Title
  658.406

  ISBN 0–566–07634–9

Library of Congress Cataloging-in-Publication Data

Price, Frank, 1929–
    Loving work / Frank Price.
        p.   cm.
    Includes bibliographical references and index.
    ISBN 0–586–07634–9 (hardback)
    1. Vocational guidance. 2. Career changes. 3. Career
  development.   I. Title.
  HF5381.P694   1995
  659.1–dc20
                                                    95–12675
                                                    CIP

Typeset in Times by Raven Typesetters, Chester and printed in Great Britain at the University Press, Cambridge.

Contents

v

Preface

The passage of time used to be tick-tocked away in the smooth flow of leisurely centuries, when work was a thing we all took for granted. Work was simply there, to be had, plenty of it. We held steady jobs in companies as stable as the pyramids and seemingly as enduring. In those days we had a future.

Until change itself changed, turning time into a frenzied and frightening helter-skelter of speeding nano-seconds. Work collapsed. Jobs disappearing in the dust of pyramidal hierarchies toppling. In these days we have a past.

We also have a present. The here and now. So how might we make the best of it? The few of us who still have jobs and the many who do not. How will managers and ex-managers alike cope with the strains imposed by the stress of pitiless change? As helpless victims or as resourceful strivers? What are we to do?

This book tries to provide some insights to guide our response to change. To turn threat into opportunity. Its first part describes how quality can be introduced into a company to provide a firm foundation for improved performance. It is simple; anybody can do it. Its second part covers some options open to those with the drive to enrich their lives by enlarging their experience – as writers, consultants, entrepreneurs – whether they still have jobs or have gone their own way.

It sets out to instruct, educate, entertain. But above all to encourage.

Frank Price

PART 1

IS THERE LIFE AFTER MANAGERIAL DEATH?

Introduction

A plague called Progress has descended on our western world of work. Jobs are fleeing to foreign parts, or being cut down. Is your job safe? Then read this story of those that were not. Lest it should become *yours*. Hear these words from one who knows, one who was a Progressive, a carrier of the plague.

I was only obeying orders. I am sorry to have been the agent of your destruction, to have ended your career in the middle tiers of the hierarchy so abruptly. Nothing personal, you understand. Like the soldier in the film *Zulu*, who stands to at Rorke's Drift fearfully anticipating the impi onslaught and asks 'Why us, Colour Sergeant?' and gets the unhelpful reply 'Because we're 'ere lad, because we're 'ere', you might ask 'Why *me*?' And get the same answer – because you were there.

You were there. A member of that endangered species the *manager*, when the tides of history chose to sweep you away, to swill you out of your niche in a hierarchy that was now itself the object of devastating attention. The pressure of this groundswell, this 'sea-change', is flattening and gutting organizations; pyramids are toppling around their occupants, squeezing out those in the middle strata who are nowadays deemed to be dispensable. That is why you were dispensed with. That is why I was required to carry out my orders, to play out my assigned role as your executioner, to have you disposed of, to render you SNLR – Services No Longer Required. Because you were there.

So now you are on the dole, made redundant by seismic social upheaval. This is what economists call 'structural unemployment'; this might afford you the consolation of describing yourself as structurally unemployed, but it will not get you your job back. Don't blame the economists, and don't blame me.

Blaming other people . . . it is one of the paradoxes of this life that we rarely hate and blame people for the things they have done to us; but we nearly always detest them for the things we have done to them. Please ponder upon this statement for a moment, think on it next time you have another acrimonious tiff with your spouse. Realize that this is the way things are, and the next time you feel anger or hatred for somebody ask yourself what you have done to them that makes you feel so bad about them. So I suppose I should feel anger towards you for having done the dirty on you by destroying you as a manager, but I do not. I bear you no malice for what I did to you. I have a deep enough understanding of the majestic indifference of inevitable historical change to appreciate that both you and I were nothing more than the innocent victims of forces beyond our control. Mere playthings in a cosmic game. The only difference between us being that you lost your job and I kept mine.

They paid me well to do my job, your bosses. That is what 'consultants' (that being the cloak we wear to conceal the axe) like me are for, to keep the bosses' hands clean of blood as we dispense with dispensable people. We are the latter-day sin-eaters, the hired gobblers of other people's guilt, the paid absolvers who atone for the sins committed by others in our name. We are the wielders of the whispering axe which is used to cut the head-count in companies with ambitions towards organizational anorexia. Companies like the one which once employed you.

Your bosses, pious God-fearing fellows that they are, virtually serenaded you with that little ditty used during the 1914–18 war to recruit deluded heroes to the killing fields of Flanders, 'We don't want to lose you . . . but we think you ought to go . . .'. So you went. I was the one who sent you, on their behalf. So that they could feel good about you and bad about me. Yours was just another head to roll and bounce on to those already heaped like turnips under the dripping block – it's your erstwhile colleagues we are talking about; you were not on your own, you know. So, you see, you are nothing special; you have nothing much to moan about. You have nothing to hate me for. Oh I know that you saw my arrival as an unmixed *curse* upon you. But you were wrong. I came as a blessing in disguise. I came *to set you free*. This is another of those beautiful paradoxes which serve to make our short stay on this planet of torment so interesting; you believe I brought you death, when in truth *I brought you life. I brought you love.* Allow me to explain.

Please understand that I am not seeking to excuse myself for what I did, neither for what you think I did, nor for what I did not do. I am not apologizing. I am not asking your forgiveness for a crime I did not commit when I beheaded you in the course of my duties. I just want you to *understand* things a little better. Like any official from the Inland Revenue I am actually here to *help* you. Having tipped you out of the sarcophagus of your job description and restored you to twitching life I want you to learn how to live it and to love it. Freedom is now yours; as you come blinking and uncertain into its blinding light I want you to learn how to use it. This is the reason I am talking to you in order to be your guide at this joyful time of your resurrection-in-redundancy. Look upon our conversation as a journey we will undertake together, a gentle stroll through the enchanted landscapes of the weird and wondrous world of business and organization. To try and put you right. To search for new opportunities afforded you by your re-birth. To show you that there can indeed be life after death, that there is no need for you to despise yourself as a helpless *victim*. But let us just remind ourselves of the nature of victimhood, so that those of you who have not yet heard the swish of the axe may learn to live without the dread of it. Let us look at the victim you already were – a slave to the system – before I came along and victimized you further by setting you free. This is how you might have progressed in *that* victimhood.

Victimhood – The Non-exclusive Club

There is a school of thought which postulates that victims become victims because they choose to do so. This adds insult to their injury. But here and there perhaps there is a grain of truth within this sweeping slander. After all, it is so easy to feel aggrieved, to cast oneself into the role of victim. Whether it is anything as trivial as six or seven games of Scrabble lost one after the other, or as serious as the repossession of your property by a mortgage lender because you had optimistically overstretched your resources in vain pursuit of gentrification, it is all too easy to feel yourself being 'got at' by a malevolent destiny.

Or perhaps you do not believe in destiny; perhaps you are one of those people who arrogantly assert, 'you make your own luck' as you enjoy the blessings which fate has chosen to bestow upon you. Until the wheel turns, and you are assailed with misfortune. Then it's a different story; your good luck was your own doing, but your bad luck you deny is yours. So it is promptly deposited, like an unwanted infant, onto somebody else's doorstep. You then strike a posture of injured innocence. Your sense of worthiness has been affronted – after all, you did nothing to deserve this awful fate which has now befallen you, so somebody else must be blamed. It's all *their* fault! Whose? That's easy. If you work for an organization and events conspire to make you feel aggrieved then it just has to be the fault of your boss. You know yourself to be good at your job, so why does your boss never tell you 'well done'? Why does he blame you for any unfortunate incident which was outside your control? Life is so unfair! (You conveniently forget that nobody ever said anything about it being fair anyway.) Why, when things go wrong, do you always get the blame? Clearly, you are being *victimized*.

This manifest injustice fills you with a burning self-righteous anger. Excellent, here is your opportunity. If you are as smart as you are smarting you can harness this anger, use it as a generator of power, transform it into a personal motivator. Keep stoking its fires with the fuel of imagined insults, fan its flames to fever heat, and in no time at all you will become a full-blown paranoiac with a bursting head of steam. Now you are ready to take your revenge on those incompetent and insensitive oafs into whose cruel authority a wicked fate has seen fit to deliver you.

At this point you come to a fork in the road leading to your retribution: one branch descends gently downhill, the other climbs upward. The fingerpost on the downward path is marked 'They'll miss me when I'm gone'. The signboard on the ascending track says 'I'll show the bastards'. These are the two pathways opened for the paranoid personality. You are free to choose whichever of these two routes takes your fancy. To what destination does each of them lead? Let us take a look . . . .

Victimhood's Vengeance

First we shall go down the descending road and see what's at the end of it. This is the 'They'll miss me when I'm gone' option. It is a well-trodden path usually taken by those victims whose feelings of persecution have driven them to despair. If you choose to join this melancholy procession, because that is the kind of depressive person your genetic inheritance has decreed you to be, then before embarking on the journey at least exercise the courtesy of 'phoning the Samaritans and advising them of your intentions. They will ask 'Can I help you?' and promptly try to dissuade you, of course; that's what they are for. But the iron logic of this 'They'll miss me when I'm gone' tactic requires that in order to be missed you will actually have to go.

But yours is a stern resolve; you've made your mind up, so begone with you. Here is how your sad little story will very likely turn out . . . .

'Oh sod it! Might as well load the car with a bottle of Stolichnaya, a flask of chilled orange juice (vitamin C promotes health), twenty high-tar cigarettes, a cut crystal tumbler and a length of flexible rubber hosepipe. Park on some lonely clifftop overlooking the eternal sea. Stick one end of the hose on to the exhaust and the other through the window. Make sure there is enough petrol in the tank and then die as I have lived, enjoying a periodic binge and a hacking cough and wishing harm to nobody. They'll miss me when I'm gone.

They won't. It won't work, not for me. Even this innocent revenge will be denied me. Knowing how capriciously Dame Fortune has teased me since I put my hand up her skirts all those years ago it will be just my luck to be tailed on to the clifftop by a police patrol, prematurely pulled from my intended coffin cherry-faced with embarrassment and carboxyhaemoglobin. On top of that lose my driver's licence for being drunk in charge. Pay a stiff fine and then be handed over to the ministrations of professional carers, budding Torquemadas who will torture me for my own good before restoring me drained, dried and blank-eyed to the gin-trap embrace of the hatchet woman whose existence has been dedicated to the daily demolition of my ego ever since that day she vowed 'I do'. She will taunt me with my impotence, remind me that not only do I not know how to live – I can't even do a half-decent job of dying like her friends' husbands did. That appalling Mr Purgatroyd from the Income Tax will resume his bombardment, sending me more of his sickly brown envelopes making impossible demands on blue-tinted forms as big as Ordnance Survey maps. I will be returned quivering to the custody of my boss who will sneeringly appraise my performance at one of those ceremonies of ritual castration he calls his Management by Objectives coaching and counselling sessions. I shall be required to work myself to death in order to earn my living.'

This is what will happen if you choose this route. Because you know that even if you depart from your company you will be remembered for no longer than the pain of toothache is remembered when the dentist is done. Besides, if you cannot be around to enjoy the bereavement of those who are supposed to miss you then where's the fun in it?

So instead you elect to climb the uphill track in search of your sweet revenge, the one marked 'I'll show the bastards'. To do this you must turn yourself into more of a bastard than those whom you intend to show. But since paranoia generates limitless suppliers of self-hatred you can easily become the most hated and successful bastard of them all. You achieve this by strenuously hating other people. Not only is this easily done by anybody who hates himself, as you have chosen to do as a career-progression strategy; it is utterly impossible *not* to hate other people while ever you harbour such a reservoir of self-loathing. Remember, you can only give what you have, and you have plenty to give.

So give it. Hose people with hatred. Spray your bosses with it, disguised as humble deference for safety's sake. Drench your subordinates with it; you will need no such delicacy with them so let them feel its full corrosive force. Spit out the venom in order that it may infect others. You are a middle manager, with managerial authority. What is authority for except to be abused? So abuse it. Be abusive. Be at all times stern of face: never, ever smile. At the most permit yourself nothing more than the occasional small indulgence of a sardonic curling of the lip, on one side of the mouth only, whenever you see anything vastly amusing such as the squirming discomfiture of a subordinate wincing under the whiplash of your tongue. Naturally, however, you are allowed to snicker sycophantically whenever your boss cracks one of his leaden jokes, as long as you preserve your mask of joylessness lest he should suspect you of weakness.

Apart from these permissible departures, these moments of relaxation, you must assiduously cultivate a deep scowl with lips compressed into a tight down-turning arc of disapproval so as to demonstrate your resolute commitment to the preservation of strict discipline. Assure your superiors 'I've got 'em under a tight rein', whenever referring to those who head into you. You will show them right enough! There will be no frivolity here!

No frivolity, yet *you* can have fun. You can be as sadistically inventive as you wish in the spewing corruption of your power. Lament loud and often the vile conjunctions of the zodiac which have caused you to be surrounded by a team of incompetent idiots, especially within earshot of the idiots. You will call this 'motivating them'. Be opportunistic in your terrorism. Suppose for instance that your company decides to recruit graduates, new blood to bring new perspective into the organization, and you find yourself fortunate enough to be landed with one, a *woman* at that. What a wonderful chance to be a right bastard has now been laid before you!

Make the most of it. Be nice to her; this will demand consider-able effort in the way of hypocrisy but persevere. Win her confi-dence. Invite her to accept a special assignment by conducting an analysis of the company and preparing an overview as seen from her newcomer's innocent-eye standpoint. Ask her to be candid and to pull no punches, to state any shortcomings that she might perceive in the organization, even to feel free to criticize – con-structively of course – her relationship with you, her immediate superior. Assure her you will value her academic objectivity and unbiased conclusions. Because you will, oh you will indeed. Soon . . . .

You are about to enjoy one of your life's little pleasures: from behind the high mahogany ramparts of your executive's desk you are about to preside over yet another enactment of that ceremony of degradation so dear to your spiteful heart. She presents her report, the fruit of three weeks of innocent labour. You peruse it, to keep her waiting, a pleasure delayed being a pleasure enhanced. This is the fore play of the torturer. After a few minutes' savouring your anticipation and her anxiety by pretending to study her report you tear it, and her, to pieces. You are sick of women clamouring for equality so you let her have some. You criticize every aspect of her analysis. You are known to be a man who fearlessly calls a spade a spade, so make use of this excuse for rudeness by asking her what the hell she means by all this bullshit about 'organizational mythology', 'leadership characteristics', 'adversarial management philosophy', 'motivational theory', and all the rest of the airy-fairy intellectual claptrap which constitutes this so-called report. Scoff at her 'book-learning', bloody business schools. Remind her that you are not a theorist; you are a man of decisive action who makes things happen. Tell her that you were denied the educational opportunity from which she has clearly derived such little benefit. You were a pupil at the School of Hard Knocks and are a graduate of the University of Life. With honours.

Turn on to her the volcanic fury of your puritan's tortured libido, its powerful feelings gone rancid after years of being bottled up in darkness and denial. You didn't get where you are today by being kind to women. Or to men. Or to yourself.

Because you hate yourself you seek to escape from yourself in the solace of work. Embrace it. Hug it to yourself as ardently as the drunkard fondly cradles his cup to his bosom. Become a workaholic and win the world's approval, spend long hours at it to the exclusion of all else. Enjoy it because there is nothing else to enjoy. Enjoy it while it lasts, until the anger and self-hatred which drive you finally claim you as victim and explode inside your chest. Freedom at last! You will die with honour, your obituary a panegyric of highest praise because nobody dares to speak ill of the dead. Except me.

Now do you begin to understand, my dear victim? Do you see the awful fate I saved you from when I cut you out of the company? You would have taken one of these two roads, had I not intervened. Both, as you see, are pathways to hell, to death-in-life. I brought you life-in-death. I saved you for better things.

So what are we to do with your new life and its new-found freedom?

First we shall give thanks that you have been spared the tribulations of becoming one of Charles Handy's 'core' employees in an organization so stripped of anything thought to be remotely superfluous that it is positively emaciated. Charles Handy is perhaps the most eminent of our management thinkers and organizational soothsayers. He accurately foretold the formation of companies employing half as many people as they used to, doing twice the work, for about one-and-a-half times the pay. At least, I think that's what he said. This prophesied state of affairs is already coming to pass. Workaholism is being hailed as a universal strategy of competitive endeavour; there are already disturbing reports of its consequences – dislocated marriages, psychogenic illness, more drunkenness and drug addiction. Praise be to the god of work. That's progress.

But you, victim so-called, have been spared this fate. So count yourself lucky.

But – what do you want to do?

Aah . . . there's the rub. What an awful question. Your only reply to it is a blank stare of complete incomprehension. Because you don't *know* what you want to do. You *never did*. Because you never needed to, you only ever did as you were told. Followed your job description, went through the motions, kept your head below the parapet, rendered yourself invisible by adopting the proper protective colouration of a company chameleon.

Perhaps it is premature to expect of you the private vision essential to a life of meaningful freedom. So if I might offer you a little guidance . . .

Since you can no longer be numbered among that industrious élite of workaholics at the core of a company you are obliged to want to be something or somebody else. But what? The Charles Handy analysis of the changing nature of organizational work offers you an alternative. You can become what he calls a 'portfolio person'.

A portfolio person is somebody with a repertoire (a 'portfolio') of saleable knowledge and skills. For example, a management consultant is a portfolio person. This newish species (the word newish used in its evolutionary sense) is, unlike the generality of middle management, not threatened with imminent extinction. To the contrary, it is flourishing. It is conventionally regarded as being a highly paid profession, you can buy books about it which

promise you the alluring prospect of being paid £700 a day – they
don't say for how many days a year. But it's an interesting career
option for you, is management consultancy.

Its practitioners hover on the fringes of companies as atten-
tively as vultures flopping expectantly around carrion, waiting to
clear up the mess. Which is what consultants do – clear up messes,
scavenge the company landscape in the interests of ecological
health, hoping for rich pickings.

So one of the options you might care to activate could be to set
yourself up as a *consultant*.

There again, you might not fancy this; whilst consultancy, as
already indicated, *can* be rewarding – in terms of pounds sterling
per hour you can be the best-paid person in the company for the
few days that you are in it – but competition between vultures is
keen. They have been known to croak nastily and peck viciously
at each other in the urgent business of ripping off a gobbet of
nourishing offal. It is possible that after your long Rip van Winkle
years in the cool catacombs of the company you might not relish
the heat of such a hostile climate, that you feel more suited to
something quieter, a little more sedate. Like becoming a writer.

Writing, like jogging, onanism and transcendental meditation,
is, more often than not, a solitary pursuit. But they say there is a
novel in every person (only one?) so maybe there is one in you
struggling to get out. Perhaps you might feel inclined to commit
the accumulated wealth of your life's experience to paper, to
endure the numbed buttocks and callused elbows which come
from overlong labours at the desk, where the only exercise you get
is drumming your fingers while you wait for inspiration or that
elusive *mot juste*. You must be prepared to fortify yourself with
the two thousand cups of tea and the ten thousand cigarettes during the three hundred days it takes to churn out your manuscript.
After that you might be able to retire on your royalties and call
yourself a *writer*.

Or if this seems to be too sedentary a way of passing time; if
after all those years in the stillness of the pyramid you fancy a bit
of action, perhaps you could set yourself up in some kind of
business other than consultant or writer. Your redundancy com-
pensation would come in useful here, as the old Viking proverb
has it, 'you cannot go for gold until you have spent silver'. True in
those days and true today; you need funds whether what you are

launching is a longship or a launderette. But you have funding, enough to cover a small-business start-up, so you might decide to become an entrepreneur, a *tycoon*.

What an interesting life is opening up for you now that you are organizationally dead! It beats working for a living, better than being a cloned salaryman. What giddying prospects present themselves to the bold and the free. To you!

What is it to be then – consultant? Writer? Tycoon?

Before we examine these options in greater depth let us consult your employment record in the job I so generously chopped you out of, run a check over your attitudes and accomplishments in that role to see what sort of future might be best for you. Let us do another flashback. You can concentrate on your dream of a golden future while I tell people about the tarnished past, about the cage you were in before I let you out.

Victimhood – Into the Cage (I)

A couple of hundred years ago, in the days before the mealy-mouthed utterances of Politically Correct speech, words went unminced. A lunatic was not described as 'mentally challenged'; he was candidly dubbed 'madman'. Unless he came from a rich or noble family which preferred euphemisms, in which case he was called 'eccentric'; his daft talk and demented posturing were tolerated until they became too embarrassing and his family lost patience and had him flung gibbering into a private asylum.

The most memorable of these was the Hospice of Our Lady of Bethlehem – Bedlam. Patients entrusted to its care underwent a remedial regime which included treatments such as being dunked into freezing water and castigated with whips. The rationale behind this curative mortification of the flesh being that if you fill the patient's body with enough pain the discomfort will drive out the demons possessing it. Modern psychiatry has not yet abandoned this rationale; similar attempts at demonic exorcism are made by clamping electrodes to patients' temples and throwing the switch. This shocking procedure represents a great advance in medical technology. Progress is marvellous to behold.

If you were a gentleman of leisure in those days you could pass a pleasant hour on a rainy Sunday afternoon by buying an admission ticket to Bedlam's spectators' gallery. One penny bought you a ringside seat close to the cage in which the patients were confined. This was a health service privatized more than two centuries before the formation of profit-seeking hospital management trusts.

From their privileged seats the dandies of the day were entertained by the antics of the lunatics; insanity, like cock fighting and bull baiting, was a spectator sport. If things were going a bit slow for your liking the expenditure of an extra penny to the proprietor of the institute – an entrepreneur to gladden the heart of any Thatcherite economist – would secure you the loan of a pointed stick. This was used to prod any indolent inmate, even those huddled in melancholy catatonic withdrawal, into a frenzy of hysterically amusing behaviour bizarre enough to tickle the most jaded of spectators' ribs.

Things are not all that different today in our work organizations. The big difference is that you are now in the cage with them and you are being paid for it. It's called management. You still have your pointed stick; it's called authority.

Do you think I exaggerate? Then look around you. If that fails to convince you that the world of the organization is sometimes a crazy place populated by some crazy people please suspend judgement until you've listened to the next little tale of managerial folly.

Case study: having a smashing time (told without breaching confidentiality bonds)

The company makes things by ramming ceramic cylinders into metal sleeves. A bit like earning your living by squeezing earthenware mugs into tin cans, only a bit more technical. A bit . . .

Their manufacturing director had heard me speak at some seminar or other, and mainly because I am as tall as he is and we seem to share the same prejudices he invited me to the factory 'to see if I could be of use'. Sales-prospecting visits to potential clients such as this virtually amount to a free consultation inasmuch as the client learns a few things buckshee if he's on the ball, but that's how the game is played.

'We've got quality problems,' he told me.

'And therefore manufacturing capacity losses and trouble with on-time deliveries,' I responded, knowing that problems reproduce with the alarming fecundity of rabbits on fertility drugs. 'What's up, can't your quality man cope?'

'I'm afraid he doesn't seem to be able to, that's why I'd like you to have a look.'

Getting political, already. He fixed a visit so that I could go poking about in the factory, escorted by the quality director (yes, director!), for an hour or two and then have a meeting with the managing director and assembled cronies. This nosing-around exercise is what proper consultants mean when they tell you they will carry out a 'full diagnostic survey and analysis of need'. This more impressive form of words justifies the unblushing presentation of their invoice and a bulky report.

Our prying around led us to a large hydraulic press, in which the ceramic cylinders were being smoothly inserted into metal sleeves, sometimes smoothly, sometimes not. 'Occasionally the cylinder outside diameter and the sleeve inside diameter are not quite right, and then they fail to go together properly,' explained the QD.

'You can say that again,' the press operator interjected unbidden, 'Too many crash-ups. How are we supposed to make bonus when we've got crap components like this lot? Tell me that!'

This was all wearily familiar territory which I had trodden a hundred times and more. So, slip into the old four-step routine of Measure, Record, Analyse, Act, and start *asking the process the right questions*. That's the trick of quality: knowing the right questions, not the right answers to the wrong questions.

In a matter of minutes we had written down the measurements of diameters of a reasonable sample of cylinders and sleeves. A quick tap-tap-tap on the keys of the pocket calculator and the results indicated two distributions of diameters with tails overlapping. A classic compatibility of mating components misfit condition. 'Looks like anything from about 2 to 8 per cent of cylinder–sleeve combinations will fail to fit.' I showed the QD this thumbnail analysis based on our recorded measurements. That's the way you do it, working smart rather than hard. Nothing particularly clever about it; anybody who can count their pay can learn to do it.

At that point there came a bang from the press and a pattering like hailstones as the ceramic core erupted under pressure into fragments which hit the reinforced plexiglass of the confining safety screens. The operator expressed his disapproval.

As far as I was concerned this crash-up might have been a thunderbolt flung by Zeus on my behalf to emphasize my contention that these components would give trouble. The operator whanged back the safety screen and started to clear up the mess, complaining loudly as workers do whenever they are being badly managed.

'Does this happen often?' I enquired. The operator nodded, 'A lot.' 'How often?' I persisted. 'A lot too often,' he elaborated. Not inclined to be numerate, this lad. 'How many times a day do you reckon, then?' I just had to know. The operator paused from his grubbing about in the innards of the machine from which he was trying to disentangle the mangled remains of the metal sleeve, rolled his eyeballs heavenward in recollection, shrugged and informed me, 'Oh, five, ten, twenty times a shift, a lot.' This may have been Maori-style counting of the one . . . two . . . three . . . many sort but it was enough. Though not yet accurately quantified this was no trivial problem; here was a big one, with a big solution waiting to be activated.

As you probably know, a problem is a bit like a racehorse – it carries its solution on its back, like a jockey. I am expert at jockey-spotting. Here was my route into the company. Solve the problem. Save them heavy money. Stick 'em a stiff fee knowing it's already paid for itself ten times over. I would take on jobs like this for zero fee plus 20 per cent of first year's savings and make a rich living working one day a week. But that is not how things are played in our game. Anyway here I was now as good as in business. They had need of me.

The QD glanced at his watch, obviously bored with the commonplace event of a press crash-up. 'Time to meet the managing director,' he said with some relief, 'Let's go to the boardroom.'

The boardroom was furnished with a long polished table flanked by big chairs with a bigger chair at its top. This layout allows for status seating: the nearer you sit to the throne the higher your rank. There should really be a salt cellar halfway down the table to mark the division between the nobility and the common gentry. There wasn't one; its place was occupied by an ornate ashtray. Good, I thought, no health freaks here, we can all be relaxed.

I was allotted an honoured position at the MD's left hand. This is historically appropriate; this is where the wandering minstrel was seated in the Celtic banqueting halls of old. It served the practical purpose of enabling the king to listen to the lay of the minstrel without craning his neck to catch the words, especially if he happened to be hard of hearing.

Pleasantries were exchanged and coffee ceremoniously consumed. I requested access to the ashtray and lit a cigarette. 'How many of those things do you smoke in a day?' the MD enquired. 'A lot,' I replied. 'We're thinking of turning our entire plant, including the car park, into a non-smoking zone,' he went on. I wondered what the hell smoking had to do with shoving pots into cans but forbore to ask. So I countered with 'Scientific research proves that nicotine promotes creative thinking.' The MD elevated one eyebrow. 'Really, whose research?' 'The tobacco companies', and I can confirm it,' I assured him, 'I am a smoker and I am a creative thinker.'

'What can you creatively think for us?' asked the financial director who was sitting, where else, at the monarch's right hand. Historically correct again: the king always keeps his chancellor close by him.

'How about umpteen thousands of pounds a year, actual figure yet to be worked out, straight to the bottom line, a ten-fold return on your investment in my creative thinking?' I promised and I meant it. 'How does that grab you?' Always talk money. Nobody really understands the mystery of money, but very few people are reluctant to talk of ways of getting hold of more of it.

'And exactly *how* do you propose to do that?'

'By the application of statistical methodology (I can use the proper jargon with the best of them when I'm baiting the traps) to the assembly losses on your presses. To get you back the cash you are currently pouring down the plug-hole. You're bleeding to death out there by the look of it.' This is what sales trainers might call 'oversell'.

At this point the QD, who was sitting well down the table conducting an archaeological dig in one of his nostrils, in search of ancient wisdom, presumably, spoke up, 'We *cannot do* statistics on our process,' he stated with the utter conviction of the totally deluded, 'We do not have any normal distributions.'

It occurred to me that his intra-nasal quest for wisdom had been fruitless. I had recently demonstrated, before his very eyes, that if you know how to distil the data of numbers, which form normal distributions, into their *meaning*, you can begin to control the process. Was he *blind*? Mentally challenged?

Did he not know – and him a man of *quality* – that a 'normal distribution' is what you get – in theory – when you take a lot of measurements – say, the tallness of a sample of men of varying heights – and see how the measurements of individuals tend to form a cluster around the average of all the measurements in the sample? There is nothing mysterious about it, nothing special; it's been known about for long enough, since 1801 in fact. It's one of the tools of the quality trade, a very powerful but often misunderstood one. The QD clearly misunderstood it.

It is nothing more than a mathematical concept, just as Π (pi) is a mathematical concept. It has to do with *relationships* between numbers. An abstract thing of the mind, with no physical existence. When did you last see anybody lift a Π off the mantlepiece, dust it, put it back and gaze upon it with gratitude because it helps us to relate diameters of circles to their circumferences? Never. Yet we casually make use of Π, so what's the trouble about making use of the normal curve? These things of the mind have no reality except in the mind. But that doesn't stop us using them to shape the 'real' world. Similarly we talk about a 'quantum leap', yet can anybody tell me where to go to watch an athlete leap a quantum? But we have no difficulty in handling the concept. So why was the QD shying away from the statistical approach? I will tell you why in a moment.

The QD folded his arms, crossed his knees, and gazed into infinity. He had said his piece, and that was that. So the MD said his piece: 'What I want here is total quality management.'

'Don't we all?' I answered, rhetorically as I thought. 'What exactly do you mean by TQM?'

'If you do any consulting work for us, and I stress *if*, I shall require your assurance that we shall have no more typing errors in the letters we send out, no more sloppy mistakes in invoicing our customers . . . that sort of thing. ATD, attention to detail. That is what I mean by TQM.' He leaned forward, 'Can you do that for us?'

No, I couldn't, but I thought I might as well make one last throw of the dice. 'No I can't, I'm not an office magician but I can help you with your manufacturing quality if . . .'

'We can sort that out ourselves.' The MD seemed confident. I wondered what he based his confidence on. He told me, 'Our Quality Director is here to attend to those things.' So he founded his confidence on his QD. Ah well, he that buildeth his house on sand . . .

'It's been a pleasure meeting you,' I told them truthfully, 'and I wish you the very best of luck,' without adding they were going to need it.

'Hang on, hang on,' the manufacturing director came to life. 'I invited this man here to tell us what he could do to help us, and believe that what he says makes sense. So why don't we . . .?'

'No point,' snapped the MD, 'We want TQM, not a lot of fancy number-juggling on the shop floor. We can sort that out ourselves.'

The QD lowered his gaze from infinity and relaxed into his chair, visibly relieved that no smart-alec consultant brought in by the manufacturing director was going to come in and queer *his* pitch.

Like all good intellectual armchair revolutionaries I am good at making decisions in smoke-filled rooms. (When the anti-smoking zealots have won there will be a business opportunity for somebody – supplying cylinders of de-toxified synthetic cigarette smoke to fill the rooms where decisions are about to be made. Turkish fragrance, sir? Virginia for madam? A whole new arm to the healing art of aromatherapy.) So I made my decision.

For an assignment to be successful there has to be an *intimate* rapport between consultant and client. They must inhabit the same world. We didn't. They believed that their process and products stood outside the laws of physics which inflict random variations on all process outcomes. They were claiming uniqueness, as if they were dwelling in a parallel universe in a different space–time continuum in which chaos reigns. There could be no rapport across this intergalactic void.

As we went through the ritual of departure the steady humming of factory machinery was being punctuated by a sound like sporadic artillery fire from a distant battlefield, as the hydraulic presses went on with their wastrels' work. This was alchemy turned upside down, turning gold into base metal.

Or do you look upon theirs as *sane* behaviour? Accepting their process losses with bland equanimity while wittering on about a few typing mistakes. Here was a quality director without direction. A vision focused on trivia. They were beyond help. This was Bedlam.

So ends this case study.

The inequality of quality

The democratic assertion that all men are equal might be an ideal shared by Thomas Paine and Thomas Jefferson, which they enshrined in the American Constitution, but it is most certainly not borne out by everyday experience. The reality is of a more Orwellian *Animal Farm*-ish sort, in which all animals are equal but pigs are more equal than others. Likewise in our industrial organizations all middle managers are in equal danger of extinction but managers of the quality function are more endangered than others. So much for quality and inequality. It seems that quality managers, like the panda and the snow tiger, should be listed in the ecological Red Book, highest risk category of all.

So whenever I use the term 'my dear victim' it is to one of these severely threatened sub-species that it is addressed; but what is said is every bit as applicable to managers from other disciplines whether or not they have yet fallen victim to the levelling axe. After all, there is no inequality on Death Row.

A little while ago I promised that we would look into the victim's pre-execution conduct in his company, to see if it could give us a clue as to what he should aim to become now that he has been released from the tedious necessity of having to attend a place of work every working day; should he aim to be a consultant, a writer, a tycoon? Which of these futures might his accomplishments best fit him for? Let us step into his past, so as to step into a possible future, by stepping into his cage.

Victimhood – Into the Cage (II)

By the time I got there the company had been going for about forty years, making bits and pieces out of metal, plastics, rubber, and servicing the automotive manufacturing and other industries. It had long ago gone through the exciting pioneering phase of company evolution, then through its crisis period of confusion and loss of control, before undergoing the organizational meta-morphosis into the boring second phase – that of rational scientific management. It is at this stage that companies seem to become bogged down in an evolutionary swamp, and quickly decay into a desperate and prolonged crisis which can persist for decade after dreary decade. In this moribund state any 'growth' is made by putting on fat, vision is turned inward (but not into insight), energy dissipated in internal conflict, and cloning occurs as the company strives to become more and more like itself. This is the time of fat cats, sly dogs and docile yes-men. Many of our country's companies were stuck in this quagmire of congealed attitudes and petrified philosophy until the tsunami wave which swept out of the East turned stagnation into turbulence. Perhaps some still are.

Sensing the imminent paradigm shift the company's bosses decided to prepare to ride the wave, to take the tide that might ful-fil Shakespeare's promise by leading on to fortune. They went shopping – they attended conferences. These flourish during the season of uncertainty, when certitude becomes a saleable com-modity.

A conference is a market place where sellers hope to meet buyers. Purveyors of instant wisdom, messiahs with maps of the one and only road to managerial nirvana, spielers of catchy slogans, wannabe gurus psyched up on their own gobbledegook … hollering their wares in deafening cacophony and confusing diversity. From this raucous rag-tag and bobtail gathering of wiz-ards and witches (in this game women are often more equal than men) you pays your money and you takes your choice. That's where they found me, flogging my home-brewed panacea fizzing with the promise of certain salvation. Which is how I came to find myself an honoured guest in their outfit.

The boss told me he was worried about certain quality problems, and took me to meet the management team, to let me get a feel for what they were up to.

They were up to all sorts. In fact they were up to no good, although they hadn't yet realized it. They were doing their best, and you can't ask for more than that, can you? Oh yes, you can. Not to do so is sometimes to settle for mediocrity, to ask for little and settle for less. As the socialist statesman Aneurin Bevan once said about his compatriots, 'The thing which appalls me about the British working class is the poverty of their aspirations.' He might have said something similar about some of our companies were he alive today. Can there be any left who would settle for the second-rate? You tell me . . . .

It didn't take long to get a very telling picture of what was going on. This is, as I said before, the 'diagnostic' phase of the consultancy assignment. It takes an hour or two. As I said, if I were a proper consultant instead of a one-man band (and don't you *dare* add 'blowing his own trumpet!') I could invite a colleague in and we could creatively and profitably stretch two hours into two weeks – that would be four man-weeks – to justify a bloated fee, like the wise men of Persia, as I am about to remind you.

The temple of Darius

Darius, King of Persia and King of Kings, had caused a great temple to be built. The mighty pillars of its doorway were surmounted by a splendid lintel stone, its face smoothed and polished to a perfect finish. Darius looked upon it, and felt a twinge of dissatisfaction. It lacked something. Its bare-faced austerity begged to be adorned. (His must have been the same impulse as that which inspires the paint spray-can graffiti artist when confronted with a naked wall.) So he summoned his three wise men, and commanded them to think up a wise saying, *which would be eternally true*, to have chiselled into the lintel's emptiness. He asked them how long their philosophical deliberations could reasonably be expected to take, and settled for a lead-time of three days within which they were to supply the words of eternal truth.

The three wise men exchanged knowing glances and conspiratorial smiles; they knew they already had the answer. But being wise they kept their collective mouth shut and the king waiting and took a three-day break. On the third day they delivered the portentous words, 'And this too shall pass away', to be duly chiselled into the stone.

You could see it for yourself but I suppose it's gone by now. That will be all about proud kings and words of eternal truth, for a while.

As I said, consultants smarter and harder-working than I am inclined to be would have done a Darius on the diagnosis, and made a lot of money. But I must be a bit stupid; money has never seemed to me to be an objective worthy of drudging one's life away for, which must be why I have never had more of it than was enough to meet my modest needs. Some people find pleasure in spending it on shopping sprees; good luck to them – I get kicks out of not buying all those many things I do not want. A traitor to the consumer society. Or do *you* believe that we should all work as hard as we can for as much money as we are able to amass? That the sole purpose of the business is profit? That the driving imperative of the organization is expansion? That of the economy endless growth? You are probably right.

Rejecting the Persian paradigm I delivered my particular brand of eternal wisdom to the boss during the first day of the association, not the third. Before I tell you what it was let me take you through the 'survey' and see what you make of it.

The Survey

Have you ever wondered about how often things come in *threes*? *Three* wise men, *three* stooges, *three* musketeers, the Holy *Trinity*, *three* men in a boat . . . and the *three* misguided men I met on the first day – the quality, technical and production managers. A trio in trouble.

They were quite forthcoming. 'We are well into SPC here. That means statistical process control, you know.'

'Really? I thought it stood for stop producing crap.' My reply got the relationship off to a good start – always begin as you intend to go along. 'Are you going to show me this SPC of yours then?'

'Of course. First we shall show you our machine capability study.' These gentlemen were really on the ball! They ushered me into the presence of a cabinet of wide shallow drawers of the sort that draughtsmen keep unfolded drawings in, as reverentially as priests leading an acolyte to the altar. Clearly we were now in a shrine. A drawer was slid open – I half expected to be vouchsafed a privileged glimpse of the venerated Mappa Mundi, or the secret writings of Joanna Southcott which once caused a Pope to fall into a faint (what was actually shown to His Holiness was a street map of Milton Keynes). Instead there was revealed in all its glory a document with lines of many colours, strings of tidy dots, clumps of numbers to many places of decimals done in fine-point calligraphy – a veritable illuminated manuscript, a product of monastic devotion to detail. It seemed to glow beneath its protective cover of sturdy acetate sheet. They gazed upon it like the adoring magi contemplating the newborn Saviour. This was their sacred rite.

'Is that it then?' I enquired, with my customary delicacy.

'Yes. We did this. It is our machine capability study.'

'Oh no it's not.' I swung the heavy transparent cover back on its hinges to get a clearer look, an act of profanity which I'm sure caused them to wince. 'It's a bogus control chart, that's what this is.'

They adopted expressions of wearied bafflement, explaining to me with the careful simplicity you use when addressing a half-wit child, 'You see these two red lines?' pointing out a pair of parallel lines running arrow-straight across the graph and straddling the strings of dots, which oscillated up and down between them. The erratic progression of these dots resembled the spoor of an in-ebriated salesman at a conference staggering in dirty shoes down a hotel corridor trying to find his bedroom door – the phenomenon know to physicists as The Problem of the Drunkard's Walk. 'These are called the three-sigma action limits. That means that 99.73 per cent of the output lies between them.'

'No it doesn't.' I just felt like being pedantic for a change, 'All it means is that 99.73 per cent of your wandering spots fall between them. In theory.'

By now they were beginning to get a bit exasperated with the obduracy of this thicko intruder who cast doubts on all they said. So they trundled out the howitzer of higher mathematics and trained it on target.

'Take a look at these mathematical formulae here', and the first round of a daunting equation burst under my nose. Missed! Then one of them began reciting the litany 'Sigma equals the square root of the sum of . . .'

'Bugger that!' – I abandoned any straining after polite dis-course – 'if this is a machine capability study where's the machine?' I knew very well where the machine must be; I just fancied asking a rhetorical question.

'Why? It's out there with all the other machines. In the machine shop of course.' Of course it is.

'Then how do you intend to use this chart? Do you plan to bring the machine into this office, or take the chart out to the machine?' They looked at each other in bewilderment, wondering what I was on about. I had spiked their gun, so I counter-attacked. 'Is the out-put from the machine to which this chart refers in control or out of control right now, this minute?'

'It's not working today.' The production man sounded triumph-ant for some unknown reason, 'It's gone down.' There is no answer to that; at least it afforded the consolation of knowing it could not be churning out junk, so best be grateful for such small mercies.

'Besides, we did this study very thoroughly only a few weeks ago,' added the quality man dismissively, 'and machines don't change their capability overnight, do they?' I don't know whether they do or not; but neither did they.

'This capability study is here as a matter of historic record,' interjected the technical man, 'we are running programmed SPC on the machine shop itself. By Computer.' By Computer! Well, that's all right then.

The boss, who had been keeping a quiet vigil on the fringe of the discussion, spoke up, 'Why don't you show him?'

We trooped over to the machine shop. I glanced around the place – not a control chart to be seen. 'Thought you said you were doing SPC in here,' I observed, 'so where are the charts?'

'As I told you in the office,' explained the technical man in his I-am-speaking-to-a-simpleton voice, 'we are doing it by computer. So that is where the charts are. In the computer. The computer is in the inspection room. In here. I will show you. You will see some *real* control charts.' I was looking forward to it, waiting to be impressed, like a bumpkin at a village fete gawping slack-jawed at a conjuror pulling eggs out of his ears.

The computer – their pride and joy, newest of their shrines to their god of gadgetry – was about the size of an upright piano. One of those that plays by itself. 'It cost us over twenty-five thousand pounds,' the technical man boasted, patting it gently as if it were a well-loved old dog. 'This is the very latest in information technology. You feed the data in, and out come the charts. Beautiful.'

The data were being fed in by two young women: one to actually press the keys, the other to recite the numbers. They were being supervised by a young serious-looking man wearing a white smock with a row of pens sticking out of its breast pocket. He turned out to be the assistant quality manager. The whole data-entry operation seemed to me to be a bit mob-handed, but this was none of my business. Not yet.

The charts were coming out. As I had been promised they were certainly all things bright and beautiful. Printed in a gridwork of blue, green and red lines; a pair of juddering styluses (OK, styli I suppose, if you're a classicist) inking in their black traces like seismographs recording a volcanic upheaval. Aesthetically pleasing, indeed beautiful, as the technical man had said.

The only trouble with them was that they were very obviously just so much graphical gibberish, so much numerical nonsense pictorially presented in lurid hues. Very pretty to behold, though. I kept this knowledge to myself for a little while, in the prescribed Persian wise man manner, and contented myself by commenting truthfully enough, 'they are certainly impressive-looking documents, these fancy charts of yours. What happens to them?'

'We send them every week to our biggest customer,' said the quality man, naming the British subsidiary of an American multinational.

'What for?' I am an acknowledged master of the daft question because, paradoxically, daft questions can eventually elicit clever answers. You can get yourself a good education by doing it.

'Well it's *obvious*, isn't it?' The quality man's voice was reaching a higher pitch; he sounded as if he was getting sick of me. No, it is not obvious, my dear victim-to-be. What *is* obvious is that what is screamingly obvious to me is obviously not obvious to you. (Sort out that bit of sophistry, it makes sense.) So I stuck the prod in again. 'Is it?' I asked.

'Of course it's obvious. The customer looks at our charts, sees they are OK, that they are a guarantee of our quality, and that's that. We only put in the computer system because they insisted on it. Americans are like that.'

'What do *they* do with the charts?'

'They file them away. For twelve years, if you must know, in case of warranty claims. We call it "traceability". We've got BS5750 you know, and you have to have traceability.'

I thought it was about time I shifted the focus of my enquiries. 'Is it all right to talk to your young women?' I asked the boss. Young women. Not 'girls'; these two were beyond pubescence and well into their golden time of nubile womanhood. Not 'ladies', that's twee-talk. Women. You do not use demeaning terms to patronize persons such as these.

'What is it you are actually entering into this computer?' I asked the one entrusted to tap the message in.

'*Shit*,' she replied. 'That is what I am entering into this computer. Rubbish. I enter it every Friday. It takes us all day. My friend reads out the numbers for me and I put them in. He watches us to make sure we do it right.'

'And what comes out of the computer?' I wanted more of this; this was the most sensible opinion I had heard today. It was more than that, as we shall see.

'*Pretty* shit,' she answered, with her refreshing candour. She knew! She knew what the managers did not know.

'Why do you do it?'

'They pay us to do it; is there any other reason?' No, but there will be soon. I am pleased that I have met *you*. I think we shall be seeing more of each other, much more.

'What makes you say the numbers are rubbish?'

'I just *know* they are. We spend all week inspecting the product, gathering numbers, thousands of them. Then every Friday we sit here and punch a few hundred of them – any old numbers from the week's output – into this machine. Out come all the pretty pictures and I just get this feeling it's all a waste of time.'

I thanked her for her contribution and turned to the quality man, 'Does the customer ever send back any of your control charts?'

'No, of course he doesn't.'

'Does he ever send back any of your product?'

'Well, yes, I suppose so, from time to time, but . . .'

The boss, who had been listening to the conversation and had a speculative look in his eye, cut in, 'Too much, too often,' before turning to me and suggesting, 'I think it's time you and I had a little chat. Shall we go to my office?'

So we went, so that I could make my verbal report on this briefest of diagnostic surveys. I will tell you about it in a minute.

In the meantime what do *you* make of this excursion into Bedlam? Do you think that I exaggerate, abuse poetic licence for the sake of a story? Please be assured, I do not. This is how it was. Do you think that this is the only little Bedlam in the world of work? I shouldn't think you do, because it isn't.

What Thomas Tryon wrote in 1689 – 'the world is but a great Bedlam, where those that are more mad lock up those that are less' – was surely true of the company we're talking about here; and maybe of a good many more.

But let me tell you what I told the boss.

[handwritten margin note: Bedlam. more less mad]

The Report

Education is knowing that you do not know. The ignorant do not know that they do know; therefore they think they know. The educated constantly seek education. The ignorant despise it; this is why their company is so insufferably boring. The company of the educated is a delight. It is the hallmark of a civilized society.

We were in the boss's office. I wandered over to his book-case and glanced at some of the many titles. To know his library is to know the man. There were some interesting authors represented here, not only the usual names of regular and established management writers, but others, less conventional. Clearly I was in civilized society here; this boss belonged to the philosopher-king variety, an educated man wanting to know more.

'I want to know more about the nature of my organization,' he said. 'Please begin by telling me about my management team.' He relaxed into his chair, ready to listen to things which probably he knew already.

'Bad news, I'm afraid,' I began my report, 'they are very hard-working men.'

'That's bad news?' he smiled knowingly, 'Tell me why.'

'Yes, they are hard workers, but so was Sisyphus who was condemned by the gods to roll his boulder up the same hill every day, except that they have condemned themselves.'

'Engaged in futile endeavour, are they?' He didn't seem to be at all surprised.

'Ineffective and wasted effort,' I agreed. 'They work hard because incompetence *has* to work hard, since it is not clever enough to work smart. They are incompetent, they lack understanding.'

'Understanding of what?'

'Well, for one thing it is quite evident that they have had some training in the statistical theory which underlies the whole body of knowledge that we call quality management.'

'They have,' he confirmed. 'They attended a short course on

statistical quality control run by consultants engaged by our biggest customer's American parent. That was a pre-condition of the commercial contract, intended to bring us into line with our customer's procedures.'

'They were well taught,' I assured him. 'They acquired a great deal of knowledge. But no understanding, no wisdom about how to use their knowledge to advantage. They learned a lot about maths and statistics, but not much about quality.'

'Von Clausewitz!' he exclaimed, 'The difference between sword-smiths and sword-men. In his book *On War!*'

'You've got it,' I said, thinking what a fine thing education can be to those who know how to make use of it. 'They are dazzled by the maths, so they do it as they did at school, parrot-fashion. Without thinking. Furthermore they confuse precision with accuracy, believing that any number precisely expressed to many places of decimals just *has* to be accurate. So they are good at being precisely wrong. Like some bomb-aimers in the air raids in the Second World War to whom precision was all, as long as the bombs fell into a tight and pretty pattern it didn't really matter if they were a mile or two off target.'

'At least the bombers knew that by doing it wrong they were saving their skins by staying away from heavily defended targets,' the boss was enjoying this metaphor, 'Our lads don't even know they're doing it wrong, they just do it.'

'Quite,' I confirmed his opinion, 'they have elevated simple control routines, that can be done by anybody with a bit of proper training, into a semi-religious ritual, accessible only to a priesthood, to themselves.'

'Tell me more,' he invited, 'I've had my doubts about what they're doing for quite some time now. It's much as I suspected.'

'Their approach is typically scientific rationalist management style. *They* do all the thinking, compile a set of instructions – procedures – and pass them to underlings who are required to carry them out by rote. Meaningless activity to keep people busy in the pretence of working.'

He switched course. 'What do you think about the computer?'

'Not much, speaking as a computer-phobe. I suppose it's OK, but I'd sell it if I were you. Computing can become addictive; every computer should carry a health warning. The so-called control charts it turns out are worse than useless. A travesty. A chart is supposed to be a *running check* on variation, to let you know pretty quickly whether the variation you are observing is natural to the process or not. It is designed to tell you when to take *no* corrective action as opposed to when you *should* be responding to the changed variation. Used in the proper manner it is a very powerful tool of quality; misused and it is worse than useless, it is misleading.'

I paused for breath and another fix of tea and tobacco smoke. He was still listening so I resumed. 'The movements of variation your charts throw up are plain crazy. They show a degree of variation that is simply impossible to achieve. Did you not notice that quite often the plots whizzed right off the chart? That's chaos, madness.'

He nodded again. 'I've noticed. I've been noticing it for months. Not having had any training in statistics I couldn't really say why I thought the plots were nonsense. That's why I invited you here. Because I just knew by gut feeling that those charts are so much bullshit.'

'Same as the young woman feeding the data into the computer.' I wanted to talk about her, 'She knows, but doesn't know how she knows. I suppose her instincts tell her, and I've learned to trust a woman's instincts. In any case, she's right. Who is she?'

He smiled, affectionately it seemed to me. 'Oh yes. She is our Karen. Our firebrand trade union representative on site.'

'Trade union rep, eh?' I had met her sort before, and was looking forward more than ever to meeting this one again. 'Usually a sign of a frustrated manager. Being denied power by the managerial route she takes it for herself, exercises leadership qualities to get herself made the captain of the opposition team. After that she virtually runs the operation at the sharp end but has the good manners to let you believe you are still running it.'

This is how things are in many of our factories, including the non-unionized ones; it's the Boadicea syndrome, one of the things you become aware of very quickly as a consultant – if you want to find the real source of power in a factory, seek out the strong woman. Find a way through the screen of managers. This is usually easy because more often than not they belong to the corporate chattering class which convenes an endless series of meetings. While they talk you get to the shop floor and find 'Florrie' or whatever her name happens to be. She is much the same person in

all of the factories, only the names they call her by are different –
same goddess under a changed appellation. She is the one to talk
to if you aim to implement cultural change. We shall speak more
of this woman later.

'Tell me, did she impress you?' he asked.

'Yes, she did. For five reasons. Do you want me to tell you what
they are?'

'Of course; this interests me greatly.'

'OK. First, she speaks with simple eloquence. She's a natural
communicator; such people as these are rare, and are to be cherished. She uses plain language, uncorrupted by any management
training jargon.

'Second, she has insight. She knows that the job she has to do
every Friday is a waste of time, and she probably resents the fact
that those who buy one of her most valued assets – her time – do
so only to fritter it away.

'Third, I admire her integrity. She has the courage to challenge
the validity of the things those in authority require her to do. In
this she challenges authority itself and its conventional assumptions.

'Fourth, her *anger*.' I paused, to refresh myself.

He was listening intently, impatiently, as I flicked some ciga-
rette-ash off the lapels of my jacket and then made a big job of
grinding out a stub. 'Go on, then, you said *five* things impressed
you; so far you've only mentioned four and they are all good
points and I like 'em. What is the fifth?'

'Ah yes, the fifth point. This is the best of them, and the one
which you will like most of all. As long as you are prepared to go
along with it.' I paused, teasing him again, ringing a bell to make
the Pavlovian dog within him slaver in wolfish anticipation.

'Are you going to tell me, then?'

'We have the diagnosis,' I said, 'No we have the plan for treatment. This is it. We will use Karen as the torch-bearer to bring
Total Quality into the company. She has *all* the essential personal
attributes and motivation. She has no training in statistical
method. That's where I come in. I teach her basic applied statistics
and statistical process control. Then I teach her to teach. After
which she will help me teach SPC to your operators, and after I'm
gone she will keep it going. This learning will enable your operators to control their own quality and their own working day. To

use the fashionable term, this will "empower" them. Empowerment following education, the only way to make it work. But immensely effective and worth the effort.' I paused again, to get my breath and give things time to sink in. 'What do you think to it?'

'I like it. But I wonder will it work,' he said. 'Let me just clear some points in my mind. You say we should introduce TQM *bottom-up*. This is not the usual way. The conventional – and recommended – way is by cascading it from the top down. Why should a bottom-up approach be better?'

I knew of companies attempting culture change by cascade training who were in trouble. So I told him, 'Because cascade training amounts to no more than standing on the top of a mountain and having a pee and wondering why so little of it trickles into the valley below.'

Cascade + Pee !

He enjoyed that. So I told him some more.

'I know an oil company, a big outfit with a fourteen-tier hierarchy. They are cascading a famous American quality system down their pyramid. So far it's still four tiers from the bottom, after *four years* of trickle-down training costing huge sums of money. Payback to date? Nothing. They've run out of pee. If knowledge were water it would have turned into stalactites long before it reached the base of the organization where the action is. Cascade training seems to me to be a sop to the vanity of those with higher status and a greater sense of self-importance than those beneath them. A kind of "me first I am a manager" attitude.'

'You're not saying that managers should not be trained, are you?'

'No, I'm not. Far from it. Cascade training presupposes horizontal splits in the organization, into status layers. I propose to divide the hierarchy vertically, into segments in which status becomes irrelevant. Training groups, for the one-day basic seminar, are composed of people of mixed ranks, and that includes directors. This approach assumes that regardless of rank people are prepared to learn together.'

This must have appealed to the Athenian component of his intellectual inheritance, 'I *like that*,' he said, 'a bit of democracy in the workplace.'

'Yes, it will make a change, won't it?'

'But will it work?'

'Why shouldn't it? It has worked in companies similar to yours.' If the *boss* had doubts it surely would *not* work; his commitment to the philosophy and to his own beliefs had to be total.

'I remember trying to learn statistics at University,' he confessed. 'I found the whole subject dry and boring beyond belief. Nothing but endless equations. Perhaps it was simply over my head.'

'Perhaps you were taught by a dry and boring lecturer, or somebody who wished to impress you with his profound learning by making it hard for you to learn it as well. To humiliate you as he had been humiliated. There are better ways of teaching it, and for better reasons.'

'Maybe, but I still feel doubt. You are talking about teaching to a workforce, with barely an O level between them, a subject which managers – many of them with degrees – find hard to grasp. The shopfloor people are not exactly numerate, you know.'

'I know *this*; they are numerate enough to count their pay. They handle arithmetic every time they play darts. They figure out probabilities better than we do every time they place a bet with the bookmaker. They're numerate enough to learn it the way I teach it.'

'And how do you teach it?'

'Partly by the Socratic system of question and answer. For instance, in the interests of explaining the statistics of the normal distribution I provide an illuminating answer to a question which puzzles many men but few women, namely "How big is willy?"'

This admission aroused his attention, as well as bringing an expression of sceptical disbelief to his face, a look of near-wonderment as if he was finding it hard to believe his ears.

'You tell them how big *what* is?' He needed to hear me say it again, to prove his hearing was not playing him tricks.

So I said it again. 'The human phallus. Willy. When it's in its priapic condition of course. You will be aware of Priapus, the Roman god of procreation? Or the ancient monument in Dorset known as the Giant of Cerne Abbas? Like that. You see, my education was in the natural sciences and it included human anatomy, physiology, and biometrics. These are subjects which lend themselves to statistical analysis. So I know about these things. At that time I was planning to become a doctor of medicine, but I switched career track when it dawned upon me that I just didn't care enough about other people's feelings to become a physician. That was before I realized that this was probably the best of qualifications for a lifetime in a caring profession. So I became a scientist instead. Science is the unembarrassed pursuit of knowledge; it is untainted by prudery or social niceties. Therefore certain aspects of knowledge which might, in polite circles, be referred to with a cautious delicacy, cause a scientist like me no embarrassment whatever. The statistical distribution of the size of willies, for instance. If *you* find it embarrassing please tell me; I would be interested in your reasons.'

'No,' he laughed, 'it doesn't worry me in the least. Anything goes, as long as it's in a good cause.'

'Like training a workforce to do their own quality, and *understand* what they are doing?'

'Sounds fine to me,' he assured me. 'How on earth did you decide upon such a – shall we say – unusual approach to making a dull subject interesting?'

'Aha, thereby hangs a tale. Would you like to hear it?'

He said he would, and ordered us another pot of tea. High-octane liquid, harvested from the hillsides of Assam, the rich fuel that powered British imperialism, beat the blitz, and energizes the imagination of those whose business is the telling of tales such as the following . . . .

Tales of willies

When I was writing the book *Right First Time* in the early 1980s it occurred to me that one way of *humanizing* the incomprehensible abstractions of mathematical statistics would be to do exactly that: to take samples of certain human dimensions – such as the tallness of men – and use them to make the point about the distribution of a sample of values about their average value into a cluster with a calculable spread. This is the essential and unavoidable basis of all genuine quality management; the key component which has been missing from much of so-called 'total' quality management since the initiative was hijacked by the human relations school. More about this mob later.

Once on this humanizing track I found myself travelling further along it, to the point of reasoning that if I were to use such anatomical features as the tallness of men or the size of their feet as an educational paradigm to make learning easier, then why not extend this approach to another prominent feature of the male anatomy. Why not? So I opened a new chapter in the manuscript with the words:

> The nimble pervert leapt out of the alley, and flung his raincoat wide in front of the oncoming woman. She stared coolly and said in tones of sad commiseration, 'Don't worry yourself about it, my poor fellow, *size* isn't everything.' This is one of those white lies which kind-hearted women use to console the doubts of men; the one which Wallis Simpson, according to palace gossip, is said to have told her priapically challenged husband 'David', the ex-King of England. This threw the exhibitionist. With a puzzled look he dropped his stare thinking to himself, 'Size? She knows? She knows something I don't know.' His introspection confused him still further, 'I don't know whether she knows or not. Because *I* don't know either . . . .'

Neither did I. Like the poor bemused flasher, who had no idea how big it *should* be, I had only the vaguest notion of dimensional normality. Yet if I were to use this chapter to make a critically important statistical teaching point then I simply had to have scientifically correct data about the distribution of the length of this organ throughout the population of all the men in the land.

I moved into my research mode. Whatever I am running down a truth my pursuit is as swift and relentless as that of a greyhound running down a swerving hare. My research began with a trawl through various medical textbooks which have spent half a century gathering dust in the attic. After all, the size of the particular feature under discussion is not likely to have altered a great deal after a mere fifty years of evolutionary influence. To no avail. I discovered some diverting, nay, terrifying descriptions of disorders likely to afflict the thing, especially if exposed to carnal delights, with vivid illustrations like the ones they showed us when we joined the Armed Services, but nothing about how big it was supposed to be. I closed the books in disgust, and moved to option number two.

This was another sensible choice of source, a very promising one it seemed at first. I telephoned the librarian of the medical faculty of a university noted for its regular crop of distinguished surgeons. He was circumspect. 'Why do you want to know?' he asked. Although I thought it was hardly any of his business I divulged my intention to write about it. 'Writing about it?' he repeated, 'Is it pornography you are writing?' Shocked by such a base notion I hastily reassured him of the creative and moral integrity of my enquiry. Still he withheld the information. Ever inventive in his obstructiveness he demanded, 'Are you a qualified person?' Qualified in what? I wondered. Chiropody, gasfitting, municipal sanitation, sheep-shearing . . . What occupation do you have to be qualified in to be admitted to that exclusive brotherhood who guard knowledge too heady to be known by lesser beings? Is there a special handshake? Do you roll up a trouser leg? Is there a code-word? I was getting tired of him, 'Yes, of course I am a qualified person,' I snapped. 'But are you a qualified medical practitioner?' This was a man who could have withstood having his toenails pulled off with pliers by a Gestapo interrogator and give away nothing more than his name, rank and number as permitted by the Geneva Convention. What the hell was he doing in a *library*, supposedly a source of information?

'No, I am not. Actually I suppose I am, a little bit, I've studied the statistics of epidemiology and occupancy theory. I prescribe a diet of nettles to cure adolescent acne, and enemas for those constipated with self-importance like you.' Clearly he had no intention of cooperating with me in my search for truth, so I rang off.

Thereupon I experienced a flash of inspiration as option number three presented itself, emerging from wherever inspirations emerge, where it had been lurking all this while, the *obvious* source of information I sought – the published research findings of the late and famous Dr Kinsey, sexologist-in-chief of America.

Americans do not do things by halves, well, not usually; they are exceedingly thorough. Dr Alfred C. Kinsey was an American professor of biology who founded the Institute for Sex Research, dedicated to unearthing the truth and dispelling the myths about sexual attributes, experiences, attitude and behaviour. I was certain that this body of knowledge held the answer to my question. I accordingly sent a draft for nearly a hundred dollars to the United

States and duly received a copy of *The Kinsey Data*. This is a heavy tome of over 600 pages of his findings tabulated in different classifications. I searched the categories dealing with anatomy, and there it was at last, the answer to my question.

Indeed, much more than that. Kinsey had learned more about this subject than any other person on the planet or throughout the recorded history of civilization. Although his research was conducted two thousand years too late to include the celebrated Ancient Roman *bon viveur*, who was so well endowed that he was accorded a round of polite and respectful applause whenever he paraded his nakedness through the public bath-houses; it covered a big enough sample of the men of America to be representative of the population. His research is of breath-taking scope, covering every possible aspect of the privy member: its estimated length, measured length, circumference, angle of slope, lateral inclination, curvature, duration, frequency of morning arousal. Not only the answer to my question, but answers to questions it would never have occurred to me to ask. This was real science, revelation, genuine American thoroughness.

Before I was able to express my answer in the statistical terms I needed for training purposes I had to analyse over three thousand items of numerical data. It took several hours a day for several days, patiently tapping it all into a pocket calculator until it was distilled into just two parameters – the average and standard deviation of the size of willy.

That concluded my research.

He was still paying close attention, watching me speculatively while I chose to waste time fiddling with a cigarette, inspecting it as if it were the first one I had ever encountered. I beamed at him encouragingly.

'Well?' he said.

'Well what?'

'How big *is* it?'

'On the average?'

'Yes, how big is it on the average?'

'Well, for Caucasians like you and me it's 6.3 inches, and the variation throughout . . .'

'Ah, yes. Yes, I see.' A fleeting faraway expression flitted over his eyes as he lost himself in a second's-worth of mental arithmetic. 'Yes, 6.3 inches you say, very interesting.' He seemed pleased with himself – I wondered whether I should do the Roman thing and politely applaud.

Instead I continued, 'And as I was saying, the variation throughout the *population* – those millions of American men – from which Kinsey's sample of a few thousands was drawn, is described by the standard deviation, the measure of a spread of values around their average value. This value, in this population, is 0.7 inches.'

'Oh, 0.7 inches. Yes I see.' He hesitated. 'What is the significance of that? What is the use of knowing it?'

A fair question, the answer to which I was leading up to. 'This. If we *add* one standard deviation to the average, 6.3 plus 0.7, we get 7.0; and then *subtract* one standard deviation from the average, 6.3 minus 0.7, we get 5.6. These two numbers tell us that the range between them, 5.6 to 7.0 includes about 70 per cent of the entire population.

'We do it a second time, *add* 0.7 to the 7.0 we just got, to give us 7.7; and subtract 0.7 from the 5.6 we also just got to give us 4.9. This gives us the *wider* boundaries, 4.9 to 7.7, which embrace about 94 per cent of the population. The thing is, you see, that the further away from the average you move the fewer values you find.

'So we do it again, for a third and final time: 7.7 plus 0.7 equals 8.4; and 4.9 minus 0.7 equals 4.2. This tells us that just about *all* the population values lie between the *widest* boundaries of 4.2 and 8.4 inches.

'Only about one man in a thousand is equipped with a Cupid's dart less than four and two-tenths of an inch long. Evidently Ernest Hemingway, the one who wrote all those macho books about bull fighting and big-game fishing, fell into this category of rarities, at least if we are to believe the kiss-and-tell testimony of some of his estranged lovers. He spent his life trying to compensate for what a niggardly mother nature had denied him, I suppose – a case of extreme physical deprivation generating literary genius.

'On the other hand we find the one in one thousand gloating beneficiaries of an over-generous natural bequest fitted with a veritable lance longer than eight and four-tenths of an inch. Frankly, I must say, in spite of the impeccable rigour of

Kinsey's methodology I found myself entertaining doubts about the veracity of this calculation, until I saw one for myself.'

'*Saw* one? Where on *earth* did you see such a thing?'

'In Pittsburgh, as a matter of fact. I decided to pass an hour or two at an all-night cinema – cheaper than boozing once you've bought your obligatory gallon of popcorn in the foyer. I went to see what I expected to be, judging by its title – it was called *Caligula* – an educational epic of life in Rome under the Caesars. It turned out to be a soft-porn skinflick; though to employ the term '*soft-porn*' seems a bit of a contradiction in the circumstances. And *there* he was, in fact there were *two* of them: the one in one thousand and the two in ten thousand! Large as life. I thought this cannot be real – it must be a sly trick of the camera, or the thing is made of fibreglass and carefully glued on, a prop of pornography, so to speak. But no, I could see no seams. They were for real. Cinematic proof that Kinsey was correct. And I suppose this is what management writers mean when they tell us we should all try to "develop our potential", make full use of our natural endowments. Actualization of self, thrusting entrepreneurism, and all that stuff.'

'I wonder where they *find* them,' he mused. 'After all, it's not the sort of thing you would find in your normal run-of-the-mill job advertisement, is it?'

'I don't know so much,' I countered. 'Think about it, and some of the jobs we expect people to do for money; imagine it, a job advertisement: "This responsible appointment is best suited to somebody who is really an absolute pr. . . . .".'

'Personnel manager,' he cut in, 'because they're useless. But, seriously, fascinating though all this is, what has it got to do with manufacturers like me? Cutting metal for a living, churning out valve spigot rods, for instance.'

'*Everything*. We are talking here about *natural variation*, are we not?'

'Yes, natural variation in human beings. That's not the same as metal rods though, is it?'

'It is *exactly* the same. That is the whole point of it. There is natural variation in the dimensional characteristics (not "parameters") of human beings. There is likewise a natural variation in the length of the rods you make. You set up the machine to make the rods. You fix the controls to cut the lengths of, say, 6.3 inches.

The specification says so. *Exactly* 6.3 inches? All the time? *Every* rod length?'

'No, of course not. We are allowed a tolerance. Hang on, I'll phone through and get the real specification for some real rods.' He dialled, chatted to somebody, then said, 'Fancy a stroll? One of the technologists is setting up a machine right now. Let's join him.'

You could tell he was a technologist: he was wearing a white smock. They used to carry a six-inch slide rule in a leather sheath trade-marked PIC in their top pocket; I know, because I've still got such a museum piece – I use it to baffle young mathematicians. He didn't need such an antediluvian wand of office; he'd got a computer. No mistakes with fixing decimal points any more; no more two times three equals sixty, or is it oh point six, where the hell shall I stick the point? nonsense. Here was accuracy, and precision to thirteen decimal places.

He had a large heap of metal rods at his left elbow. He was taking them, one by one, and measuring their lengths on a special jig with a dial gauge on it, before adding them to a second heap at his right elbow. Well organized, like every technocrat should be.

'Doing a lot of measuring aren't you?' asked the boss, eyeing the heaps of rods meaningfully.

'Got to', said the technocrat, 'Got to make sure none is out-of-specification.'

'What is the spec for rod-length?'

'Ten inches, exact, tolerance plus and minus ten thou.' He selected another rod, fitted it into the gauge and keyed the number into his computer.

'How long was that one?' asked the boss.

'Plus eight thou', was the terse response.

'Looks like a long job you've got yourself here,' I sympathetically informed the industrious young technocrat. 'Have you got any dial calipers I could borrow to measure a few?'

I measured a handful, about two dozen, of the rods already measured by the patient technologist. The boss wrote the numbers down on a handy scrap of paper; I did my bit of jiggery-pokery on the pocket calculator.

'Does your numbers-engine do any stats analysis for you?' I asked the lad.

'Fully programmed,' he said proudly, 'sum of squares, averages, correlation coefficients . . .'

'Does it give you the average value of your entries?'

'Yes.' He keyed for the average and chanted from the display '10.1976324'.

'You get 10.2 then, near enough. How many have you measured?'

He tapped another question into his altar of knowledge. It answered '376'. '376', he reported accurately.

'That's a lot. I've done 23 rods and my average is 10.24, same as yours, near enough. What's your standard deviation?'

Again he interrogated the inanimate electronic genius before which he was squatting. '1.046!' he said, and suddenly blushed, and shame-facedly added, 'I think it's wrong.'

Not a bad conclusion for a bright young man with a bright new degree with honours.

'I make it four thou, as near as dammit,' I told him, 'can you roll up the input data, to see if we can find the oddball that's screwing your results?' We found it. Numbers accidentally transposed during key-in, easily done.

'By the way,' I added generously, 'if your tolerance *really* is ten thou either way then your machine can't make it. It needs at least fifteen thou either side for comfort.'

'What do we do about it, then?'

'If you can't change the laws of physics you change the specification,' I advised him unhelpfully.

The boss escorted me back to his office.

'I'm impressed,' he said.

'You're supposed to be,' I advised him. 'I'm impressive. That's how I get my work. I save you effort. I save you money. That's what I'm *for*. That's why you will gladly permit me to put my hand into your till, because you'll know that I am putting in more money than I am taking out.' This was a contractual promise. No cure, no fee, grease my palm and I will open the gate to let you out of your Bedlam. I will bring you peace of mind. I will bring you quality. With love.

PART 2

KEYS TO THE GATES OF BEDLAM

What Should be Done

We were sitting in the boss's office – hub of the wheel whose spokes were the channels which carried his authority to lesser wheels cogged into its rim. An organization which was supposed to run like clockwork because it was built on a mechanical paradigm which Isaac Newton himself would have found mighty pleasing. We were about to begin dismantling it. Because it didn't work any more. It had run out of its time.

There would be casualties, victims; there always are.

'Let us recapitulate,' said the boss, 'review the plan which is emerging from what we've talked about so far.'

Suits me, I thought. No need to interrupt him; he was doing fine.

'We shall introduce TQM – total quality management – into the company by educating the workforce in statistical process control so that they can look after their own quality. Yes?'

'We shall do this in a series of one-day seminars, attended by up to twelve people at each seminar, to be drawn from various *segments* of the company rather than segregated into status-layers.'

'Correct,' I nodded encouragingly, adding, 'and you yourself will attend the first of these, and bless all others by being there to open them.'

'There will also be a short programme of separate seminars for the management team, to look at how they manage, and to increase their awareness of organizational behaviour and development.'

He was sorting it all out quite nicely, I thought.

'Following the initial seminar to the work-groups on statistical process control – SPC – there will be on-the-job training in its practicalities. You will do this, with whomever we appoint from the workforce to help you. Yes?'

'That's right,' I confirmed. 'In this way, there is no transfer loss. Nothing spills out of the bucket.'

'Bucket? What bucket?'

'If you send people away on a course, they go there, as it were, with an empty bucket. Somebody fills it with liquid called "knowledge" piped out of a big tank called a business school or whatever. The recipients carry it back to base but spill a lot on the way home. By the time they get back the bucket is half-empty, or half-full, depending on whether you're a pessimist or an optimist. Either way there's not much of it left, and it cost you a lot of money to put the bucket under the nozzle. Do it as we are going to and they lose nothing. In fact we keep on drip-feeding the bucket.'

'Sounds good,' he conceded.

'I'll make it sound even better,' I promised. 'It will not only cost you *much less than half the price* of sending people away for training off-site; I can assure you that within two weeks the whole programme will be *paying for itself.*'

'How will it do that? Pay for itself?' If you really want to catch the interest of a captain of industry tell him you can make some *money* for him. Money. The proposition you cannot refuse; the cloak to cover idealism sometimes – righteousness made rewarding. Develop his workforce, not only at *no* cost, but at a profit while doing so and a steady return thereafter. Short-term gains sustained into long-term dividends. Irresistible.

'It will pay for itself by pulling in some of the slack which exists in just about every business system.' I gave him the benefit of my experience. 'In my experience there are always gains to be made by *reducing variation*. In the use of raw materials for instance, by learning how to make more out of less.'

'For all practical purposes,' he went on, 'we are about to teach our workforce how to manage itself.'

Yes. *Our* workforce. Once I am in with a client my identification with the company *has* to be total. I am *in* the company, not *of* it, but the bond of shared objectives must be unbreakable. Until the time comes when I must leave, of course, then it is a sort of bereavement. But *until* then, as the boss said, it is *our* company.

'What will the managers do then?' he asked, with a mischievous glint in his eyes.

'Not much.'

Our meeting to hear my so-called diagnosis and recommendations for treatment had run its natural course. Time to wrap up.

It takes a day or two to set up a series of seminars in a company 250-odd strong. This lull gives you time to wander around the organization meeting people informally while sniffing the cultural atmosphere. You can have a lot of fun doing this: as well as gaining an insight into the company you can begin to pick out the people who will be your heralds of the new order – those who work to 'develop their potential'.

This notion that one of the duties, yea, the delights, of the manager's job is to cultivate the talents he finds lying fallow in his subordinates is very much a middle-class projection on to working-class subjects. It's a splendid idea. Doing it, or even talking about trying to do it, can make you feel good, fill you with a holy glow of self-satisfaction.

So the act of developing people makes you feel good. So it should. But not *everybody* wants to be developed. In my experience about one in fifty or sixty people would rather you left them alone. They don't want any do-gooder poking into their lives, to 'enrich' their working day. So you leave them alone; concentrate on those who want it.

And many of them are *clamouring* for the chance to give more of themselves to their work. Desperate to be more developed, yearning to find some scrap of meaning in lives given over to endless drudgery whose only purpose seems to be the grabbing of a little cash. Or do you believe that man can live by bread alone? That money is the measure of all things in a monetarist universe? This is a miserable idea; even dogs know better.

So while we were preparing for the heady excitement of the seminars to come, I mooched about the place, dropping in here and there; this casual roaming around is an essential part of reconnaissance, of 'getting to know you'.

I thought it time to get to know the top team a bit better, starting with the quality manager. But before we talk about it let me tell you about Prussia, in Northern Germany, in the years 1900 to 1914. I know that Henry Ford claimed that 'History is bunk'. What else would you expect from a greasy-fingered mechanic? Anyway, if what he said were true then it debunks his own statement, so it's false, and history is not bunkum. So we will use this snippet of history because it happens to be useful today.

It is to do with how the Prussian military High Command selected officer candidates. Have you ever attended a WOSBY? A War Office Selection Board? To see if you are fit to become an officer. No? I did, once. Well, an Admiralty Selection Board actually. When I was in the Royal Navy trying to make the best of having been dragged screaming from the bosom of my adoring family, taken by the press-gang to serve King and Country, along with all the other young men who were called up through being unlucky enough not to have flat feet. There was a small group of us, chosen because we had demonstrated OLQ ('officer-like qualities'); by not chewing gum or wiping our noses on our cuffs, I suppose. We prepared ourselves well for the Selection Board, mugging up on naval history, absorbing the patrician prose of the out-of-date copies of *The Times* newspaper which was our prescribed reading. Practised speaking in clipped accents.

Came the day, *carpe diem*, as Horace said, seize the day. Into the interview room, one by one in alphabetical order of surname. A long table with heaps of gold braid the other side, half a dozen admirals and captains, smothered in colourful medal ribbons. One solitary straight-backed chair facing that lot.

The first of us went in. He had prepared himself well. They mildly asked him their first question: 'What day is it today?' He hesitated. Was it Empire Day? Or St George's Day? Or, heaven forbid, *Trafalgar Day*? No, it was Thursday, and he had forgotten. An admiral was obliged to remind him. He came out again. It's the little things in life that so easily trip you up. But, back to the Prussians. I am indebted to the *London Review of Books* for the following account.

A digression: Bismarck's boys

The War Office Selection Board operated by the Prussian Junkers' caste during the first decade of this century was elegantly simple. Candidates were judged on two mental qualities. On *intelligence* – were they stupid or clever, and on *industriousness* – were they lazy or hard-working?

You will see that from this two-factors system four classifications can be derived:

1. Lazy and stupid
2. Lazy and clever
3. Hard-working and clever
4. Hard-working and stupid.

Each candidate was assessed by a squad of generals wearing, one imagines, 'pickel-helms', those helmets with a spike on top, and bristling moustaches with ends waxed into points like darning needles. Whichever of the four categories the candidate was accorded governed his future as a career officer, as follows:

1. Lazy and stupid – would make a damned fine regimental officer.
2. Lazy and clever – ideal material to become a general; shove him into the fast track.
3. Hard-working and clever – perfect qualifications for staff officer.
4. Hard-working and stupid – worse than useless, will only cock things up. Shove him back into civvy street.

How very un-English is this way of praising some people while condemning others. Fancy *sacking* somebody for being *hard-working*! Just because he is stupid.

We don't do things the Prussian way; we know better. We even use our words differently, load them with a different emotional burden. Take the word 'clever'. If we say of someone 'my, my, but he's a *clever* one that one is', what are we saying? We are implying that he is shifty, sly, too smart by half. We say it in a tone of mixed admiration and disapproval, with a kind of grudging respect. But we don't like him, and we would never trust him. We would *never* promote him. Because we see him as a *threat*. Cleverness provokes hostility.

So really clever people are obliged to conceal it by pretending to be stupid. This is a form of protective colouration. This makes it difficult for teachers such as me to distinguish between the genuinely stupid and the counterfeit version. But we have ways of doing it.

So anybody who is seen to be 'clever' is doomed in our managerial mythology. What about the verdict 'lazy'? This is another killer. 'Oh dear, poor old so-and-so, he seems to be firing only on two cylinders these days.' Said of somebody who chooses to sit and think, rather than hurtle around the factory with flames scorching the flying tails of his smock as he energetically tries to pass off mindless vitality as real work. Said in sad tones of head-shaking bewilderment that this once-active colleague has degenerated into sluggish idleness. Said, with gloating treachery pretending to be heartfelt concern, in the presence of the victim's boss. Said by his friends.

So anybody who is both *clever* and *lazy*, who in the Prussian military would have been tipped for future *generalship*, is in our industrial ethos condemned to despised obscurity, passed over for advancement.

What about the ones who are *stupid* and *lazy*? The potential 'regimental officers'? They gravitate into jobs whose titles include the word 'co-ordinator'. This species of idler used to proliferate in the larger institutions until they were shaken out of the tree by the typhoon out of the Orient. Since the job of actually doing nothing is in itself a sort of hard work they recruited assistants. Being stupid does not mean lacking cunning, or having a finely attuned sense of survival. These people built themselves 'jobs' as impressive – and as essentially insubstantial – as the false fronts of sheriff's offices and Last Chance saloons on the film set of a spaghetti western. Two-dimensional illusions of four-dimensional work. (*Four*-dimensional? Yes, three in space and one in time.) Most of those people must by now be in the legion of the white-collar unemployed. Victims. Perhaps they have metamorphosed into consultants.

What about the third category, the *hard-working* and *clever*? They are still with us. Thank heaven.

And the fourth category, the *hard-working* and *stupid*? So are they, alas. It is in this swarming shoal of busy misfits that I trawl for my victims. Fishing is pretty good, these days. It's an ill wind . . .

That's an end of this digression. Let's get back to my wanderings and wonderings in the company.

I drifted, seemingly aimlessly, into the quality man's office. Which of Prussia's four categories would he fit himself into, I wondered? I had already identified the boss as a true general, a clever loafer happy to leave the active work to his staff officers while he surveyed the commercial battlefield from his commanding heights. But what about his men, and his women? Of what mettle might these be?

The quality man was sitting at his desk. It's time I named him, so let's call him 'Joe'. His assistant, the deputy quality manager, the lad I had seen supervising the entry of data into *the computer*, was sat there as well. Shall we call him 'Kevin'? (I make these names up because whenever I write I am not writing about a *particular* person.)

So, Joe and Kevin were conferring. 'Having a meeting, is it?' I let myself into the office and draw a chair up to the desk.

'We're writing another procedure,' said Joe, adding amiably, 'Would you like to see it? It's the procedure that shall determine first-offs acceptance stroke non-acceptance of items of product at band-saw start-up in accordance with the requirements of traceability of records to meet the provision of British Standard 5750.' He paused, for breath, and handed me a sheaf of A4 notepaper. Seventeen pages. Small handwriting. About four thousand words already, and still scribble, scribble, scribble like Mr Gibbon patiently scratching out *The Decline and Fall*.

'Who gets this,' I asked, '*when* it's done?'

'The saw operator, and the line inspector.'

I'll bet I know what they do with it, an' all. 'Are they supposed to read it?'

'No, they're supposed to follow it,' Joe explained.

There was a sudden heavy banging on the door. It burst open, and a young woman breezed in waving a piece of paper. 'Sign this please.' She passed it to Joe. Joe read it, and passed it to Kevin. Kevin read it, signed it, and handed it back to Joe who studied it closely before handing it back to the woman.

I had already met this young woman during my factory stroll. She was on the despatch section, where things were put into boxes along with a document called a Certificate of Conformance. That was the piece of paper she had just brought in to be signed. After she had fled the office to return to her urgent affairs we returned to our discussion.

'Lot of *words* in this procedure of yours Joe, don't you think?'

He looked pained. 'Lot of words? Have *you* ever tried to write a specification? It's not easy. I've been on a special course.'

Another hammering on the door and she was back waving another piece of paper. The same ceremony was re-enacted. Joe read it, passed it to Kevin who signed it, passed it back for Joe to read again and restored to its rightful owner, who disappeared as swiftly as she had arrived. Back to the despatch area, about two hundred yards away.

'Anyway, Joe,' I picked up the conversation, 'I didn't come here to talk about specifications; I came to discuss the SPC seminars with you.'

'Oh yes. The boss has told me about your ideas. Going to teach statistics to the workforce, aren't you?' He sounded a bit sceptical. 'Won't work, you know.'

'Why not?' I was looking forward to his explanation of the folly of my ambition when suddenly she was back into the office. Again! 'Sign this please,' she gave her password.

This was too much. 'Oy, oy, oy!' I burst out, 'What the bloody hell is going on here? With your "sign this" every couple of minutes. What *is* that bit of paper anyway?' I asked, even though I already knew.

'This is a C-of-C; a certificate of conformance,' Joe informed me. 'It has to be properly signed by a proper person in proper authority.'

'Why can't *she* sign it?'

My perfectly reasonable question caused a look of horror to come over his face, a mask of disbelief. 'Why . . . can't . . . *she* . . . sign it?' He repeated aghast. 'Because *she* is not a proper person to sign it, that's why.'

I was in Bedlam yet again, so I started some prodding with my pointed stick. 'Who *says* she's an improper person who isn't allowed to sign things?'

He leapt to his feet and clawed at the bookshelf behind his chair, pulling out a file so heavy he had to use both hands to let it slam on to his desk. 'I'll tell you who says she can't sign it. BS5750 says, that's what, look here . . .' he riffled through the hundreds of pages, then announced triumphantly, 'Clause eighteen dot three dot one. Here it is. I shall quote: "Certificates of Conformance of all items of product despatched shall be signed by the Deputy Quality Manager"; that's *him*,' and he stabbed a finger in Kevin's direction before continuing his quote, ' "or in the absence of this officer of the company they shall be signed by the Quality Manager", that's *me*,' he added unnecessarily. 'That is why *she* can't sign it. Does *that* answer your question?'

It did. I tried another one, quietly, a sly prod this time. 'Kevin, why exactly do you have to sign these certificates?'

'Well, er . . .,' he glanced at Joe, seeking guidance in answering what must be a trick question. 'Well, I sign to say that the things in the box have been OK'd by quality.'

'Good, I see.' I went on in a quietly reassuring tone of voice. 'You sign to say the things in the box are OK, without actually seeing the things in the box?'

'Well, yes, it's procedures, you see.'

'So, you don't really *know* what's in the box?'

'I don't suppose so really, if you put it like that.' He furrowed his brow in concentration, and came up with his answer, 'But *she* knows what's in the box!'

'I know as well, Kevin, and you don't know. I was out on the shop this morning, before you got here. I *saw* what was being put in those boxes. You didn't. Do you know what it is you are actually signing certificates of conformance for? I'll tell you what is in the boxes – ossified dog turds, that's what.'

'Don't talk daft!' Kevin was quite rightly angry with me, 'I know what I'm signing for because she tells me what is in the box, and I know I can trust her.'

'Trust her?' I administered what I had imagined would be a death-stroke of unassailable logic. 'Then why do you not trust her to *sign* this bit of paper seeing that you do not know what is in the box and she does know. Change the procedures; add her name to the list of those empowered to sign!'

'Can't be done,' decreed Joe, 'Sorry, but she is not a proper person under the terms of BS 5750. Not an officer of the company.'

There is no answer to that, not to people like Joe. I had already decided to invite the young woman when I had spoken at length to her that same morning, to take up the torch of quality later on in the drive.

'Joe, let's you and me take a stroll on to the shopfloor, show me what goes on, eh?'

He had already started inscribing page eighteen of his procedure. 'Sorry, I *must* get this done – can't Kevin take you round and show you?' Kevin looked alarmed at the prospect, and quickly demurred. 'But I've got those customer's returns to look at. You said you wanted the rejection report on them today.' I am familiar with the feeling of being personally unpopular. It comes with the job. But I am hard-faced. That also comes with the job. 'Come on, Joe, the boss said you'd show me your quality set-up, ready for the seminars.' That got him to his feet, muttering darkly.

He took me on a tour. To meet his team of eighteen women, he

called them his 'lady inspectors'. They were very, very busy. Each
at her little bench with its stackable boxes made out of plastic.
Every box laden with output. Each woman writing her little report
on her discoveries. A trickle of reports coming to Joe every hour,
the trickle growing into a stream and then into a strongly flowing
river of raw data in which Joe was floundering and going under.
Poor old Joe.

'We've got good reporting procedures here,' he assured me.
'We keep track of everything.'

Once you find yourself being taken on a conducted tour of
Bedlam you might as well have a look at all the loonies in their
distressing variety: the prancing maniacs, the gibbering buffoons,
the weeping melancholics.

We came upon a woman with tears running down her rosy
apple cheeks. 'Why is this woman crying, Joe?'

'She's not *crying*; she's inspecting these components.'

'She doesn't seem very happy about it.'

'She's not.' He addressed the weeping woman, 'How many are
out of specification today?'

The component being examined was a small plastic cone
whose point was missing, cut into what we mathematicians call a
'frustrum'. Each cone was about an inch or so high, and the frustrum face about half an inch across. The woman was putting these
one at a time under the ball-point of a dial gauge, twiddling them
around and sliding them about, watching the flickering needle on
the dial gauge while she did so. That is why she was red-eyed and
weeping: eye-strain. Although anger and frustration could have
been an equally likely source of her tears.

'Four out of five,' she said dejectedly, as if it were all her fault.

Was I hearing aright? Four out of five being rejected as 'out of
specification'?

'We make these for a very demanding customer,' Joe told me.
'A *German* company.' Prussian, perhaps? 'The top and bottom
surfaces of the cone have to be parallel within four thou. We have
to make five thousand to get one thousand good ones. It's a difficult job, is this. Our sales director says it's a loss-leader.'

A loss-leader! Where's he come from, this sales director?
Kwiksave No Nonsense Superstores? They use loss-leaders to
pull the punters in, but *here*? In an industrial operation making
engineering bits and pieces? Loss-leader? We are not talking

baked beans here.

'What do you mean, Joe, they have to be parallel within four thousandths of an inch?'

'Taper, we call it. Top and bottom faces of the cone should be parallel to each other, but can be up to only four thou out of parallelism.' All highly technical stuff, this. All rubbish, as well.

'But Joe, Joe my dear chap.' I was being hyper-considerate, 'Don't you see, isn't it obvious, that the upper surface is itself *undulating* like a range of hills? It is not flat. It cannot ever *be* flat, because when you apply heat to a plastic shape such as this its differential shrinkage inevitably results in ups and downs to the upper surface. It is impossible to make a meaningful measurement of *taper*. You can get any reading on the gauge you want, it's all meaningless.'

'Impossible or not, our sales director says that's what the customer wants, that's what the customer pays for and that's what we do.'

Here was yet another of the many places where I could put my hand into the till of the company and leave a lot more money in than I took out.

'How big is the business, Joe? Pounds sterling per year in sales of this item?' It turned out to be many thousands.

'For every thousand quid's worth you sell, you produce and then sling down the drain another *four* thousand quid's worth.' I explained. 'Does that make sense? Or is it madness?' I could earn my keep for a year's consultancy on this job alone. Simply, *and* easily.

'There's nothing I can do about it,' he protested. 'I get my orders, to work to the specification. That's what I do.'

He did. He worked very hard. His 'lady inspector' worked so hard she was sacrificing her eyesight on the altar of his obedience to the twin deities of 'the customer' and 'the spec'.

The company was diligently bleeding itself to death. If this company had been a sinking ship we would have an entire crew not baling water out, but baling water *in*, as fast as they could go.

I wonder what the Prussian High Command would have made of Joe. Bismarck boy of the year?

Next we come on to a HOW TO DO IT piece: how to teach the obscure and daunting statistics to a crew of ordinary folk like you and me, in a manner which is not too hard to grasp.

How to Do It

This is an account of how to conduct the one-day seminar which forms the basis of the strategy of introducing TQM into a company on the back of SPC. So really it ought to be part of the text dealing with one of the victim's options – how to be a consultant – but it fits just as neatly here.

This is a *practical* approach. Anybody who wants to teach quality in his or her own company will find this of use. I have sold this day a thousand times. My clients have picked it up; to my knowledge there are many men and women who have used it as a starter to their own consultancy work, both within and without their parent companies. It uses the book *Right First Time* (please see Recommended reading) as its basic learning aid. Since its publication in 1984 this path-finding work of practical philosophy has been, and still is being, used by innumerable clients to improve their quality performance. Among them a Far Eastern steel company who bulk-bought 1,500 copies in one go to provide an educational blitz on its workforce; a household-name confectionary corporation who made it mandatory reading for all its managers worldwide; various universities in America and elsewhere; many business schools. It has been translated into other languages; had sections of its text photocopied tens of thousands of times . . . in a word, it has been of widespread use. It could be of use to you, too.

In some respects it flies in the face of conventional wisdom which says, among other things, that when you are launching into TQM don't expect any payback on your investment for at least two years. Two years! This has become a 'magic interval' in the conventional literature. I have met these magic intervals before; I used to run a shark-fishing operation at one time (more about this later in the book) and so I used to read the angling journals. Whenever they reported the capture of a shark they nearly always used the statement, 'after twenty minutes of play the fish was brought to the gaff'. Always the same 'twenty minutes'. The period seemed to have become a fixation with angling correspondents, or with sharks, so I became one as well, and reported the reality of what experience showed me. Likewise with the introduction of TQM into companies. Why the reporters' fixation with 'two years'? That's a hell of a long time to wait to recover the costs of a quality endeavour; and these costs are not unknown to be more than substantial sometimes.

Why wait two years? The world might spin off its axis and be hurled into ruin, or some mad despot might wreak havoc with a home-made nuclear bomb while you wait for your return. Two years is too long. Shall I tell you what will happen, as you spend your money and wait patiently for a bit of profit, for twenty-four months? I will tell you. *You will lose interest.*

Interest, not in the money-lender's sense, though you are certainly losing that as well while you keep funding an operation that is all promise and no payback. Interest in the sense that you will become bored into total apathy by the long wait. The entire initiative will slide to a stop, because it isn't showing itself worthy of the investment.

Ask yourself who benefits from this long wait. It certainly isn't you. If you are using one of the bigger consultancies they will expect you to sign a contract extending well into the future to 'indicate your long-term commitment' to the quality programme; and with it your long-term commitment to stumping up their fees. Fair enough. Business is business. But their promise of deferred gratification – the longer you wait the better it will be – lets them off the hook of having to produce any tangible, measurable results, in terms of money earned out of the programme. So you might find yourself having fun by joining the rain-dancing that TQM so easily degenerates into and at the same time losing sight of the original aim of making some money out of it.

From the moment an outside helper enters your premises his ambition should be to make himself redundant. Never mind about two years. The introduction and implementation of TQM doesn't take two years; it takes forever. So make it pay from the start.

The quickest payback in my experience was a lot less than the notional two years; it was two days.

This one-day seminar is geared to start making savings the day following. If anybody tells you it can't be done, tell them it has been done and is still being done. But no need to take my word for it; you can do it all for yourself. The culture change begins with you.

This strategy of using a one-day event to detonate change consists partly of the old-fashioned 'talk and chalk' style of teaching, so deplored by modern pundits, who stress that learning should be 'experiential'. Anyway, come to that, this day is of itself a learning experience. A mixture of the passive, when the pupils sit and listen; and the active, when they engage in participative pursuits. It assumes zero knowledge of statistics on the part of the participants.

The statistical basis of the seminar is stripped down to its fundamentals, reduced to a simplified system which works in practice in the real world of work. There is no arranging of data into convenient cell-groups – this was a trick we had to do before the advent of the pocket calculator, to boil down a mass of data into manageable form. Here and there people still teach that data should be grouped, because doing so 'knocks them into a normal curve'. It doesn't. The normality is intrinsic to the process. This obsolete method is now nothing more than confusing and redundant clutter. Remember, in the words of von Clausewitz, we are not teaching people to be sword-smiths; we are showing them how to use the sword.

Let's do it . . . .

Seize the day

The boss had agreed to devote an entire day to this seminar; he was there. With him were his three functional managers – quality, technical, production – the chief accountant, the purchasing manager and the woman named Karen accompanied by five of her colleagues from the shopfloor. Twelve in all.

Twelve is about as big a group as you can comfortably cope with. I have held this seminar for far larger groups from time to time but they tend to curdle into cliques. Twelve is better, and anyway, there is a sound Biblical precedent for keeping the team to no more than a dozen.

In some companies this mix of rank causes a bit of embarrassment, squirming discomfort even, and sheepish inhibition, but there are ways of breaking the ice. This group was easy with itself, the boss was an approachable person, held more in affection than in awe by his workforce. Even so, I started them with the ice-breaking warm-up exercise, as follows.

Communication – or talking to each other

This activity is taken from the training compendium *50 Activities for Unblocking Organizational Communication* by Dave Francis, published by Gower (see Recommended reading). This is Activity 30 from that compendium – 'The Yi calendar'. (It is reproduced in full in the Appendix.) The objectives of this exercise are:

● To study communication processes in problem solving.
● To develop skills in discriminating between relevant and irrelevant information.
● To develop skills in structuring information.

The Exercise Brief which I read out to them ran as follows:

The Yi people, who number nearly five million, live in South West China in the provinces of Sichuan, Guizhou and Yunnan. They used a unique calendar until recent times. The members of your group have been given certain true information and you are required to determine the number of months in a Yi year. You may share the information you have been given orally, but may not show your cards to anyone else.

Listed in the exercise are thirty statements about the Yi people and their calendar, such as 'All the Yi months are the same length', 'The Yi year is the same length as the Gregorian year.'
Before the seminar each of these thirty statements was printed on a postcard. One statement per card. Total of thirty cards per pack covering all thirty statements. I had four packs, on different coloured cards.
A pack of thirty cards is dealt to the team, just like you would deal out a hand of playing cards. Because thirty cards is too small a number to make a game with twelve people, I asked the pupils to divide themselves into two teams.

They did. Six managers in one team, six of the workforce in the other.

'Do you want to mingle a bit?' I invited them, 'As you are it's six of them versus six of us.'

'Six women playing six men,' Karen cut in, 'Leave it that way, eh?' Why not?

So the blue postcards were dealt out to the six men – they got five of each, of course – the white cards to the women. Same information on both sets of cards. They were reminded that they could only exchange information by talking to each other; they were not allowed to table their cards face-up; they could otherwise tackle the exercise by whatever method took their fancy.

The managers promptly arranged their chairs around a flipchart, appointed a scribe and began talking.

The women went into a huddle.

I lit a cigarette and sat back to enjoy the goings-on. The cigarette serves an extra purpose. If a team fails to produce the answer – how many months in the Yi year – by the time I've smoked down to the filter then we have here a real problem in communication.

One of the managers asked if it was OK to use a calculator. I said yes, noticing that they were constructing an intricate decision-tree on the flipchart in various colours, with its alternating yes and no routes.

The cigarette still had over an inch of white paper unburnt when Karen wagged a finger towards me and hooked me into the huddle, which by now had stopped its mumbling. She whispered a number into my ear. It was correct.

One of the managers noticed. 'Has she got it?' he enquired.

'Not by herself,' I reminded him, 'She and the team have arrived at the correct answer, though.'

The men's team had been fairly noisy compared with the women's. I had been listening to them shouting false clues at each other; now one bawled out, 'I've got it, it's . . .' and he shouted a number. It was wrong. The women jeered. Then another managerial voice announced with conviction and relief that they had now worked it out, the number of months in the Yi calendar is . . . and he stated the correct number. I stubbed out the fag.

This is an exercise that has never let me down. It has never failed to reveal useful information about individual and team behaviour. As you sit and watch and listen you begin to appreciate how deeply habits of communication and miscommunication are ingrained. How personality traits dominate actions, sometimes even to the disadvantage of the group. After all, the company is at times an arena of gladiatorial egos, diverse, powerful, interesting, bullying, self-interested. All useful material to the would-be change agent.

This episode serves to remind us that any manager who is about to expose himself to the ego-threat of being 'beaten' by those of lesser rank must first of all have a strong self-image. He must even have the courage, as Winston Churchill said, to be prepared to make a fool of himself. This is the humility of true strength, not the easily broken brittleness of mere vanity.

One of the managers collared me at coffee break and took me to one side, complaining that he felt it was a bit thick, being asked to play games in front of the workers.

'You shouldn't have asked if you could use the calculator, Joe,' was my unsympathetic response.

With the ice broken and the channels of communication opened up we could get on with the real business of the day – teaching statistical method to the non-numerate. How do you get such potentially boring information across the educational divide? You build a bridge. What do you build the bridge out of? Humour and fairy-tale, cobwebs of immense strength.

Your purpose is to implant the *concept* of the normal distribution into the listeners' minds. Embed it deeply, until they become so familiar with it they feel an easy confidence in using it. Strip it of its regal majesty. Drive out the fear of mathematics.

The normal distribution has other names: it is also called the normal curve, the bell-shaped curve, the Gaussian curve or distribution (named after Johann Karl Friedrich Gauss, pronounced "gowce", German mathematician, 1777–1855, whose name is also commemorated as the unit of magnetic force).

To make certain that this *vital* concept is driven home you do what actors are taught to do: first you tell them you are going to tell them, then you tell them; then you tell them you told them. So this is how I get the message across, and I offer it to you, in the sincere hope it may be of good use to you. This is the three-step sequence in action. Starting with a fairy story.

Step 1: Tell them you are going to tell them

In the year 1917 the Americans decided to join in the war which raged across Europe between 1914 and 1918. They agreed to send their legions of soldiers to help the British and French forces overcome their German enemy.

Apparently until this date American soldiers had never been supplied with metal helmets. Realizing that this war was a battle of machines, with bits of hot metal shrapnel flying murderously about over the battlefield, the American top brass decided that their men must be issued with tin hats. So the government set about issuing contracts to metal-bashing companies to manufacture several million helmets. But first they had to answer *one* question: 'How big are the heads of our servicemen?'

It was vital to get the answer to this question right, lest soldiers should be issued with over-large headgear, which would lend them the aspect of metallic mushrooms, growing in the trenches; or undersized tin hats that perched perilously on top of their scalps, affording no protection.

Now if you or I wished to know the size of human heads we would do the commonsense thing: go to a hat-maker, and say, 'Mr Feynmann, you supply hats to the men of America: stetsons, trilbies, boaters, homburgs. How big are their heads? And he would have told us. Governments don't do things this way.

The American government appointed a man called Walter Shewhart, an engineer and mathematician, asking *him* to find an answer to their question.

Mr Shewhart knew that it would be utterly impossible to measure the head size of *every* soldier, yet every soldier had to be fitted with a comfortable helmet. How was he to find the answer?

He also knew about Karl Gauss. Knew that Gauss's mathematics on the normal curve had been gathering dust for over a century. Knew that this held the secret to his answer.

So, using the idea of the normal curve, he took a random sample of a few hundred soldiers, measured their head sizes, wrote down the numbers, analysed them and came up with the answer. How? Like this . . . .

You might think that this is just a silly story, and you might be right. But it does its job. So please listen to the rest of it.

You must be standing at the flipchart to tell this tale, so you continue your story:

> I want you to imagine that when Shewhart measured the heads of the men in this sample, he cut them off. Then according to the size of the heads, he skewered them through the earholes on to a series of metal rods arranged horizontally a bit like an abacus.

At this point you execute a swift sketch onto the flipchart. You draw to the left a vertical post, and from it extending to the right a series of equally spaced horizontal lines, about eight or nine, saying . . .

> These are the rods on which Shewhart will arrange the heads according to what size each of them happens to be. Like this, all heads of size 7 go on to this rod, $6\frac{7}{8}$ on to the one below, $7\frac{1}{2}$ way up here, 7 again back on the rod for that size. And so on.

So you build up an assembly of about fifteen to twenty 'heads', drawn simply as circular faces as if drawn by a child. If you fancy yourself as a bit of an artist, as I do, you can stick a pair of eyes, or a nose or a few buck-teeth on to the 'heads', to liven them up and to indicate they are all looking this way.

When you are putting the 'heads' on to the rods you cheat. You create a centrally clustering display. Most of them you stick on to the size 7 rod, then the higher and the lower you go from this the fewer you put in. You are cheating in a good cause. Soon you will no longer need to cheat, but for the time being you must carry on.

Let us suppose that you stick a sample of twenty-six 'heads' on to the grid, like so:

Size 8	=	1
$7\frac{3}{4}$	=	2
$7\frac{1}{2}$	=	1
$7\frac{1}{4}$	=	4
7	=	8

$$6\tfrac{3}{4} \;\; = \;\; 3$$
$$6\tfrac{1}{2} \;\; = \;\; 5$$
$$6\tfrac{1}{4} \;\; = \;\; 1$$
$$6 \;\;\;\; = \;\; 1$$

You say to your pupils:

Notice how most of the heads happen to be size 7. Notice also that the bigger you go the fewer there are, and the smaller you go the fewer there are. Notice further that the biggest head that Shewhart found in his sample was size 8, and the smallest size 6.

Do you think Shewhart told the government he had got the answer to their question 'how big are soldiers' heads?' yet? Passed on this information? No, he did not. Because he knew that his sample results were not yet *information*; they were still raw *data*. To turn data into information you must *analyse* it. And it's easy.

Shewhart knew about Karl Gauss, and his mathematics. So he took the knowledge, dusted it off and used it. He knew that the biggest size in his sample, size 8, was not the biggest head in the population. Somewhere out there was a man of the sort scientists call 'dolichocephalic' with a head as long as a stallion's. And at the other extreme a man with a head smaller than the size 6 in his sample, a 'brachycephalic' with a skull like a cannon-ball. But *how* big was the biggest, and *how* small the smallest? Gauss could tell him. But we will do it this way. I want you to imagine that Shewhart measured *every* head in the US Army. Cut them all off. Stuck them all on to his abacus, like so.

You must move into a frenzy of inscribing heads on to the chart. Stacking plenty around the size 7 but making sure you place one at size $8\tfrac{1}{2}$ and another at size $5\tfrac{1}{2}$. You build them into a symmetrical array, a bell-shaped curve characteristic of the normal distribution. You are still cheating, remember. In a good cause. Next you tell them:

Imagine now that Shewhart took a huge hosepipe, and draped it around this distribution of heads on the extreme right of the abacus, so that it touched the left temples of all the outermost heads. Like this.

And you take a thick felt-tip pen of vivid colour, and with a triumphant flourish you draw in a most beautiful smooth curve – the Gaussian distribution.

You remind them that Shewhart did it a different way; he got the same *information* from the *data* provided by his very small sample. By analysis. He used the Gaussian normal curve to PREDICT the existence of head sizes bigger than and smaller than those in his sample.

I am telling you all this so that you can pass it on to your people. If you want them to *understand* SPC instead of mindlessly spotting dots on to charts, or feeding crap into computers and getting pretty crap out.

Is this story of Shewhart's heads true? No, of course it isn't; I made it up. A convenient fairy story to make the first step in a three-step operation to drive in the idea of statistical distribution.

For all I know you might think yourself too high and mighty for this sort of childish nonsense; fair enough, sorry if I've patronized you. But I will tell you this: there are thousands of people in Britain and in other countries, and in India to my certain knowledge, who have benefited from this childlike approach. Please, do not knock it; just count yourself lucky that you are not as educationally deprived as many of our workers are.

You have now completed Step 1, 'Tell them you are going to tell them'. Now to Step 2.

Step 2: Tell them you are telling them

You are about to do much the same as you did with the fable of Shewhart's heads, only this time it's no fairy tale; it's for real.

Ask your pupils how tall they think the men of this town (city, area, county) are. How tall is the tallest and how short is the shortest, do they reckon? Ask them if they believe it possible to answer this question, not by measuring *every* man in the area, but by using the heights of the few gathered together here into a *sample*.

Tell them you will predict these values from this sample of 'us' here, and that you are so confident of getting it right, because you know the power of Gaussian predictive capability, that you will write the answers on a piece of paper right now and seal them in an envelope. On the paper you write 'Shortest = 5 ft 1 ins, average height = 5 ft 9 ins, tallest = 6 ft 5 ins', and you don't open it until the end of the exercise, when you compare it with what you get from the sample you are about to analyse.

There is some risk in this; you are taking a gamble. If your party includes some lanky young man built like a giraffe, or a dumpy bloke with bandy legs, this could skew your statistical predictions. These oddballs could make you go wrong. If they do you just turn it to advantage by making some kind of learning point out of it. Anyway, does it really matter if you make yourself look a bit of an idiot now and again? No. Relax, take it easy. Have fun. Now you can open the envelope, and read aloud the values you wrote on the paper you sealed in it.

Step 3: Tell them you have told them

This is a reinforcement phase. You can, if you feel generous, tell them (your pupils) that since they have looked at variation in the head sizes of men, and the heights of men, you will now regale them with a naughty story about the variation of . . . yes, you guessed it, willies' tale. It's up to you. This is only a way of giving them a breather before the third driving in of the message of the Gaussian curve.

A couple of ways of doing this come to mind. You can buy sets of plastic rods, similar in size to drinking straws. They are produced to known population variation parameters. I used a box of 250 whose lengths had an average of 6.2 ins and a standard deviation of 0.2 ins. You can use these to do a 'machine capability survey' followed by a 'process control' operation.

I used boxes of other rod populations, averaging 6.0 ins, 6.4 ins and 6.6 ins, so as to be able to ring the changes in a simulation of a process running in and out of control.

That is that, then, the three-step hammering in of the normal curve, basis of SPC, cornerstone of TQM.

'As somebody who struggled with statistics at university,' chipped in one of the managers, 'I was fascinated to see how you would teach it. For the first time in my life I begin to understand it.'

That was pleasing to hear, but I thought I'd better issue a caveat that access to statistical method did not afford us entry to a world of absolute truth. For instance, if we have a batch of, say, ten thousand rods, and we ask ourselves what is the average length of *all* ten thousand, then to find out we would have to measure *all* of them. However, we could state the average length of all rods as being the average length of a sample of rods, plus and minus calculable limits of error. We could be *near enough*; for all practical purposes we could be as good as spot-on.

'You are demeaning the work of quality,' was Joe's verdict, 'You make it look as if anybody could do it.' He was, of course, right.

'Machine capability surveys are part of my department's functions,' the technical man protested. 'I wonder what we will be doing once *they* (pointing to the women) are doing them.'

'Yes,' the boss agreed mildly, 'I've been wondering about that as well.' I hadn't.

So we filled the rest of the day with more work, which you know – as Parkinson, was it?, told us – always expands to fill the time available. This was meaningful work. We sent somebody out to bring in a box of the output of a machine.

'Let's survey the capability of this machine,' I suggested. 'How many items of output shall we take as a sample from which to deduce the capability of this machine to cut rods to the correct length?' Many numbers were put forward; we settled on a sample size of twenty-five.

'Why twenty-five?' somebody wanted to know.

'Because its square root is five, and that's handy for doing necessary arithmetic later on, and because if you take more, what you gain in precision by taking a bigger sample costs you a disproportionate amount of inspection effort. Let's work smart, not hard.'

'I don't know why you're bothering with all this lot here,' contributed the production man, 'This is output from my best machine; it's a waste of time, this is.'

'Never mind, let's do it anyway; see what your best output looks like,' I suggested.

'What for?' He was becoming quite indignant, 'There's nothing wrong with it, if you don't believe me ask quality; they know.'

'We're not implying there is anything wrong with it,' I explained courteously, 'It's just that we need the output of a machine as *training material*, and this is as good as any. What is your objection?'

'If you must know, I object to being *in* here. Talking about heads and tails. I've got work to do, I have – *real* work – out there. Leave quality to quality, that's what I say. Let me get on with production.' It was a truly heartfelt plea.

'Aw, shut up moaning, I'm enjoying this. Let's get on with it,' interjected one of the women, the one with black eye make-up; I believe it's called the Boris Karloff look.

'Yes, let us get on with it. I am enjoying it as well, thank you Doris,' the boss brought the issue to a conclusion.

The team did all the measuring, the recording, the analysis using pocket calculators and then had to ponder the action. The machine was found to be incapable of producing output to the specified tolerance. What now?

The production man, even though he had been sitting in the quiet of a seminar room all day, had contrived to achieve his customary dishevelled look. Tie pulled loose and askew, shirt neck unbuttoned, smock speckled with dirt, hair wild, eyes ditto – the aspect which says to the world, 'Look how *busy* I am!'

'What do you mean?' he challenged, 'Not capable! That's the machine we use to make the stuff for our major customer. We control the quality of it with the computer. Don't we, Joe?'

'Even so, according to what we've just found out there's a lot of output outside specification, according to our sample.' Karen made her contribution, she was learning fast, 'Unless we're idiots,' she added provocatively.

'I'm not an idiot,' claimed Doris Karloff, and I had no wish to doubt her. 'Neither is any one of us. That output is wrong.'

I thought it time to quantify the claim. 'She's right; there's anything between 3 and 10 per cent of rods oversize. You are giving metal away, free, to the customer.' To recover this free gift would fund the quality initiative for a month or two, it occurred to me.

'I think it's better to use these paper charts that we put our own spots on,' it was Karen again. 'They tell you what's happening *while* it's happening; they should give us time to do something about it. Better than that bloody computer.'

'From now on we no longer use the computer,' decreed the boss. 'We no longer send nonsense charts to a customer who clearly can never have looked at them.'

'We'll do it ourselves,' said the women.

(And of the best leaders, men say 'we did it ourselves', according to the old Chinese sage; the boss was being a 'best' leader.)

'If you do that,' it was Joe the quality, about to lay down the divine law, 'if you have these girls doing their own quality like you've just said, then you will be in contravention of BS5750.' He said it in a kind of 'repent ye sinners lest fire and brimstone shall consume ye' tone of voice, slightly hysterical.

On that apocalyptic note the seminar ended, the managers went back to managing, and the team of women grasped their new 'empowerment'. (The word really means 'delegated authority', but don't tell anybody.)

What's so special about giving power to a group of workers, women workers? Is it an attempt to redress a history of over a thousand years of patriarchal injustice, inflicted by men on women? Is it a sop to feminism, something the wimpish 'New Age men' might do, pandering to women so as to win their approval for that most ancient of reasons – getting a leg over? Is it to move in the wind of sociological fashion?

It is none of these things. It is a lot simpler than any of them. *It is no more than a way of inviting a work team to do more work.* Whether the team is male, female or hermaphroditic makes no difference.

'No, no!' you will protest, 'It is *not* a way of inviting them to work harder. It has to do with job *enrichment, developing* the *full potential* of the individual.'

Of course it is; you are right. You are also wrong. Such benefits are *incidental* to the prime purpose of the movement, which, I repeat, is to get more work out of the workers. There is nothing wrong in this. But don't let us become starry-eyed with idealism; let us desist from occupying the moral uplands of do-goodery. Let us not congratulate ourselves that we are generously handing *power* to the workforce when we invite it to manage itself more than it has in the past; that we are somehow graciously relinquishing our managerial authority to our subordinates, stripping ourselves of our own power.

To the contrary, as managers, we are strengthening our power by sharing a little bit of it with the workers; reinforcing the grip our managerial *will* exerts upon their subordinate behaviour. The slave masters have hung up their whips and put away their Scriptures; they no longer bawl their orders, they give readings from manuals of industrial psychology instead. The slaves' shoulders no longer smart from the lash; the whip which drives them is now swinging within their skulls. There is still cane to be cut in the plantation, but now, thanks to legions of psychologists whose work is the contemplation of other people's work from a position of leisure, work is 'good for you', it is 'natural', it is 'good for the soul', it 'develops potential', it 'actualizes'. All the better to cut the cane with. To keep the slaves busy in their slave towns.

What *slave towns*?

They grew during the early years of the Industrial Revolution, terrace upon terrace of brick hutches accumulating around the old market towns, like barnacles clustering on a ship, or a fringe of shanties encircling a metropolis. They were built to be the barracks of the workforce, within easy walking distance of the factories, mills and mines. (Easy meaning anything up to five or six miles.) Within easier staggering distance of the pub, and plodding distance of the chapels of sectarian non-conformist religions thrown up with the terraces in inculcate docility, resignation and respectability to this new breed of people – the landless peasantry turned into the landless proletariat. Schools were included in the architectural plans, their purpose to break in the rebellious young, train them into habits of deference to authority, and educate them sufficiently in the rudiments of writing, reading and arithmetic as artisans, clerks, and in other menial positions.

Time itself, which had once been ordered by the dictates of agriculture into seasons; by the church into holy days; was now divided into shifts. Time, its passing hitherto proclaimed by the chiming of church clocks, was now marked by melancholy blasts on the factories' hooters, dolefully summoning the labourers to their toil. It was later to be thinly sliced into minutes and hundredths by Scientific Management.

Within the mills and factories discipline was enforced by overseers. Listen to the two following accounts of factory life.

Vignette: 'Hush, hush, whisper who dares'

No, unlike Christopher Robin, in the song of the little wimp, nobody is saying prayers. This is nothing so twee. Imagine a long tank about twenty feet by five feet by four feet deep. It contains a sour liquor, a mixture of acids. Ranged down each of the long sides of the tank are women. They are there to suspend metal components into the acid, in order to clean them of surface impurities before they are taken to be coated with vitreous enamel and baked in the furnace. One of the women, a newcomer, lifts her head from her work and makes a comment to her neighbour, who responds by looking alarmed and rolling her eyes wildly in the direction of the end of the tank. There stands the overseer. He wears a bowler hat, his crown of office. A collar and tie, his chain of respectability. He also wears an expression of implacable severity, after the manner of Robert Louis Stevenson's 'stern-faced priest', of a church of supposed *joy*. He is vigilant.

'*Keep . . . silent!*' he barks.

This little incident took place in 1921 in a factory in one of the slave towns. Unfortunately its owners drowned themselves in a sea of malt whisky just a little too early to take advantage of the manufacturing opportunity afforded by the outbreak of war in 1939. Their premises still endure, the chimney cold, the roof removed. The hooter now preserves a deathly silence.

But things have changed, you say, workers are not treated like that any more. No?

Visualize a large room filled with sewing machines: this is the garment industry; we are in a factory which makes underwear for famous-name High Street emporia, who enforce strict quality standards. At every machine sits a woman, head down. On one side of each woman stands a pile of semi-finished garments; she takes them one by one and speedily does something to them with her machine before adding them to the heap on the other side of her chair.

Our attention is caught by one who appears to be doing acrobatics in a sitting posture. As she goes through her work-cycle her shoulders rotate and her elbows gyrate in swooping motions; she rocks rhythmically from side to side. She has the aspect of someone practising peculiar swimming strokes at high speed. She is an 'elasticator', who is fitting the extensible thong which ensures that knickers are capable of staying up by supporting their own flimsy weight. When the bell rings, permitting her to leave her machine, she swims down the aisle with shoulders and elbows still rolling through compulsive muscular habit.

Or see another of the toiling women: her machine sews a different stitch which demands a different set of movements. To reduce the pile of work on her left-hand side by converting it into a pile on the right she has to adopt a different choreography. If the elasticator's dance is a ballet, this woman's is a march. She stamps the pedals of her machine alternately left, right, left . . . her head nods to the pace, her hands twitch to its timing. She is 'bar-tacker', whose job is to secure stitched seams to save them from being too readily pulled apart. When she leaves her machine she will stamp up the aisle nodding and twitching as she goes, like a shell-shocked soldier marching to a private drum.

The women keep their heads down, working. One of them dares to attempt a conversation, shouted to her neighbours over the subdued roaring of the machines and the frequent 'mooing' as some women accelerate their machines to full throttle to maximize bonus. This verbal act of rebellion stimulates a different sound, the urgent and resolute clip-clop of the steel-tipped heels of the supervisor's shoes as she quicksteps down the aisle. You can tell at a glance that she exercises authority. Her eye is diamond-bright with discipline through her fly-away spectacles; she is whiplash lean, like a gynandromorphic American lady executive, her voice so sharp a man could shave with it. She uses its cutting edge to scythe down disobedience. '*Keep . . . silent!*' She delivers an expert slash to the vocal cords.

This incident is not an example of the human relations class of 1921, though it probably went on just the same then; this was in 1994. In a slave town in industrial Britain.

Why have I bothered you with these little vignettes? There is a reason. It is to do with culture, and cultural inheritance. But before I explain myself further, let me ask you a question.

Do you prefer your statistical process control to be blatantly and proudly *statistical*? So that your charts are regarded with near-reverence and the compiling of them an exercise in the mysteries of higher mathematics? Some people do. They find the skeletal statistics on offer in this stripped-down system *too simple*; they don't find them impressive enough.

They're not supposed to be impressive. Just as an assassin's stiletto might have an impressively engraved blade but still do no better a job than the matt-black steel of a commando dagger, fancy statistics might be beautiful to behold, but will work no better than this minimalist version. You are not selling *control charts*. They are nothing more than tools. But, if your aesthetic sense demands embellishment then this approach is not for you.

It is for those who wish to control their processes, and products or services, in a simple and straightforward way. Furthermore, this is more than a 'tool', as a Swiss army knife is more than a device for sharpening pencils. This is a system which can be added to, built up into a more comprehensive quality function, for those who want it.

But back to what I said a couple of paragraphs ago, about our *cultural inheritance*. What is the most powerful gift that six generations of authoritarian management, of 'strict discipline', of '*Keep silent!*' have bequeathed to us? And how does it affect our efforts to implement total quality management? I will tell you . . .

The spinster's child

In his world-famous *Fourteen Points* Dr W. Edwards Deming makes Point Eight: 'Drive out fear; so that everyone may work effectively for the company.' He makes it as baldly as that! We all applaud this deeply humanistic injunction and each of us thinks he knows what Dr Deming really meant, and we interpret his words to suit ourselves. But this is what he actually said: drive out fear.

What a hope! What an idealistic and unreal hope. Fear is there, deeply embedded and endemic in our work (and social) organizations. But it's treated rather like the way we treat the spinster's idiot child howling in the vicarage attic: we all know it's there but we politely ignore its caterwauling, and converse of more genteel things, like motivation, enrichment, actualization. The idiot love-child keeps up its banshee wailing and head-banging spasms, and still we try to ignore it, but it *will not go away*.

This is the taboo subject, *fear*. Fear and its vicious twin, *bullying*. Sworn enemies of TQM.

People have tended not to speak about it; they just keep on eating the vicar's cucumber sandwiches, so to speak, and talk of trivial things whilst resolutely turning a deaf ear to the squawks and gurglings and thuds dimly to be heard coming from the soiled prison in the vicarage roof.

Of course it will not go away. It has been there for two hundred years or more, fattening on a diet of other people's self-esteem. It still stalks the corridors of our companies:

Headline – *Daily Post*, Monday, May 30, 1994

'More than half of UK workforce bullied.'

A survey carried out by Staffordshire University, questioning a sample of 1,137 people, found that 53 per cent had been bullied, and 78 per cent had seen bullying going on.

The only surprising thing about this is the fact that anybody should find it in the least bit surprising. How anything so widespread and so habitual as bullying could remain so long unremarked is itself quite remarkable; almost as if there has always been a tacit conspiracy of silence about it – the thing that dare not speak its name.

It is a topic which so far has received scant attention in management literature. In the torrent of management books roaring off the printing presses these days there is, as far as I know, only one which directly addresses the subject of fear and how to 'drive it out'. This is an American publication, product of the home of political correctness (PC), written by two authors who clearly are charming and well-mannered people whose prose style tends to be like American mustard – so bland you need to pile it on thick. Their book makes some eminently sensible observations, and suggests ways of dealing with fear. However, a search through the index revealed that three words, which I reckon are crucial to tackling the problem of fear in the company, were omitted. They are: bullying, courage, love.

What was that? I hear you ask, did he say *love*? Yes, a dirty word, is love. Just about the most besmirched word in our entire vocabulary, I shouldn't wonder. So let us talk about it, and about courage. Let us see if we can get the *measure* of its meaning . . . with another little story . . . .

Charly's tale

A few days ago I was sitting here at my desk, filling an A4 pad and an ash tray, when the 'phone rang. Any excuse to stop work; any excuse to break the silence of this life sentence in solitary confinement called writing. It was Charly.

He said he was a graduate of Cambridge University – Engineering I think – on secondment to a machinery manufacturer doing a project on total quality management. In order to complete his assignment, in the next two weeks, he was required by his boss to submit a report stating exactly where TQM stood now in the company, plus a plan to improve it by 100 per cent in the next two years. (Notice the magic interval again? Twenty minutes to gaff a shark, two years to capture TQM.) He said he had a problem. I agreed. He asked what should he say to his boss. I suggested sod off. He said he daren't; his boss was a stickler for measuring things, a man who demanded facts.

Facts. 'Give me facts,' said Gradgrind in Dickens's *Hard Times*, 'You there, girl number 34, what is a horse?'

'A horse is a quadruped', answered little Cissie, girl number 34, 'Sir'.

Gradgrind nodded approvingly, 'That is a fact.'

So I said give him some facts. Measure those things that can be measured – scrap rates, line rejects, customer returns, delivery delays – give those to your boss. Facts.

Charly said this would not do. The boss wanted a measure of total quality management.

I said tell him with my compliments that TQM is made of things that are beyond measure. Of courage, love, justice, beauty ... Concentrate on these, work at them, but don't waste your time trying to measure them.

I had been of no help to Charly. He rang off, and I went back to my lonely labours of turning dreams into words and money into smoke.

So ends Charly's tale. His boss wanted him to measure things. Do you like measuring things? OK, measure . . . l . . . o . . . v . . . e – love.

There are ways of measuring love, and they are all lies.

'I love you,' says the swain to his lass.

'How much do you love me?' she wants to know.

'A million billion miles,' is his barmy reply.

'Is that all?' She wants more.

What he really means is he fancies her, and she knows it. This is adolescent lust calling itself love; it is to be expected – it is play-time.

'I love you,' says the proud and possessive husband, 'therefore you will please me by doing as I ask.' This is love as an act of conquest, an army of occupation holding its garrison in the loved one's head, dominating, demanding submission. This is not love; it is psychic parasitism. It is despicable. It happens.

'If you really love me you will do so-and-so . . .' This is love as blackmail, the sale of approval, a kind of do-as-I-say-and-I'll-give-you-a-kiss game played by those whose self-esteem is so fragile they court the good opinion of their spouse and others. This is a state of arrested moral growth stuck on the 'need for social approval' level of the Maslovian needs hierarchy.

'But for my love for you I could have been a brain surgeon', or a ballet dancer, or a star of stage and screen, or any other fantasy object. This is the 'if only' form of higher moral blackmail. *If only* I hadn't met you, therefore you, and you alone, are the architect of my miserable life's misfortunes. It's all *your* fault.

'Do that and I won't love you any more' – another variant of the approval-for-sale game, generally used by timid mothers to quell rebellious brats.

'I am your mother. I brought you into the world and I love you, my only son. If you love me you will not get married to that hussy. You will look after your poor old mother.' This is mother love, sometimes the most pernicious love of them all. She idolizes her boy, which is to say she turns him from a human being into an object of veneration, the poor lad. Makes him into a moral Peter Pan of permanent dependence. This is mother as the gelding goddess, murder of the soul masquerading as mother love. There is a lot of it about.

These examples of love have nothing to do with love; they are transactions in guilt. Instruments of control exercised by one person on another, of judging people and finding them wanting and using it against them.

Love does not judge; it accepts. Love makes no demands on the loved one; it invites.

We are not speaking here of this abused little word in its

modern tarnished form. We are using it more in one of its Ancient Greek forms; I am told that they had seven different words for it where we have only the one. Perhaps their term *agape* – the love of brother for brother, brother for sister, sister for sister – is the most appropriate one for our discussion of love – or its absence – in the workplace. Because love and the lack of it form a key factor in bullying, which is a generator of fear; and fear is the adversary of TQM.

'Drive out fear!' said Dr Deming, as if fear were some evil demon of possession dwelling in our minds. It is, of course, but how is it to be exorcized? With whips? More fear? To be driven out by an even greater fear? Hardly; such a cure clearly would be worse than the disease. How then? With love?

Let us surmise that the bully is a bully because he feels unloved. It is my experience, of the many bullies I have known, that the bully hates himself. With no love of self there can be none to extend to others. Oh sure, bullies are able to feel *pleased* with themselves, but that is not love; that is vanity, self-approval. Love neither approves nor disapproves, it accepts without judgement. Approval of self is to do with the vanity of the *ego*.

The ego is that identity you made for yourself, with your own approval, out of the raw material of experience as you went along. A bit like the scarab beetle gathers dung unto itself. This monument to yourself which you built for yourself is a construction of vanity and greed, cracked with guilt. This is the thing you transcend when you finally choose to accept yourself.

I see I have once again all too readily drifted into the misty seas of mysticism. Time to get back to work. Before we go please permit me one more act of indulgence. Allow me to offer you just two words of what I believe to be wisdom:

Accept yourself.

Stop criticizing yourself, stop moaning. Stop playing 'if-only'. Stop playing 'but for you'. Stop regretting. Trust tomorrow. Cultivate courage.

Courage. As I seem to recall having said before – but it will bear saying again – where there is no fear there is no need of courage.

Fear is there. Fear is here. Fear is just about everywhere. It always has been, and while there are people who feel themselves to be unloved because they have chosen to deny their own love of themselves to themselves, there will be bullies. Such people will always find some way to bully others. They might seize the easy, almost accidental, opportunity to wield authority by becoming parents. Not wishing to spoil the child they do not spare the rod. Tormented themselves, they torment their offspring. This is tragic; this is true. Whenever a child is mutilated or murdered who are the first people the police – in their vast and sad experience – turn to with eyes of suspicion? The parents.

If the self-loathing bully finds no outlet, or insufficient outlet, in the sacred grove of parenthood, he seeks the authority bestowed by being promoted at work. Then he can shout and bawl at people. Try to make them as afraid as he is. Try to transfer his aching burden of self-loathing and fear on to the backs of his subordinates. Such a little droplet of unrequited love can grow into an outpouring of hatred, of bullying.

Bullying is psychological rape.

Bulling is the perverted use of power.

But fear is everywhere. How is it to be driven out? Not by a legion of Demings and his disciples. Yes, he meant well; we applaud his noble sentiment. Seeing that he forebore to tell us how to do it we must work it out for ourselves.

How do we drive out fear? Consider . . .

The boundaries of a tyrant's authority are *never* drawn by the tyrant. He will press continuously to extend them ever further. The limits of a tyrant's authority are *always* set by the tyrannized. When they have had enough of it.

How do they do that? By calling meetings to discuss the nature of fear? By conducting attitude surveys of guaranteed confidentiality and anonymity to find out who is bullying whom? By being meek? Let me give you a clue; let me tell you another story. An autobiographical one.

Vignette: 'Don't you *dare* shout at *me*!'

I am an expert practitioner of the art of shouting. As a youth in the service of an imperial power I was trained by professional shouters, the Chief Gunnery Instructors of Whale Island, the Royal Navy establishment HMS *Excellent*, in Portsmouth. I practised, under their tuition, in echoing drill sheds on dusty parade grounds, hollering drill orders from one side of a vast emptiness to a squad of men diminished by distance at the other. They called it 'developing power of command'. They were the direct descendants, professionally speaking, of Stentor the Greek warrior of the Trojan wars, whose voice was 'as powerful as the voice of fifty other men'. They instructed me to 'bring the voice up from the belly', to employ the diaphragm to expel air from the chest in a thunderous roar. The pressure of wind within you pushes your eyeballs forward in their sockets, inflames your cheeks, bloats your temples, but by God, you have learned how to make yourself heard. After that they sent us abroad to bellow at the 'lesser breeds'.

When they let me out and I got a job in civvy street I thought I had done with shouting. So when I found myself being *shouted at*, by a boss who had been denied the learning opportunity afforded to me, but had tried hard to teach himself, being *humiliated* by this hectoring oaf in front of a roomful of witnesses to my dressing down my training took over and I involuntarily shouted back.

He had risen to his feet to deliver his outburst. As a Stentor he was clearly nothing more than an enthusiastic amateur. To save him embarrassment I cut into his tirade; I leapt to my feet, stood to attention with my thumbs down the seams of my trousers, raised my chin truculently and roared, 'Don't you *dare* shout at *me*!'

It worked. There was a stunned silence, like the one you get the instant after an aeroplane crash or a motor vehicle collision. Then he sat down. We continued the meeting in the normal tone of voice. The ghosts of those gunners who were my mentors must have applauded their pupil's fine performance.

Nobody ever shouted at me again. The boundaries of one would-be tyrant's despotism had been marked by one he had tried to tyrannize.

How do you drive out fear? You do it for yourself, by yourself. It can be a dangerous and a lonely game. Don't expect to make friends by doing it; if you are courageous enough to shake off the tyrant's yoke don't expect your colleagues, who still chafe under its weight, to praise and admire you. Far from it; they will more

than likely be deeply envious and resentful. Why? Because your
self-liberation will only further remind them of their position of
abject servitude and their gutless acquiescence to it. Do you think
the slaves still shuffling in the chain gang will feel affection for
one of their fellow prisoners who has had the nerve and the luck to
shake off his manacles, to manumit himself from bondage? Your
friends would rather see you fail, laugh at your struggle to be free
of the tyrant, gloat if your efforts lead in the beginning to humiliation and punishment. Once you have broken away from the bonds
which still bind them, they will curse the memory of you. Either
that, or mythologize it into one of the factory fairy tales, as the
Golden Prince on the White Horse.

Whatever you do, once you are free, do not attempt to free
those you left behind in bondage. Why not? Because they *love*
their shackles. They *adore* the tyrant. They *relish* the taste of the
lash. They make a virtue out of their necessity.

Have you not noticed this deep strand of masochism that runs
through the character of Western civilization, a Germanic need to
be disciplined? To be dominated by higher authority? What else
do you think is the psychological mechanism by which humour-
less authoritarians find themselves elected to the highest office of
the state?

You speak of the need for change; of introducing a more open
style of management in our businesses, but do you *really* want it?
Are you *fit* for it? If somebody hands you your 'freedom', will you
know what to do with it? . . . Are you sure?

Have you ever been present in an organization as it is taken, by
change agents, through the exciting, exhilarating trauma of transformation from a closed authoritarian managerial climate, dominated by the disturbed personality of a dedicated autocrat, into a
more democratic open style of management culture? What would
you expect the principal sentiments, that you might hear
expressed after the upheaval, to be? Delight? Gladness that the
tyrant has at last been deposed? I shall tell you what you would
hear, as I heard it.

'Aha,' shaking their heads as if expressing regret at the passing
of mortal man's years. 'You can say what you like about old Jack,
he was a proper bastard, but at least you knew where you stood
with him.'

The old Jack they were referring to is, of course, the toppled tyrant. They *miss him*. He brought *order* into their lives. He brought *meaning* to their miserable existences. These are slaves you are listening to here, *born* slaves who by some act of insane self-delusion actually believe themselves to be 'free'. Because a slave owner has told them so.

Their natural home is in the cluster of hovels huddling in the shadow of the castle walls. They swear fealty to the overlord, in return for his protection. They offer the bended knee in exchange for being 'looked after'.

Are you still sure you want to introduce the benefits of TQM into companies in order to do all those goody-goody things it tells you about in the management books? All that 'actualizing potential', 'individual empowerment', 'teambuilding' stuff? Do you still believe your greatest talent to be the liberating of the talents of others? Hoping to make the world of work into a better place? Trying to build a New Jerusalem in those dark Satanic mills? Struggling to depose tyranny and enthrone fair play? Justice?

I sincerely hope so!

But don't expect the acclamations of a grateful multitude. Don't anticipate having honours heaped upon your worthy shoulders. Dream not of being laden with riches as your reward. Your work, like virtue, will be its own reward; and *it will be enough*.

You can take heart from history. To strengthen your sense of purpose listen to the words of Horace. Horace who?

Quintus Horatius Flaccus Horace, Roman poet and satirist. Son of a manumitted slave (a manumitted slave is 'sent forth from his master's hand', released from his bond), from whom he inherited a small estate which he forfeited through joining the wrong side during a civil war. Reduced to poverty he was driven to writing verses. I know the feeling well. He expounded the 'philosophy of the market place'.

This market philosophy is singularly appropriate to our free-market economics of today. Let us take one of the quotations of this most quoted of Roman sages, to see if it might be of use to us:

> The man who is tenacious of purpose in a rightful cause is not shaken from his firm resolve by the frenzy of his fellow citizens clamouring for what is wrong, or by the tyrant's threatening face.

'. . . rightful cause' – encouraging the personal growth of those whose talents are oppressed by antiquated management systems.

'frenzy . . . for what is wrong' – those who oppose change and seek to perpetuate the status quo because they are its current beneficiaries.

'. . . the tyrant's threatening face' – anyone in authority who is hostile to your idealistic endeavour.

'. . . tenacious of purpose . . .' – stick at it!

'. . . firm resolve . . .' – your determination, fired by your *anger* at seeing power abused, to bring a measure of justice into the oligarchy of work.

Oligarchy? Perhaps it would be best to expand upon this little theme of rulership. We live in a democracy; it may not be the best way to run a country, but so far nobody has found a better one. We work in an oligarchy. The moment we leave democracy – where the rulers are ultimately answerable to the ruled, to the electorate – and step through the factory gate or the office door we enter an oligarchy. This term means 'rule by the few'. Our rulers are no longer answerable to us, the ruled; they are answerable only upwards, to higher rulers. This is a power structure riddled with the opportunity for the abuse of authority. Wherever there is opportunity there are opportunists. Remember the Prussian paradigm of stupid–clever–lazy–industrious? Who is impelled for one reason or another to get promoted? The hard-working, because our collective belief mindlessly applauds 'hard work'. How is 'cleverness' seen in our conventional wisdom? As undesirable. In consequence guess who gets into positions of authority more than most people – you've got it, the stupid who work hard. After that the turds and the nerds are in command.

The Prussian officer-cadet selectors were right in their assessment of the stupid hard workers; they threw them out. We promote them into positions of power.

There they wreak havoc! They bully. They terrorize. They lay waste. They kill.

But again we can turn to the words of Horace for consolation:

'Brute force without wisdom falls by its own weight.'

The stupid–industrious are without wisdom. But they are not without animal cunning. Left to fall under their own weight and they might stand for too long. They have to be given a push. This is one of the things that change-agents are for.

I have the uneasy feeling that a phrase I used a few paragraphs ago might have caused you to raise an eyebrow in disbelief. That bit where I spoke of tyrants who '. . . wreak havoc . . . kill'. Kill? A bit over the top, you perhaps think. Let me give you a few examples from memory.

A manager was summoned to a meeting of the entire management team – his colleagues – to be introduced to the man newly appointed to replace him. This was the first intimation he had had that his job was at risk; from now on he was an assistant to the new man. *Fait accompli.* Public humiliation. How do you think his colleagues responded to this? They hailed their newest colleague, and turned cold towards their superseded friend. He was now down in rank, one layer lower than they were in the hierarchy. He might have been turned into a leper by the way they treated him. So he became unclean. He went sick. Developed cancer. His hair fell out. He died.

Here's another one.

A sales manager had enjoyed a long and easy relationship with his operations director, who was suddenly sacked. His replacement, from within the organization, was an infamous bully who took sadistic delight in tormenting his subordinates. The salesman, who had been capturing business by fixing selling prices so low it was impossible to make the business pay, went into paroxysms of work. He spent nights wrestling with the complexities of pricing calculations, spinning in giddy circles on his computer, hyperactive to the point of incoherent hysteria. The more he worked the harder the new director chivvied him. In a state of near-permanent shock his complexion bleached to a ghastly pallor, his lips purpled, his features bloated. The life went out of him, his *post mortem* said it was heart failure.

That's enough of these depressing tales of the things men can do to other men, and get away with. These are mere anecdotes; they 'prove' nothing.

Belief

So here is a piece of scientific research, some non-anecdotal *facts* from which you might be able to 'prove' something. Let us find out. I quote from the research paper since it is now in the public domain; it is to do with the connection (if any) between *belief* and *disease*. This is sound medical research in a paraphrased version:

Would you believe it?

The study of drug use and abuse has become an industry in itself. It has produced some interesting findings. For example, there is a research report which looks into the effects of *belief* among those people taking certain drugs. A sample group of users was asked whether they believed that using the drug would give rise to fatal disease as a consequence. About a quarter of the people in the sample said they believed that there would be no ill-effect from taking it. Three-quarters of them said they thought it would lead eventually to illness and early death, but intended to keep on using it anyway.

This sub-group was asked if they believed it harmful as a result of their own experience, or because conventional medical wisdom and media opinion said so.

After a lapse of a dozen or so years the death rates of the three sub-groups were compared.

Three-quarters of those in the first sub-group, who believed the drug would have no long-term effects, had survived.

In the second sub-group, those who from their own experience thought the drug *might* cause fatal illness, nearly seven out of ten had survived.

Of those in the third sub-group, however, who based their beliefs about the dangers of the drug on medical opinion and media information, only one in ten survived.

These are significantly different proportions of survivors among the three sub-groups.

These results suggest, and the evidence points to it, that *fear*, the *belief* that the drugs will have fatal consequences, is a more powerful killer than the drug itself.

What we are actually talking about here, both in my two little tales of death and in the account of the drug research is *voodoo*.
Voodoo? Yes. The power of the mind to kill. The venomous thought which poisons its thinker. The *fear* which murders its victim from within. Surely you didn't think that voodoo is something confined to the Caribbean islands, superstitious nonsense about Zombies and the un-dead. The thing which killed the most patients in the research study was the *belief* that the drug was a killer and the *fear* that it would kill them. It was *not* the effects of the drug itself.

Do you *believe* in the validity of this research? Do you agree with its implications that fear is a more potent killer than the drug in question – that the evidence points to this conclusion? *Proves* it?

The report makes a further interesting observation which backs up this contention: about 98 per cent of psychiatric patients take this drug, yet it has been established that schizophrenics suffer less drug-related disease than the general population (of drug users). Presumably these patients are immune or indifferent to general opinion about the alleged effects of the drug.

The drug, it seems, is quite innocuous compared with the fear of some of those taking it. Fear, however, is clearly very bad for you; so bad that you can die of it. There should be a government health warning about it.

So why don't you relax, and fearlessly smoke a cigarette, for that – as you probably guessed – is the 'drug' – tobacco – which is the subject of this research report.

If you happen to be a dedicated non-smoker you probably believed the validity of the findings of the report until I mentioned smoking. Now you might think I tricked you into drawing a false conclusion. I did not. If this is the case, you tricked yourself. If you now deny the validity of the research and its inescapable consequences it is because it conflicts with your deeply held beliefs – your prejudices no less, and all the anti-smoking propaganda we are daily bombarded with. You usually demand 'scientific objectivity'; that is what you got here. Its evidence still stands and points to a conclusion which some people might find disagreeable for no other reason than the fact that it is at variance with their opinions, with their beliefs. Such is the power of belief: it is able to distort reality. Even worse, it is able to create its own reality. You can live by it or die by it.

Anybody who has ambitions to change the way organizations behave – or rather, the way in which the *people* in organizations behave – is advised to take a long and deep look into this phenomenon known as 'belief'. Because this is the only place where lasting behavioural change can be brought about. To alter behaviour you must first alter the belief which underlies it, because we all act–behave as if what we believe to be true is really true. We have our own beliefs, from which we build our town 'truths' which thereafter condition our attitudes and behaviour. Let us take a few perspectives on the nature of this thing called belief.

Belief: how it is used

It is in the nature of mankind to 'explain' things. All things. Things as diverse as the question 'why are we on this planet at all?' to 'why do bubbles form on the inside surface of a glass of beer?' via 'why is an arrow-poison frog coloured black and yellow?' and a million other phenomena we feel the need to 'explain'.

The test of any 'explanation' is how well it fits in with the opinions of the person 'explaining' it. If it is congruent with his existing framework of knowledge then it is a 'correct' explanation. Consider some examples, some apparently trivial; others not so.

Belief: a lot of horse

A few miles from where I live there is a tract of pastureland which used to be locally famous as a mushroom field, until the farmer discovered chemicals. This ancient field had never felt the plough; it had lain undisturbed from time immemorial. In due season it yielded massive crops of mushrooms, so prolific that the fungi seemed to jump out of the turf as if by magic on a humid summer morning.

This field was part of a stud farm, where the farmer bred shire horses. To assist him in this endeavour he kept a stallion, to delight his brood mares, eschewing the new-fangled fleshless tinkerings of artificial inseminations. Stallions are not to be messed with; any sensible person steers well clear of any large animal which is 'entire' and therefore likely to be touchy with testosterone, especially avoiding the vicinity of its rear end if it happens to be a gigantic horse. Only an idiot would risk closeness to such an unpredictable creature.

So that is what the farmer employed to tend to his stallion – a village idiot. This was a man who, as folk wisdom said, had been 'touched by God'. God must have been a bit heavy-handed in this case. His anointed one was bent in the back, had a hump, and a face of near-Neanderthal cragginess. He dragged one of his feet. He had one sterling quality which rendered his services invaluable to the farmer: he was utterly unafraid of the stallion. Whenever he 'walked' it, the look of equine savagery which usually lit the horse's terrifying gaze was replaced by an expression of almost comical disbelief as it quizzically regarded the stunted manikin who was daring to order it about. So it obeyed him, with a touching docility, completely dominated by his idiot self-assurance.

We addressed the idiot as 'Corny'. As if his crippledom was not itself a heavy enough burden to bear, his doting and disappointed mother had saddled him with the forename 'Cornelius'. Village lore had it that he had been accidentally dropped into the font by a drunken vicar during his christening ceremony, and this immersion in holy waters had endowed him, like Achilles before him, with fearlessness. He certainly had no fear of the horse.

I met him in the mushroom field, at daybreak after a heavy fall of dew. The air singing with insects and the mushrooms seemingly leaping out of the grass.

'Mornin', Corny,' I greeted the apparition in its tweed ratting cap, a shooting jacket donated by the farmer who was about twice his size, corduroy trousers that stank whenever he stood with his back to the fire in the pub, and monstrous boots that would have taken him to the bottom if he had ever fallen into anything deeper than the infamous font. 'Plenty of mushrooms today,' I observed.

'Oh yes,' he nodded, as far as it is possible to nod when your chin is already permanently on your chest. 'It's the stallion, you see.'

The *stallion*. No, I didn't 'see'. So I enquired further, 'The *stallion*?'

'This is his field. He makes the mushrooms.'

The sun was climbing, the pinky mother-of-pearl dawn light turning brassy with the promise of heat, the thin mist lifting. The world was unreal. '*He* makes the mushrooms?'

'That's right,' Corny explained, anxious to enlighten this ignoramus. 'As he moves in the field he spills his seed upon the grass. It turns into mushrooms. That is where mushrooms come from.'

The prospect of a horse committing the sin of Onan had never occurred to me, and interesting though it was it seemed best not to pursue it. I pondered Corny's 'explanation'. It was perfectly adequate as far as he was concerned. All he wanted was a few mushrooms to fry up with the breakfast bacon; what did it really matter to him how they had got into the field in the first place? He had 'explained' the mystery to his own satisfaction.

His explanation would not have satisfied a mushroom-grower; his is a different frame of reference.

Before you scoff at this story of a simpleton listen to the next one . . . .

Belief: a lot of bull

I was in a plastics processing factory. They melt thermoplastic material, squeeze it through a shaped die, to impart a specified cross-sectional form, pass it through a water trough to cool it, then saw it into convenient lengths. These become trunking through which cables are passed when electric wiring is being fitted into a building. Because they remain in full view on the wall of the room being wired, because they are a permanent fixture, they have to look right. As the company told me, they must be 'aesthetically pleasing'; no scuffs or scratches on the visible surface. No blemishes to detract from their glossy beauty.

The company had a problem: far too much of what they made was condemned as junk because its important surfaces were deeply scratched. So they took it straight from the extruder and ground it up before trying again. This is the classical bottle-to-bottle hook-up I told you about in *Right Every Time*. It's a different slant on the same episode (plastics processors are not the only people who recycle their raw material). It's about the same people.

Anyway, they were scratching and reworking far too much of the output – the question was 'why?' The boss said that the most likely way to find an answer to this question would be to consult the two technical wizards who overlorded the extrusion operation, Mike and Desmond.

I went on to the shop floor and introduced myself to Mike and Desmond. They were standing with an air of proprietorship, by the delinquent extruder, dressed in baggy boiler suits but wearing collar and tie to mark their higher-than-operator status.

They showed me a specimen of extrusion salvaged from the previous day's output which had already been sent to the grinder, to begin its conversion journey over again. This was their evidence of rejectability, retained in order to prove the rightness of their decision to any doubter. 'Do you see these scratches?' They indicated the score marks running longitudinally down the length of the otherwise gleaming public face of the extrusion. 'Rejectable, does not meet our aesthetic standards. Cosmetic defect,' they pronounced.

'Where do the scratches come from?'

'There is *grit* in the cooling water. In the cooling tank. It gets into the extruder die, and scratches the plastic, do you see?' This was a very generous explanation. Too generous.

'Then stick a filter in the water circulating through the cooling tank,' I suggested, reasonably enough as I thought. But no . . .

'There *is* a filter in the line,' Mike explained patiently, 'we are not stupid, you know.'

'Then stick a filter with a finer mesh into the line,' I persisted.

'No, you don't understand,' explained Desmond. 'This grit is not very big,' he demonstrated by rolling his index-fingertip on to his thumb, 'You can only just feel it like this.'

'How big do you reckon it is, twenty thou, ten thou, five thou . . .?'

'Oh now, about ten thou diameter at its biggest,' he was still rubbing his finger-end on to his thumb by way of emphasizing the magnitude of the offending particles of grit.

Grit is heavier than water; it sinks. The vulnerable face of the extrusion which required an unblemished finish was extruding from the top of the die. I would have expected the grit to damage the extrusion in the lower part of the die, where its effect would remain hidden and so be non-rejectable. I explained my theory to the double-act. 'Turn the die upside down,' I recommended.

'Can't do that,' they shook their heads, 'Securing bolts not made that way.'

'But if the particles of grit are lodging in the top of the die, as they seem to be, and you invert the die, the top of the die will form the bottom of the extrusion and you can scratch it to hell and it won't matter.'

'Haven't we just told you that it is not possible to mount the die the wrong way up?' Mike and Des exchanged a significant glance, one eyebrow each raised, slight shaking of head, which said, 'Oy oy, we've got one here!'

'Show me that scratched piece again please,' I said, thinking that there is always more than one way of skinning a cat. 'Let's go into the engineering shop; they've got a twenty-times projector in there, I understand.'

We trooped into the workshop. I asked for a hacksaw and sawed through the extrusion in the region where it was most deeply scored, then mounted it and looked at the twenty-times lifesize image of the sawn face on the screen.

'Shall we measure the depth and breadth of the scratch?' The 'scratch' showed like a Rift Valley on the flatness of the extrusion's surface. 'Over forty-thou wide, and thirty deep,' I read off the measuring gauge. 'With rounded edges, fire-polished. What do you make of that for a scratch made by a little boulder of ten thou diameter, my lads?' Another 'belief' bit the dust.

'Well, well,' said Des, 'Fancy that! Marvellous, innit?'

The only marvel about it was the fact that they had been getting away with it for so long. The so-called 'scratch' was an 'unfill' streak due to material shortage passing through the die. You can make this happen either by dropping the pressure at which you feed hot plastic into the die, or by pulling too hard on the haul-off which pulls the extrusion from the die. A straightforward matter of balancing two input factors. Nothing clever; plain common sense.

Whenever Mike and Des were called into the plant outside regular hours they were paid a call-out fee, plus double time while they worked 'antisocial' hours. Oddly enough the extruder tended to start producing 'scratches' about half an hour after they had clocked off, and they always rectified it before the pubs closed. Coincidence, I suppose.

Or perhaps a lot of bull.

Belief: how it is misused

This little section on 'Belief' began by stressing mankind's need to 'explain' things. Things such as:

1.   Why are we on this planet at all?
2.   Why do bubbles form on the inside surface of a glass of beer?
3.   Why is a poison-arrow frog coloured black and yellow?

Let us look at some explanations, or should it be 'explanations'?

1(a)   According to the first book of Moses, commonly called Genesis, 'In the beginning God created . . . . . . Let us make man in our image . . . a sixth day.' Myth of 'special creation'.

1(b)   According to Academician Oparin of the old Soviet Union, life was formed when a lightning flash electrocuted a puddle of primeval slime about 350 million years ago, to produce a glob of jelly from which we all 'evolved'. Myths of 'spontaneous generation' and 'evolution'.

2(a)   Small imperfections in the surface of the glass act as nuclei which stimulate the formation of bubbles.

2(b)   Some of the dissolved gas evaporating out of the liquid is drawn, by surface tension effect, to the wall of the glass.

3(a)   Science says to indicate that it is poisonous.

3(b)   I say it's because poison-arrow frogs are painted black and yellow; therefore I identify this specimen as a poison-arrow frog. As do other frogs.

This is in the same league of superstition as the one about the coral snake. Why is it banded in red, blue, black and white? To show that it is venomous? Then why is a black mamba (equally venomous) black? Or a green mamba green? Their bite isn't exactly harmless, yet there is no colour warning of danger.

Stallions, mushrooms, extrusions, bio-origins, bubbles, frogs

... all 'explained'; and all 'explanations' equally nonsensical.

Does it matter? Not one little bit. It only starts to matter when the same sort of explanatory thinking is used to 'explain' the things that go on in our industries and our businesses. *Then* holding a wrong belief can be as dangerous as the belief that marijuana is bad for you.

To illustrate this I think I might tell you yet another horror story from the crowded memory of cock-ups that seem to have filled my years. If you find the prospect wearisome you can always skip it.

Belief: a lot of broken glass

You meet a good many hard men in my job; but these were the hardest of the hard. They were Scousers, Liverpudlians, men of acerbic humour employed by a famous glass manufacturer. Seven or eight of them slumped resentfully in their chairs, angry because their boss had required them to attend a quality seminar *on a Saturday*.

'It's sodding Saturday today,' one of them opened the proceedings. 'We wouldn't *be here* today but for that swine next door.' He jerked his thumb over his shoulder to point out his boss who was sitting at his desk in the next-door office through the partition.

'Neither would I,' I agreed, 'Do you think I'm spending all day Saturday with miserable buggers like you because I *want* to?'

This seemed to mollify him a little.

'You're supposed to be here to teach us SPC, aren't you?' another spokesman, a positive thinker, joined the debate, 'Well, it won't work. You can't do SPC on our product.'

Their product was a glass disc with a little hole it its centre, a bit like an old-fashioned gramophone record. They cut them out of flat sheets of glass, hundreds a day. Their boss had told me that after they had cut them they were passed downstream to an edging machine. This was a very expensive, state-of-the-art piece of apparatus. Trouble was, it kept having crash-ups. Then they had to call the main labs at Headquarters and ask for help from an expert who took hours to get there and do a repair. They were losing time, output, money and customers' goodwill. It was happening far too frequently and nobody knew why. But everybody was fed up with it.

'Why can't you do SPC on your product?' I asked the logical positivist. 'All that you are doing is making the same disc hundreds of times a day. That's a *natural* for stats process control.'

'No,' they were adamant, 'You can't do it, so we won't do it.' The collective had spoken, the militant mob united in its opposition to somebody who wanted to exploit them by showing them a new technique.

'What shall we do all day then?'

'Nuttin!'

'We can't just do *nothing*,' I pleaded, 'Come on lads, I can't sit here all day in idleness and then send my invoice in, especially while your boss is next door. Be reasonable. I'll tell you what, let's *pretend* to work.'

They found this proposition quite acceptable. So I asked them to fetch in a crate of discs, about forty or so, chosen randomly, and then do what they usually did – measure them.

'Show me how you do it,' I invited.

'We take each disc,' he said as he took one, 'We use these calipers, measuring to thousandths of an inch,' he waved the instrument at me. 'We check around the disc until we find the biggest diameter, then until we find the smallest, and we write them down. Then we work out the average of the two, and if that's inside the tolerance, we say it's OK. If it's not, we adjust the cutting size.'

'Please do me a small favour, gentlemen,' I asked in my best voice, 'Take just one measurement anywhere on the disc and tell me what it is, then search for your largest and smallest and tell me what they are. I'll write them all down.'

This was leisurely pretend-work. It took us nicely through to coffee-break, by which time I had compiled four columns of figures: the instant 'snap' measurements, the searched-for biggest, the ditto smallest, and the average of these two. All kids' stuff really.

After coffee one of their crew did his arithmetic bit. He worked out all the average diameters and then calculated the average of all the averages.

I had already done the same, the average of the 'snap' – instant – measurements was near enough the same as the laboriously compiled number they had arrived at by their tedious double-measuring route. I informed them of this happy outcome.

'By the way,' I added, 'you are working thirty to forty times harder than you need to.'

This must have been happy music to their ears, so I elaborated, 'The instant diameter measure takes less than five seconds. Your way it takes two to three minutes; I've timed it. Yet the results are the same.'

'Furthermore, it you analyse the measurements you will see that among the output of discs which you have *not* measured there will be some – three, four, five, six in a thousand – which are too big for the edging machine, and will therefore cause a crash-up. This will remain unknown to you, the way you do things now, because the first you know of a crash-up is exactly that, a crash-up. This is also the last thing you know, because when the machine jams on an oversize disc it smashes the disc, destroying the evidence. You may be working hard, but you are not working smart.'

I excused myself and went outside to take a breath of fresh air at a place near the waste glass skips where I had previously observed a scattering of cigarette stubs. I had left the lads in serious discussion.

'Hey, Frank!' One of them greeted me jovially when I got back, 'Me and the lads have just been having a serious discussion, and we think SPC will work OK for us. What do you think?' He smiled encouragingly.

'It won't work,' I shook my head dolefully, 'As you said this morning, none of us would be here wasting a Saturday except for that swine next door. No, SPC won't work here.'

'Aw, *come on* Frank.' It was all matey first-name dialogue now and plaintive begging, 'You just showed us it works. Show us how to do it.'

'Say please,'

So I told them. I had changed their *belief*. Now they could do it.

When I went back to take another crew the following Saturday the boss – the swine as they called him – told me there had been *no crash-ups* on the edging machine all week. Such is the power of SPC. But before it, such is the power of belief. As I said, it can kill people; it can cripple business endeavour. This is an important subject of great interest to reformers like us who wish to make work into a more rewarding and satisfying activity. We will be looking further into the nature of belief later on. In the meantime, back to the seminars in the client's factory.

Seminar Follow-up Work

If you teach people a new skill it is good to get them using it straight away. Lest they should forget it. The first of our training groups had been shown how to use SPC to reduce the variation in a manufacturing process, by taking action when they should take action and leaving things alone whenever they got false signals from the process. Stop them knob-twiddling. This team was now to put its new knowledge to work, tackling a real problem with a price-tag attached to it. The result of their project was to be measured in terms of the *money* they might make.

This is vitally important. Start small. Start slow. Aim for a *little* victory to begin with. Gain the confidence that *small* success will bring. A bit like a terrier being trained to catch rats . . . .

Vignette: the rat-catchers

Ratting used to be one of our rural sports. You harvested the corn in golden September, carrying the grain-heavy sheaves from their stooks in the fields into the stackyard at the farmstead. There they were stacked ears-inward into a structure like a straw house which was roughly thatched to keep the rain out until the arrival of the threshing engine months later. As the rain stayed out the rats went in. To them it was a place of security, warmth, comfort, and un-limited food. Until threshing time.

When the threshing engine arrived – a thing of boxes, belts, pulleys, chutes, wheels, noise, dust – the stack was taken down from the top, layer by layer, and the sheaves fed through the machine. Straw came out of one chute, chaff out of another, grain out at the back. The rats stayed put, lurking in the lower layers of the stack, no doubt hoping that the machinery would go away and leave them in peace. Soon only a few layers were left unthreshed.

The dogs were brought in. Now, in those days the rat-catcher didn't simply release a dog to tackle a rat: one bite on the nose from a fighting rat and the terrier would be terrified of rats for the rest of its life. The dog had first of all to be encouraged, taught that catching rats is not really such a dangerous pastime. To inculcate this canine courage the rat catcher always caught a few rats in a cage-trap, kept them alive, and used them to teach young dogs. He did this by doing a bit of rough and ready dentistry on the rats. Holding the rodent in a thickly gloved hand he would extract its incisor teeth with a pair of pincers. These teeth resemble chisels; they are capable of inflicting severe damage to the sensitive nose of a dog. The toothless rat was then dropped into an empty barrel, and the apprentice terrier dropped in after it. The dogs soon got the hang of it, enjoyed the fun.

The fun really started in earnest in the stackyard the instant the rats decided to bolt from the lowest layers of sheaves. They exploded from the base of the stack in their hundreds, flying in all directions, pursued by terriers, farm dogs, and farm hands wielding cudgels. Terriers trained on toothless rats move with lightning confidence: little success leads to greater victory.

It's the same with training groups. One taste of small success to cut their teeth on is enough to instil the confidence to overcome bigger things. A defeat to begin with can destroy confidence and credibility.

Adopting the skeletal techniques of SPC unadorned with any fancy formulae, the first of the group began to recover raw material costs to the tune of a few thousand pounds a month. This sum doesn't sound much in the context of several hundred thousands a month company turnover; but it was 'for nothing', straight on to the bottom line with no extra expenditure. It might not be much of a saving, but I'll bet *you* wouldn't refuse a few thousand pounds a month for just a bit of *smarter* work.

The training sequence of one day in the lecture room, with three half-days of on-the-job coaching, was extended to two more training groups. Now we had three groups operational – enough to manage at this stage.

The temptation at this point is to set up a multitude of teams. *Teams*?

'Teambuilding' is dear to the heart of the conventional wisdom of those TQM consultants who jumped on to the bandwagon from a 'human relations' background.

Human Relations is what personnel management nowadays calls itself. As a function personnel management is a genetic descendant of the regimental officer mentality. (Prussian classification, you may recall, is lazy and stupid.) The function grew, just after the last war, as a job-creation scheme for demobilized officers from the armed services.

Failing completely to see that this new function afforded an opportunity to provide a balancing service between the Us and Them, the traditional warring factions of industry, the personnel function aligned itself with the ruling caste of bosses. In doing so it missed a marvellous opportunity to catalyse improvements in our national industrial relations arena of conflict. Such is the way of snobbery, the power of belief.

Arriving into civilian life with a service tradition of proceduralization (one of their own awful words), personnel people saw the writing of procedures as the route to solving problems. So they transplanted the services attitude, in which there is a written procedure to govern the performance of near enough *every* activity, into our businesses.

This is a generalization, but true enough to be valid comment. So I shall take it further. Finding that the endless writing of procedures, followed by endless interpretation of same, followed by endless disputation about the alleged infringement of same, is not the most interesting or praise-worthy way of passing time; they searched for something more.

Therefore the practitioners of this bureaucratic business tried to gild their drab lily by adding other bits and pieces to their dreary function. They adopted things like 'psychometric testing', 'personality profiling', and other interesting side-lines to break the bureaucratic boredom. The more enlightened of their colleagues who had strayed into the profession began to address genuine 'people' issues.

Imagine their delight upon making the discovery that TQM is 'about people'. What an opportunity presented itself! A whole new, brightly painted bandwagon, seemingly destined to roll into an eternal future, for them to jump on. Jump on they did. Reasoning, or rationalizing, that TQM is about people, and we and *only* we are the people people, they jumped on to the wagon and claimed it as their own. The results can be hilarious.

They arrive in a company, their presence probably partly funded by an unsuspecting quango doling out dollops of public cash, and set about one of their favourite activities – teambuilding. They are good at it.

In a factory of about two hundred people they can quickly field over fifty teams. This means that many people are obliged to belong to more than one, two or even three teams. Never mind; the workers love it. At last they are being allowed to do what managers have always done – have meetings. Here they quickly discover that as a way of passing working time it sure as hell beats working. Talking, in a strange new jargon, is encouraged, and found to be a fun thing. You can chatter all day in manager-babble without actually saying anything, leaving plenty to chatter about tomorrow. Each team is allocated a 'project' to talk about. 'Tasks' are assigned. 'Criteria' are discussed. 'Comfort zones' explored.

Nobody has time to do any real work any more; they are too busy 'self-actualizing', experiencing 'experiential learning', looking into ways of 'auditing' this and that.

This is rain-dancing. I wandered into one of these so-called TQM programmes once. Its lead consultant graciously informed me that if they thought (('they' being him and his team of shamans) they could do with 'a bit of SPC' they would send for me; in the meantime could I keep my snout out of the trough while they got on with the bringing of true salvation to this heathen organization. They were the bearers of 'job enrichment', I was told, cultivators of 'job satisfaction', husbandmen to 'actualization'.

I don't believe in job satisfaction as something which will stimulate somebody into doing something. In my time I've met many a one satisfied with his job; so satisfied he is happy to spend a lifetime polishing the seat of his trousers as a long prelude to an equally comfortable pension. His sort figure high on my list of people to be taken in the tumbril to the block. (A tumbril is a dung-cart commandeered as transport for the condemned.)

I seek out job *dissatisfaction*. The persons seething with frustration. You only need to find two or three people of this mettle in an organization of two or three hundred to begin to make some powerful, and *profitable*, change. They are the 'cocky' ones; the 'trouble-makers'; the 'agitators' . . . this agitation you witness in their discontent is akin to what you see on the nature films on television. They show you a finely sculpted little capsule suspended from a leaf. It is a chrysalis, you are told. It begins to twitch and tremble, becomes agitated; there is something inside desperate to escape the confinement of the constraining sheath. You are watching the phenomenon called 'metamorphosis' – something beautiful is striving to be made manifest. The casing splits, and from it there emerges a butterfly.

You could equally well be watching the struggles of a badly underused employee struggling to escape the stifling confines of a job description. Part of your work, as change-agent, is to look for such imprisoned talent, and secure its liberation.

Your work is to help bring about this metamorphosis, this transformation of potential into actuality, of promise into power, of talent into accomplishment.

Forget, for the time being, teambuilding. That can come later, in controlled and gradual stages. Concentrate in the beginning on finding and developing those who are suffocating under the existing set-up: the odd-balls, the mavericks who kick against the stones on which others compliantly stub their toes.

The woman called Karen was one of this type. She and her team were easy to teach, because they were keen to learn. They were taught how to look at process data and turn them into control information. The running of the operation was handed over to them. They were asked to make it pay. They were asked to do what they had always been doing, only to do it better. Their programme was anchored firmly to the ground by calculating pounds sterling saved by using SPC.

But this was not TQM, you might protest. Did anybody say it was? Is an acorn yet an oak tree in which a defeated monarch might cower from his enemies? Give it time. It may not be TQM, but it's not rain-dancing either. Please don't expect too much too soon; do that and you will be disappointed, like the four out of five companies who have invested heavily in cash up front for a TQM programme only to find it fizzling out after the opening outburst of razzmatazz.

Look upon the company as a vat of sweet grape-juice which you want to turn into a wine of TQM. What we are doing here, with our multi-status segments of the company being trained one after another, after another, until there are three manageable teams up and running, is inoculating the vat at three points with a pinch of yeast. You cannot turn it into wine overnight; only the Messiah could pull that useful trick. Patience is called for, for a few weeks, until each of the three inoculation places has started to fizz and spread. Soon the entire vat will be bubbling with a heady ferment.

Speaking of yeast, I have a friend who helps me to understand things; he's a sort of philosopher, who chips a few words into my writing from time to time. He calls himself Aaron Godman; he contributed a few paragraphs to my last book, *Right Every Time*. In a bit I'll take a rest from writer's cramp and pass the pen to him. He can tell you a thing or two about yeast. For the time being let's get back to what happened after the seminar was up and running.

After a lapse of a couple of weeks, to let them enjoy their little victory and get used to handling the tools of SPC, I called on Karen and her team to check progress. Now you would think that when presented with a work system which delivers more OK output for less raw material, the management team would be happy enough to leave well alone, would you not?

You would be wrong. The abbreviated charting system, which had worked fine, had been replaced by something as complicated as the treasured Mappa Mundi in the quality office. Karen advised me that she was fed up, that the system she and I had installed was considered too simple by the management team, who had replaced it with a better one. Which didn't work. The management team kept fussing around asking why. They were blaming her.

Whenever managers feel deeply threatened a strange behavioural change takes place. Just as a beheaded chicken will scutter around hysterical but headless, frightened managers do likewise *before* they have lost their heads. Well, no, they have lost their heads, in the sense of having lost their wits, but they are not organizationally decapitated yet. Even so, they rush around, causing confusion. Death throes, do you think?

They had to be restrained. The boss issued an edict reaffirming the way we were doing SPC, reminding them that we would do all of this but *no more than this*!

The SPC teams went on doing as they had been liberated and trained to do, making more money for the company and ultimately more for themselves. Preparing their organization for a future as a preferred supplier to big Japanese names. Made possible by an inspiring boss, an inspired workforce and a reduced managerial head-count. I will now address those whose heads rolled – those who think of themselves as my victims.

To My Victims – To Your Futures

Now that you believe yourselves to be dead decision time is upon you. You now realize how lucky you were to be released from the Bedlam they paid you to inhabit, and that as one door slammed shut behind you other doors presented themselves.

Which of these new doors will you open? Each leads to a new life. Step through one and you can be a writer; another will lead you into a kind of tycoonship (tycoon-*boat*, actually, as you will see); the third will take you into the rich pastures of consultancy. I shall describe all of them to you. I know what lies on the other side of those doors, having passed through all of them in my time.

Rejoice! You now have personal control of one of your most valuable gifts – your personal time. 'Time is money,' they say. They are wrong; it isn't. If time were money you could bank it and earn a day of interest for every month invested; and the rich could live forever. The freedom to dispose of our own time is one of our greatest riches. Now that you no longer sell your days because nobody wants to buy them any more you are rich indeed. What will you do with the 28,800 seconds of time that now are yours each day instead of your employer's?

Wish them away? As you used to do when selling them to the highest bidder? Let them wither by ignoring them as soon as they arrive, harking back to an Arcadian past or fantasizing forward into an idyllic future, instead of grasping the moment? Beat them to death with frantic work?

Or, now that your life at last belongs to you – thanks to me – will you try to learn how to live it in the only time there truly is – the here-and-now, this *instant*?

Do not lament the past; it is gone. Do not seek to carve the future; it is not here. Instead, live today and trust tomorrow.

While you contemplate the opportunities afforded you by your resurrection I shall take a break. After forty thousand words into the narrative I've got writer's cramp. I shall take some time off.

I shall go and sit on the pew. It came from an abandoned chapel.

It is a seat of hard discomfort designed to keep a congregation awake during the Sunday dreariness of long sermons. It is the sort of furniture that should be fitted in seminar rooms during the graveyard hour after lunch. From this ascetic perch in my garden I shall watch the swallows building their nests in the rafters of the outhouse, listen to their burbling chatter and catch the faint sounds of distant hymn singing leaking from the timber of a pew steeped in a century of worship. You are at liberty to dispose of time in ways like this when time is your own.

To keep you company in my brief absence I shall hand over to an old friend of mind; let *him* talk to you for a bit. Some of you, those who have read the book *Right Every Time*, will have met him before.

The idiot's tale: 1

> Life's but a walking shadow, a poor player
> That struts and frets his hour upon the stage,
> And then is heard no more; it is a tale
> Told by an idiot, full of sound and fury,
> Signifying nothing.

A tale told by an idiot. That's life. I am an idiot. Here is my tale.

My name is Aaron Godman. This is to signify, with no subtlety whatever, that I am exactly what my name says I am, an enigma – a being who is half-God and half-man. A demi-god, one of the lesser gods of our infinite universe. As such I was ordained '. . . a priest for ever after the order of Melchizedek', Melchizedek being the King of Salem, of peace and salvation. Part of my job is to guide those who do not know what they are searching for and yet who search for it passionately.

A long time ago I met the author of this book, and finding a vacancy amid the rubbish that littered the spacious vault inside his skull asked him if I could move in. He said I might as well, so I shovelled out some of the dusty detritus that he called his education, and took lodging there. I am a paying tenant; he and I share a symbiotic relationship.

Through his sensory systems he supplies me with immediate experiences of life incarnate, enabling a spirit-being such as myself to enjoy the pleasures and pains of the flesh. In return I guide his search; bring him to knowledge, wisdom and the great oceans of ideas. He is filled with ideas these days; you surely didn't think him capable of finding them by himself? I take him on journeys of discovery, then he writes about them, because he too is trying to be an idiot.

I found him one day relaxing under his walnut tree. He sits there because nothing grows beneath it. Like the Javanese upas tree or an authoritarian boss, nothing is able to flourish in its poisonous shade.

He was quietly nodding off to the drowsy hum of the honey bees filling their hives with nectar, and in between cat-naps steadily emptying a bottle of his own nectar, distilled in Poland. Since I was sharing his senses I knew he was dreamily enjoying his drink, but just by way of a bit of desultory conversation I asked him if he knew where alcohol comes from.

'This came from the off-licence,' he told me.

'Yes, we know that, but would you like to see not only where it originated, but *why*?' I knew he would be unable to resist it. 'Come with me, on a little trip, and I will show you.'

'What will you show me? Will the journey be worth the effort?'

'No effort needed,' I assured him. 'Just let your mind move on its own, free itself of the artificial shackles of space and time, move faster than light – because ideas are instantaneous and outside the "laws" of physics – expand into Infinity and Eternity.'

'Where shall we be going, in our search for the origins of alcohol?' he wanted to know.

'To the experiment of the six-day wonder.'

Being a demi-god is a trade that has to be learned, like any other. You have to serve a long apprenticeship. So I took my day-dreaming vodka-sipping host to the time of my final exams. To a cosmic laboratory.

'Your task', said our tutor, Rex Mundis, a fallen angel with a wicked sense of humour, 'is to take these bags of inanimate dust and phials of liquids and breathe life into them to create a bio-mass. You will then use whatever you have created to populate one of the as yet lifeless worlds in the firmament. The one chosen for you is a minor planetary body which will later become known as Earth, or Gaia the Beautiful. You are required to fill it with teeming life-forms which you will then bid to go forth and multiply.'

He looked around benignly but mischievously at the expectant faces of the tyro-divinities before him. 'You have six days to do it,' he told us, 'On the seventh you will rest.'

We would-be demi-gods began breathing life. Dust was getting everywhere. One of us decided it might be better to wet it a little, turn it into a kind of malleable clay.

'Who is breathing life into what?' asked Rex Mundis, 'You, what is it you are going to bring into being?' With deft hands the pupil he was addressing was sculpting his lump of raw material into a four-legged creature with a very small head on a very long neck, grotesquely disproportioned.

'What's *that*?' Rex wanted to know. 'It looks utterly ridiculous.'

'I'm going to call it a giraffe,' its creator told him, blushing with embarrassment. Rex shook his head, bemused.

He turned his attention to a group of ten or so godlets gathered around a conference table. 'What are you lot up to?'

'We have formed ourselves into a design committee. We have brainstormed our creative ideas within the prescribed parameters and have arrived at a consensus. Desk research tells us that our product will fill an identified market niche.'

'What is it you are creating?'

'A horse.'

Rex stared hard at their design, '*Horses* have *humps*?' He shrugged his shoulders and turned away.

Then a row broke out between two of the apprentices, a squabble over who should create what from the list of remaining options.

'*I* want to create Man,' shouted one, a bossy type, to his adversary who was comparatively puny. 'In *my* image. It would be too cruel to cast him in *yours*!'

'That's not fair,' wailed the puny pale one, 'That only leaves the uni-cellular organisms for me. Bloody amoebae and bacteria and shapeless globs of protoplasm. What is a demi-god supposed to do with *simple* things like those?'

Rex Mundis took him to one side, a sly look in his eye, and whispered something to him. The puny one smiled knowingly, nodded and said to his opponent, 'OK, *you* create Man. In your own marvellous image, and *I'll* do the crap job that nobody else wants to do. The single-celled simple things for simple-minded demi-gods like me to make. Like *yeast*.' He sniggered and shot a knowing look at Rex Mundis, who smiled.

So the cocky one came to create Man; his simpleton friend created nothing so grand.

'Look at that!' the cocky one proclaimed on the evening of the sixth day, 'Behold and see that it is good.' The newly created man was strutting about, as cocky as his creator.

'Here, drink this,' the puny one handed the man a phial of thin liquid. The man drank it straight in one go and banged the phial on the table.

'More!' he ordered, 'Give me shum more!'

'What *is* that liquid you have given my noble creation to drink?' demanded the cocky demi-god.

'It is the *excrement* – the *waste product*, the *filth*, of the single-celled organism called yeast which was all *I* was allowed to create, thanks to *you*.'

By now the man was well into his first, but by no means his last binge. He was reeling about waving his empty phial, shouting, 'Fill it up!' He cut a most undignified figure as he drowned his honour.

His creator wept. The yeast maker gloated, 'Your creation will forever thirst for the wastes of mine. This is my vengeance on your arrogance.' Rex Mundis, fallen angel, smiled happily, and slipped into the incarnate form he found most comfortable – that of a serpent.

We returned to sit under the cool canopy of the walnut tree. 'What did you think of that, then?' I asked my host. 'You are now drinking the metabolic waste of one of the simplest organisms on the planet. The product of one godlet's revenge upon another. How does that grab you?'

He took a long swig, and dozed off, chin sagging, mouth agape, lips dribbling, softly snoring. So I gave him a nudge. He started, wide awake, 'What do you want?' he asked.

'Fancy another little journey into the comic cosmic unconscious?' I invited.

'OK, where are we off to this time?'

'Into the desert, in a *manner* of speaking; you will see what I mean.'

We found ourselves in a wild place. Hard stony ground. It was dark, with only the thinnest of red streaks low on the jagged black edge of the horizon to herald the coming dawn. We were with a mass of people, some gathered around fitful fires of crackling thorns, others wandering aimlessly about. An omnipresent background noise, which sounded like the whining of a keening wind, and a sound like stones being rubbed together, could be heard.

'What's that noise?' asked my host.

'Wailing, and a gnashing of teeth.'

'Why are the people wailing and gnashing their teeth?'

'Because they have nothing to put between their teeth. They are hungry. Hence their lamentations.'

'Where's all that milk and honey he promised us then, eh? That's what I'd like to know,' lamented one of the hungry ones.

'Oh yerse,' added another of the famished multitude, ' "Follow me out of bondage", he said. "Come with me to Canaan," he said. If this is Canaan give me bloody Egypt any day.'

'You're right there, mate,' agreed another of the belly-aching throng, 'At least they fed us there; I could murder a bowl of that maize porridge right now.'

'We wouldn't be in this mess if we hadn't listened to him,' reflected yet another complainant. 'Serves us right really. Who in their right mind would pay heed to a fantasist who listens to voices coming out of burning bushes?'

'I blame his mother for hiding him in the bulrushes. He would have been drowned but for Pharaoh's daughter. God, I'm hungry.'

'Hungry! *You're* hungry?' another contributed to the collective discontent. 'What about me then? One sodding locust in three days, that's all *I've* had, and you say *you're* hungry.'

The chorus of complaints went on, the famished people bickering among themselves, looking for somebody to blame for their misfortune. Who better to blame than their leader?

'Who are these people, what are they doing here?' my travelling companion enquired.

'They are the Children of Israel, wandering in the wilderness, on their way to their Promised Land. They are reaching the extremity of their endurance.'

'I can't stand much more of this,' a weary voice came out of the half-light of dawn. 'If we don't find something to eat very soon we shall very likely starve to death in this *god-forsaken* wilderness. If any of us survive it will be a *miracle*.'

The sun lifted its edge over the saw-tooth rim of the land. The plain was flooded with a fiery light. In its glow every rock and every stunted bush were seen to be smothered in what seemed to be flakes of snow.

'*Snow*? In the *desert*?' said a child of Israel in total disbelief.

'Hoar frost,' explained another, 'Frozen dew.'

The flakes glistened; the entire landscape was luminous with iridescence as far as the eye could see.

The multitude fell silent, awed by the glittering majesty of the spectacle of a jewel on every stone and twig.

'Eat ye of the manna!' a great voice thundered over the hushed tribes. 'Gather it unto ye, sufficient unto the day thereof.'

That's how prophets used to speak in those Old Testament times; today they use a different jargon, they speak of 'nano-second nineties', 'de-layering', 'process re-engineering', but it's the same old proclamation of salvation being peddled by modern manna-mongers in the true Mosaic tradition.

'Manna?' my host eyed it speculatively, 'What is it, *actually*?'

'A complete food, *actually*,' I enlightened him. 'Kind of iron rations for those at the end of their tether. Got all the vitamins, proteins, minerals, carbohydrates, trace elements, everything you need. Sort of emergency rations supplied by the Ancient of Days to chosen people.'

'What's it taste like?'

'Why don't you taste some and find out?'

He gingerly selected one of the manna flakes, about the size and shape of a peeled almond; it glowed softly in his fingers. He popped it experimentally into his mouth, rolling his eyes upward in concentration and making exaggerated chewing motions with a pouting mouth like wine-tasters do to impress those of us who guzzle our vintage down our untutored gullets.

'Tastes like yoghurt,' he nodded approvingly, 'clean, fizzy, sharp. Yes, Bulgarian kormaksar yoghurt, fermented goats' milk. I like it.'

'Try some more then,' I invited, and he scooped a handful and crammed it greedily into his mouth, 'Only this time think of . . . say . . . a slice of roasted Welsh lamb, with mint sauce.'

He chewed, smacked his lips appreciatively, 'By God, you're right! It changed texture as well as flavour. A miracle food is this.' He helped himself to another cupped handful. As he ate his eyes suddenly took on a crafty look, 'Hey,' he confided, 'You could package this and make a fortune.'

'No you couldn't,' I disappointed the entrepreneurial oppor-
tunist in him, 'Very short shelf-life, you see. It only lasts a day. At
sunset it turns into maggots. But the A of D sends you another harvest the following morning if you have real need of it.'

'A of D?'

'Ancient of Days,' I reminded him, 'My ultimate all-powerful,
all-knowing ever-loving boss. And yours.'

We returned to the shade of the walnut tree. A voice hailed from
the house jolting him from the reverie of his dreamtime.
'Teatime,' the strident voice of blissful domesticity advised him,
'Been dreaming again?'

'In a *manner* of speaking.'

Hello, I'm back. My scribbling fist is rested, so I can take up the
pen again and let the words flow from its point. *I* don't write these
things you know; don't blame *me*, blame the pen.

What did you make of the Aaron Godman chronicles? With
him being one of the lesser gods you expect him to speak in
parables whose meaning you have to unravel for yourself. He is
not nearly so complicated. He embeds no morals within the fabric
of his stories; the stories themselves are the message.

Take his first one about yeast. All he is saying is that a little
drink now and again to relieve stress is good for you. He is giving
you his semi-divine permission to indulge in that well-attested
practice of relaxing with a drink at weekends.

There is nothing wrong with this. There are many splendid
exemplars. According to the memoirs of his medical advisers
Winston Churchill went through the Second World War in a haze
of brandy, champagne and Havana cigar smoke. And look what he
did! Apart from such small errors of judgement like incinerating
whole cities of men, women and children; and carpet-bombing the
strategic target represented by the medieval city of Dresden into
rubble, he led the nation to victory. Feel free therefore to lift your
glass *without guilt*. You are in excellent company, observing a
hallowed tradition.

Same with Aaron's manna tale. It tells you that you can trust
tomorrow. There are times when you think the lesser gods, whose
purpose is to torment and try us, are goading you too hard. You

despair, and indulge yourself in the melancholy reflection that things are so bad they could not possibly get any worse. But they do get worse. Just as you are about to capitulate in the face of a seemingly implacable destiny the Ancient of Days intervenes, admonishing the lesser gods, telling them, 'You try my children too far!' You are about to be provided for . . . .

Things suddenly change for the better. A cheque drops through the letter-box: you are no longer destitute. An awaited letter arrives: you have got that new job. Something, anything, happens and it fills your heart with gladness and gratitude. The A of D is at work on your behalf.

I once asked Aaron Godman about the Ancient of Days. 'What *sexual* persuasion is the A of D?' I enquired.

'Can't you think of *anything* but sex?'

'Yes, I can think of tobacco and alcohol,' I admitted, 'Sometimes it makes me feel *guilty*, and I vow to give them up.'

'And become a non-smoking teetotaller like Adolf Hitler?' he retorted. 'Do that and you'll be invading Poland within a year. Too much abstinence can be bad for you. It can send you barmy. There should be a government health warning about it.'

Righto then, my dear victims. You believe yourselves to be dead. Now you will resurrect yourselves. You can become manna-gers.

You will begin by blaming neither yourselves nor me for your condition. You are at liberty to blame the lesser gods and their leader Rex Mundis, whose sole purpose on this planet is to make our lives miserable. You will be glad that their ultimate boss – the boss of bosses, the Ancient of Days – used me as the instrument of your escape from your years in the wilderness of Bedlam. You are being redeemed. Give thanks to your redeemer.

Blaming is pointless. It is an 'if only' game of futility and regret. Have done with it. I know that you are unused to freedom of decision and action. You say to yourself, 'What do I want to do?' and you receive no answer. This is because it is in the nature of hierarchical work in our organizations' mad-houses to be obedient rather than innovative. These are places where you do as you are told, within the boundaries of your job descriptions. You have never had much chance to answer the 'what do I want to do?' question because you never had to ask it. Now you must. You must reinvent yourself. Fashion a new persona. You will have fun in your new career of manna-gement. Build yourself a new monument of yourself for yourself.

Let us look at some of the options open to you. The list is as long as your imagination makes it. Let us consider the possible futures we mentioned: writer, tycoon, consultant. There is no particular preference in the order in which we do it. In fact you are not confined to doing one to the exclusion of the others; you can mix your careers from now on. Indeed you can even mix these careers if you are still employed by somebody else, but I will elaborate upon this theme later on. In the meantime let us begin with the genesis of the harlot.

PART 3

OUT OF BEDLAM

Option 1: Genesis of the Harlot

Let us suppose that you wish to explore the possibility of becoming a writer. Somebody once asked Somerset Maugham, the famous novelist and short-story teller, how you actually become a writer. His reply was, 'Very much in the manner in which a woman becomes a harlot. First you do it to please yourself. Then to please other people. Finally for money.'

Dr Johnson had already made a similarly mercenary point, 'Only a blockhead would write for anything except money,' he reckoned.

If you were fancying becoming a man of letters for reasons of artistic idealism, maybe this emphasis on money dirties your dream of creative integrity. On the other hand perhaps it whets your appetite.

One of the things about writing is that *it looks so easy*. You pick up a book, dip into its pages, and find yourself being drawn deeper into the flow of the prose: such an *easy* read! Does easily read mean easily written, do you think? As the young man I met at a conference seemed to believe.

I was doing what some people do at conferences during the morning coffee-break – those who aren't 'phoning base to make sure they're being missed, or faxing head office to prove that they're sitting at the guru's feet – balancing a saucer in one hand and a cigarette in the other, talking to the woman who had organized the day and wishing I had an extra hand to manipulate the cup, when the lad appeared at my elbow.

'Skewze me,' he demanded, with a truculence I attributed to his natural shyness, 'You're Frank Price, aren't you?'

Breaking off my conversation with the event organizer, with whom I was hustling for a little business, I admitted that I was indeed he, and asked what could I do for him. He needed confirmation of my identity.

'That fella that wrote that book *Right First Time* – that Frank Price?'

I nodded, 'That one.' He was beginning to be a bit tedious.

'Humph!' he sneered, '*I* could have written *that*.'

For a fleeting instant I was tempted to reply, 'Well, why the hell didn't you?' or 'Of course you could, it's rubbish! Even *you* could write that.' But I didn't. To do so would have amounted to an unkind put-down so my good breeding prevailed. I thought it more generous of spirit to agree with his boast and told him, 'Yes, you could have; but you didn't so now shove off and do it.'

He could have too. I don't know if later on he did write, but there was nothing to stop him. Writing a book is easy. All you have to do it to put one word after another on to paper. Or into a word-processor if that is your mode of working. Then another word after that. Followed by seventy or eighty or a hundred thousand more.

Trouble is, it takes *time*. You are able, thanks to the miracle of the mind, to conceptualize your words and phrases *instantaneously*. If it were possible to transfer them immediately on to paper you'd have a book as big as *War and Peace* in a matter of minutes. You cannot. You are obliged to do it the hard way, either with a pen or a keyboard. So slow! Creativity crippled by the sluggard flesh. Eternity ticked off by a clock. So *many* words to be written! So little time to write them.

Already, the time which is your own, because you no longer sell it by the hour or by the month to an employer, is starting to trickle through your fingers. 'Better is a handful of quietness than two hands full of toil and a striving after wind', warns the Preacher in Ecclesiastes. Yet here you are, already planning to fill at least one hand with toil, to strive after the wind that puffs up the bubble of reputation. All is vanity. All that isn't greed, anyway. I suppose writing for money adds up to a bit of both. The point is, though, that it all takes time.

The only question about your ambition to become a writer that now remains is whether what you hope to do turns out to be a better way of passing time than what you used to do as an employee of somebody else. Choose this as a career and you will be opting for the solitary existence of the monk illuminating a manuscript in his cell. A Trappist order of silence, because there is not only nobody but yourself and the dog to talk to; even if there were you could not permit yourself the derailing of your train of thought which even the briefest conversation will cause.

No more will you be able to indulge in the pleasures of social-
ization that you so used to enjoy at work. All those lovely meetings, where you sat with a look of earnest concentration on your
face as you concentrated on keeping your initials out of that
column on the right-hand side of the minutes headed 'Action
by:—'. No more of those 'could you spare a minute in my office?'
invitations from your boss to assuage his desperate need for an
audience. No more summoning your subordinates in to counsel
them on their shortcomings as they sit on the edge of the chair
with knees together and hands clasped in lap, wearing an expression of uncomprehending apology like an artificially inseminated
cow.

No more meddling with the five-year rolling strategic plan
which really amounts to nothing more than a continuing promise
to do something tomorrow because you are unable to think of anything sensible to do today. *Now* today is *yours*; you are going to
have to think of something to do *now*, never mind about the 'time
horizon' so dear to the hearts of long-distance strategic planning
pundits. *Your* time horizon doesn't extend much beyond teatime
anymore. Soon you might settle into the sweet langour of the true
aristocrat – 'How pleasing it is to do nothing, and then to rest' –
and find your days passing agreeably and your nights peacefully.
The promised 'one hand of quietness'. What more could anybody
ask for?

It's not enough, is it? There is more fun to be had in chasing two
handfuls of wind. Besides, it doesn't take an Irish wag like G.B.
Shaw to tell us that hell is an everlasting holiday, or folk-wisdom
to remind us that the devil finds work for idle hands. We *work*.

Why do we work? Even those of us who have more money than
could be amassed in a thousand lifetimes of labour. Because we
must. Because there is something demonic within us which must
be got out if it is not to do us damage. We *must* work. We found
life too boring in the Garden of Eden.

But what sort of work? Anthropologists who have studied the
peculiar behaviour of such strange tribes as the Arunta in
Northern Australia, the Jivaro in Amazonia, and other 'primitive'
people report that even they, in their natural paradise of the noble
savage, are obliged to work. For about three hours a day. They
pick food up off the floor, pluck things to eat off the trees, grab fish
out of water. This is their work. Or it used to be until the white

man came along, and taught them the 'dignity of labour'. This was done by expelling them from their homelands into ghettoes; setting them on as wage earners in the mines; then taking their wages off them in return for the things they used to get for nothing. This was done to prevent the devil finding work for idle hands.

Your hands will no longer be idle now that they have nothing to do. As God said to Adam, while running him up a leather suit, 'It's *work* for you now, my boy.' Now that you too have been ejected from the mad paradise of the organization by the pyramid flatteners and the anorexists it's work for you as well. Real work. Not ceremonial pretend-work of the sort that many of us have spent lifetimes doing for the sake of a salary. Real work that people will pay you real money for, that is your game from now on. No more smart shirking; attending conferences at somebody else's expense, or playing computerized business games for monopoly money, or wining and dining greedy acquaintances on a company plastic card in the interests of 'customer relations'. From now on it's your own money you are playing with; it's *your* bottom line; from now on you pay your own bills.

This can come as quite a shock. To those, like you have now become, newly weaned from that nipple of everlasting nourishment known as the salary cheque, the question of where the next meal might come from can be traumatic. Who will provide for you now?

Nobody. Unless you can persuade them to part with some cash. The only way you can prise anything out of them – your new customers – is to offer them something worthwhile in exchange. Seeing that you have elected to regenerate yourself as a writer you had better start writing.

Easy . . . you just write one word down after another . . . again . . . again . . . .

OK. If it's so easy do it now. Write down your *first word*.

You don't even need any capital to launch yourself into this business. A few measly pounds will get you half a dozen foolscap pads and a bundle of red and blue biros. You make use of colour. The first draft goes on to the paper in blue script. You then make corrections, deletions, additions and other alterations in red script. The resulting palimpsest (by the way, you could do worse than invest in a good dictionary while you're about it) is the document you will deliver to your typist, who will be called upon to untangle the intricate web of red arrows and things written in balloons in order to get your precious prose into saleable formation. Unless your typing will be done by a slave-worker impressed from within the labour pool of your own family you will have to pay for it as well.

OK, then, take up your blue biro, open an A4 pad and look at the first sheet of lined paper. What do you notice about it?

It's empty. Empty, vast and white. An Antarctic of paper, so indifferent it feels hostile. Not a sign of life. Just an inert and cold stillness. Pure and undefiled.

Go on then. Write something. The famous first word. Or have you got that fashionable affliction of the intelligentsia – writer's block – already? Are you hoping that the 'phone will ring to give you an excuse to stop working? (Stop? You have hardly started yet. Only another hundred thousand words to go to complete your novel.) Do you suddenly find yourself fancying a cup of tea so you think you will take a break and brew up? Hoping that the doorbell will ring and you will be able to welcome the doorstep evangelists sent from America to serve their apprenticeship as insurance salesmen? Wish that a bluebottle would buzz in through the open window so that you could rain erratic blows on to the pane in pursuit of it? Wish that *anything* might happen to set you free from this awful drudgery of doing nothing?

Nothing happens. You are on your own now. Like the solipsistic (told you you'd best get yourself a dictionary) poet you too can now claim to be the master of your fate and the captain of your soul.

Break the spell. Brainstorm yourself out of inertia into action. How? Grab that dictionary, open it at random and blindly stab a finger on to the page. What is the word you are touching? This is the word which will release the flow of your words.

I've just tried it. I stabbed 'diagonal'. Diagonal . . . Pythagoras, the square on the hypotenuse is equal to the sum of the squares on the other two sides. Prove it. Can't. Couldn't when I was a kid, can't now, but I can use it. Make a 3:4:5 triangle out of wooden slats, use it to square the corners of the shuttering for a concrete foundation I am planning to lay down. Triangle. Bermuda triangle. Tripod, stands firm. 'Standing firm on the heaving deck of a destroyer on escort duties in Bermudan waters' . . . and your story begins.

You can write the rest of it for yourself. It's easy from now on, now that with one word you have breached the dam that was holding your infinite reservoir of words at bay. Now you can feel them flowing. It's an unalloyed joy. And you actually *get paid* for doing this? Well . . . we'll see . . . .

You have now become a writer. A solitary life it is. A lonely life it is not. For companions you have a host of marvellous phantoms, a teeming population of powerful ghosts to entertain you. They are things of the mind. They are known as 'ideas'.

But maybe you are a *materialist* who feels a certain discomfort in the company of ideas. Perhaps in your youth somebody went to work on you with a bludgeon of bundled ideas whose purpose was to knock down and out any ideas of your own. This is called 'education'. *Education is the sovereignty of the ruling mythology.* Before we go on to explore the wonderful worlds of ideas, with my lodger Aaron Godman to guide us, we had better make a detour into the realms of education. Let us slip down the by-road that loops off the main narrative, which is about *ideas*, and take a look at this thing called 'education'.

About education

The subject of this tract is not only to lay open the true source of all the evils and disorders under which this country labours, but at the same time to point out a sure and adequate remedy. The source of all these has been traced to the present erroneous and defective course of education; and if that point be proved, it will necessarily follow, that there can be no hopes of amending these evils, till there be a change in that course.

This quotation is paraphrased from 'A Plan of Education for the Young Nobility and Gentry of Great Britain. Most humbly addressed to the Father of his People, by Thomas Sheridan AM, in 1796'. (It is taken from a first facsimile edition limited to 250 numbered copies, produced by Swan Books of Southwold, Suffolk. Copyright 1987, Ronald Fletcher.)

Two hundred years after Sheridan made this appeal to his sovereign nothing much has changed, except that today's educational needs would be directed at managers rather than 'the Young

Nobility and Gentry' whose leadership has long since been usurped. Defective education continues to be the source of the 'evils and disorders under which this country labours'.

Is this really the case, do you think? Is the state of our managerial education the source of our troubles? In *your* experience? It certainly has been in mine. I seem to have spent the better part of a lifetime being entertained by the antics of the inadequately educated people who often get promoted into positions of authority and leadership in our industries. I was offering them education, though it didn't seem to do some of them much good, which meant I could keep on flogging the snake-oil medicine. That's business: when managerial hypochondriacs embrace their suffering the quack-doctors prosper.

For example, the time donkey's years ago when I found myself working for Bedlam plc. It was fascinating and quite unbelievable; like finding yourself in a jungle keeping company with howler monkeys, gibbering chimpanzees, placid great apes, screeching parakeets . . . where they got things Wrong First Time, and second time . . . . It was a hilarious, enlightening and incredibly enriching experience. It is my intention to share it with you in my next book, already on the stocks and provisionally entitled *The Misfit in the Madhouse*. Bedlam was then enjoying a boom-time during which economic inflation in two figures ensured that the mere holding of large stocks of raw material was a sure-fire way to make money. Even half-wits could do it, and half-wits did.

Their raw material was plastic, their technology based on materials science – the behaviour of polymers, the stuff of organic chemistry and applied physics. Yet when he was asked 'what is a polymer?' their technical manager, who had been a bus conductor before joining Bedlam as a spanner-twirling tool-setter, replied 'It's that stuff in those bags,' pointing to the pellets of polystyrene. He regarded this as a satisfactory definition. His boss, as amiable a fellow as you would ever be pleased to meet, who promoted fools, took this as expert testimony from a man elevated to managerial office because he was a 'hard worker'. The fact that his frantic hard work had its origins in ignorance and lack of education eluded the boss, who accorded him a touching loyalty. After all, working hard is what it's all about!

This lack of education in the fundamentals of the technology typified just about the whole of the plastics processing industry at that time. So much so that when Japanese assembly plants first set up in the UK and tried to source plastic components indigenously they were unable to do so: the knowledge-gap in their potential suppliers made it impossible to meet quality standards. No amount of management education is of much use in situations such as this where technological understanding does not exist. Neither is any management consultancy intervention of any use unless it is capable of addressing the technological shortfall.

But things have changed since then, yet in some ways stay the same. Bedlam's managers, typical of British management in general in those days, were too uneducated to see themselves as uneducated so education was the last thing they thought they needed. Education? Book-learning! They despised it, and rejected offers of it. They prided themselves on being 'practical' men, men of 'experience' who knew how to get things done, fast. And wrong. Nowadays the reverse holds true: surveys tell us that managers rate the acquisition of a sound managerial education as their number one priority. No longer is learning despised, or knowledge reviled, or theory mocked.

So education is as important today as it was in Sheridan's eighteenth century. Is it really? How much of it? Let us look at a little trilogy of three tales by way of shedding light on these questions. They are: the Roman; the Wheelwright; and the A-Team.

The Roman

You and I, being educated folk, are aware that the earth is not flat. The uneducated, though unaware that our planet is a spheroidal body rotating in orbit around a minor star, also know that the earth is not flat: they point to the mountains and valleys as self-evident proof that it isn't flat. The Romans of two thousand years ago did not know that the earth is a spinning orb, but they could see that it was not flat, apart from here and there on the great plains. Yet they gridded their sprawling empire with a network of roads connecting their scattered garrison towns and all leading back to Rome. Each road following the shortest practicable distance between the two points it was built to connect, to facilitate speedy movement of military and commercial traffic. These highways are with us still: you can fall in behind the legions on the long tramp from

Bath to Lincoln following the Fosse Way; or hike northwest on Watling Street on the trek from London to Chester; or plod along a hundred others. They are all laid in their proper directions, near arrow-straight to their destinations.

This was a spectacular accomplishment, for an uneducated people. How did they do it? Could you, an educated person, do it?

I will now pose a conundrum to you, one that is to do with these Roman roads. A serious riddle which occupied several weeks of learned correspondence in the *Sunday Times* of years ago, and which has not yet been satisfactorily answered. Here it is . . . .

The Roman's riddle

When the Roman military surveyors were required to mark the track of a new road from one place to another, how did they know *in which direction to go*?

Try putting yourself, with your educated modern mind, into their position. Suppose you are billeted in London, on the River Thames, and you are called upon to build a road from London to York, on the River Ouse. Communication between these two sites is confined, until you complete your road, to a shipping lane up and down the east coast between the estuaries of the two rivers. Starting from London, in which direction do you deploy your corps of pioneers to lay the metalled track? Conversely, your opposite number in York is required to head his highway towards London. In which direction does he start to dig?

This is not an idle question; it is a real brain-teaser, especially for the educated. So tell me how you will answer it, using only those facilities available to your uneducated Roman fore-runner.

Use a compass, you say? You don't have a proper compass, but you do have a sliver of magnetite lodestone which aligns itself in the north–south direction when you dangle it from a string. York is northward of London so follow the lodestone?

Or the Pole Star, that indicates north, and do your navigating by night?

Refer to the Ordnance Survey maps? Sorry, they are sixteen centuries into the unborn future. Calculate a course by knowledge of the latitude and longitude of London and York? Sorry, there is neither long nor lat; these cannot be expressed without degrees of a circle, and these are in the future beyond your Roman reach.

Or follow the shadow of the noonday sun? Stick a pikestaff in the sand and mark its shadow, growing shorter by the hour until the sun is at zenith, then lengthening towards evening. Shortest = north!

None of these will work. If you follow the pointing lodestone towards magnetic north it will lead your road into the sea near Blackpool; if you pursue the shortest shadow or the Pole Star towards true north you will land up in Grimsby. Either way you have missed York by many miles. Call yourself a military surveyor? You are a fake and a failure. Dismissed from service!

But you *do* call yourself a problem solver. All our managers call themselves that. So solve this one. Use your imagination, forget your modern education, and produce a *plausible* solution to this problem. If the Ancient Romans could figure out how to do it, surely *we* should be able to.

I have worked out a solution which meets my criterion of plausibility, using nothing more than the Romans had to hand. If you can do the same, and feel like testing your answer you can always tell me about it by 'phoning 01745 570408. The first caller whose solution is as plausible and practicable as mine will be awarded a prize, probably a bottle of malt whisky, or champagne. I shall be the sole judge of the contest, since I shall be the sole provider of the prize. But I don't mind gambling a few quid just to hear your answer. Tell me, how did those old Romans know which way to go? But allow me to give you a kind of oblique clue, in the form of an anecdote from the food industry.

'Simple Simon met a Pieman, driven to despair . . .' Well, not a pieman in actual fact, but a *biscuit* man – a firm of biscuit producers, being driven to despair by a big manufacturing problem. Their main product line – malted biscuits – had suddenly ceased to taste of malt. All output was being side-tracked back into the input end of the process in a classic bottle-to-bottle hook-up. Warehouse stocks were quarantined pending the outcome of tests to determine at what point in time the taste had disappeared. Anxieties were expressed that stock might have to be recalled from supermarket shelves. The situation was critical, the problem pressing, in urgent need of solving.

Problem solving is one of the intellectual delights of management; it is so much more dramatic than problem preventing. 'These problems are sent to try us,' say the managers with the weary resignation of men shouldering a burden that only they can carry, while inwardly gloating that here is yet another situation which will permit them to demonstrate their indispensability and thus bolster their fragile job security. Solving problems is a legitimate way of showing off. So they showed off, attacking the problem with the tools at their disposal. When your only solution is a hammer all your problems are nails, so you hammer away at it. If your solution is an axe, then you hack at it with gusto. If your analytic tool happens to be a spade, you dig deep.

The managers addressed the problem, each with his own special tool. The chairman of the tasting panel set up a series of what he called 'organoleptic' tests. The chemists submitted the malt to gas chromatographic analysis and scanned the tracings in search of essential oils in parts per million. The formulation team recalculated the recipe. The operations director had all 'processing parameters', as he called them – times, pressures, temperatures, oven ventilation, belt speeds – verified.

All to no avail. The malted biscuits resolutely refused to taste of malt: the problem solvers had tried everything, yet still the solution eluded them, for three days and nights . . . .

Then Simple Simon happened along, with his bright new MBA from a nearby university, doing his 'industrial secondment' to find out how the real world works. Everybody was too busy problem solving to notice him, so he wandered about wearing an ingratiating expression and making tentative overtures to become involved, like a guest who's come to the wrong wedding. The only people who had time for him were the line operators, so he talked to them.

Until the operations director noticed and took pity on him, and invited him to sit in on the problem progress meeting where the problem solvers shared their bafflements, showed each other miles of concertina-folded computer printouts and sheaves of maltsters' certificates of conformance, which they perused with earnest scowls to show commitment. After they had all had their say, and got no nearer the solution, the ops director addressed Simple Simon, who was acting invisible on the edge of the gathering. 'Have *you* got any ideas? New mind brought to bear and all that . . .' this voice trailed off, without hope.

'It's the bucket,' said Simon.

'The bucket? What bucket?'

'The bucket they use to tip the malt extract in at the mixer.'

'What about the bucket?'

'It's a *new* bucket.'

'Listen 'ere, lad,' the ops director directed, 'We are here to solve a critical problem, not to talk about ironmongery!'

'The new bucket replaced the old bucket when its handle fell off. Three days ago,' Simple Simon explained. 'So somebody gave the operators a new bucket. It is half as big as the old bucket. The mixing plan says that one bucketful of malt extract goes into the mix. So the operators tip in one bucket, like they have always done. But only half as much malt.'

The ensuing silence was broken by somebody asking 'Who's this bloody know-all?' Who indeed . . . ?

. . . Simple Simon, following the advice of William of Occam, fourteenth century theologian who invented 'Occam's razor' and the slogan 'Keep It Simple, Stupid!' Try the simplest things first! You should bear this in mind if you try to find an answer to the riddle of the Roman roads. KISS!

The wheelwright

Even as a lad I found woodworking an engrossing activity. So whenever the journeyman wheelwright Mr Greensmith, a wiry old man who followed work as faithfully as international capital flows towards slave labour, was summoned to the farm to mend a dray or a tip-cart or a milk-float I gave him my closest attention. I recapitulated part of the social history of mankind, regressed to the role of man the tool-using animal. I loved tools. Mr Greensmith had a chest filled with them. He taught me that tools are neutral; no better than his knuckly hand and watery eye made them; that a chisel, for instance, simply does not care. Used on the one hand by a chimpanzee or on the other by a Chippendale and in one instance you end up with an ape whose fingers are bleeding or on the other with a rosewood cabinet. Either outcome is of no consequence to the chisel. This is true of all tools, including the tools of quality and management. They are there. They do not care. They are no better than their user who makes use of them. Many managers are unaware of this, believing that the mere possession of tools is enough to achieve success. So they collect managerial tools, and never make a wheel.

I can make a wheel; Mr Greensmith taught me. We made one to

replace a wobbly wheel rickety with a century of wear on one of the tip-carts. We went to the sawmill and brought back twenty-five pieces of timber; twelve billets of seasoned ash as straight-grained as an arrow, for the spokes; twelve blocks of vinegary-smelling oak to be cut into the curved felloes ('fellies', we called them) to form the wheel's rim; and a block of waney elm big enough for the beheading of a monarch, its grain so tangled as to render it unsplittable when shaped into the hub, or 'nave', of the wheel, with its central axle-hole, and its twelve mortices cut on the slant to accommodate the tenoned spokes with their secret wedges, and to impart a dished form to the finished wheel. Not so much an artefact as a work of art, nearly five feet in diameter.

We took the wooden work of art to the forge. The blacksmith, though no doubt unable to state the coefficient of linear expansion of the wrought-iron strap he was about to anvil-weld into a circle, measured the wheel's circumference with string, added a bit for weld overlap, deducted a bit for contraction, and formed the strap into a completed rim. Then a fire about six feet across was made in the yard, and the entire hoop heated until it was judged to be expanded enough to be picked up with long tongs and hammered on to the smoking charring oak of the rim. It was shrunk on to the wheel in everlasting encircling embrace by quenching it with liquor from the 'bosh', a metal tank with an open top hard by the anvil, which served the double purpose of a place to pee and a coolant in which to dunk hot horse shoes. This ammonia-rich stale urine was believed to impart hardness to the surface of iron; it probably did, as a primitive form of that treatment of metal surfaces known to metallurgists as 'nitriding'. Waste not want not.

The wheelwright and the blacksmith, each sublimely unaware that pi=3.1415927 . . ., unacquainted with any notion of job satisfaction or worker motivation, yet able to make a wheel. The wheel was bolted on to the axle of the cart and that was that. The job was done. Because these were people who *did* jobs, not people who *had* jobs. There is a world of difference between a job that is done and a job that is held. Theirs was a *pre*-industrial pattern of work; they did whatever job happened along. If the market for wheels slumped the wheelwright turned to his nice little earner – he made coffins. Or went haymaking. Or did whatever varied tasks presented themselves and to which his skills and inclinations were suited. Yet they lived.

This is fast becoming the *post*-industrial pattern of work, with fewer people *having* jobs and more of us *doing* jobs. The wheelwright and the smith were yesterday's equivalent of today's 'portfolio people', taking jobs as they came. As you will very probably soon be doing, as many of us have been doing for years. The purpose of education is to equip ourselves for this strange and daunting new world of no-jobs. There will still be *work* to be done. All the work is a *process* of converting inputs into outputs; anybody wanting to work will have to answer the question, 'How can I be of *best service* to this or that conversion process?'

Imagine that any conversion process is exemplified by a herd of dairy cows whose purpose is the conversion of grass into milk. How will *you* serve it? Bearing in mind that all true discipline emanates from the process itself and its needs: the farmer does not 'own' the herd; it owns him; he must husband it with devotion. This is true of any work process. Will your role be that of wheelbarrowing manure and tending to the milking parlour in daily attendance on the herd? Or that of the veterinarian making periodic visits to many herds? Will you be serving the process with high-level or low-level inputs? The choice is yours, education the deciding factor.

The A-team (Karen's gang again)

There was a touch of harmless pride in their decision to label themselves 'The A-team'. They rationalized it by saying that the A stood for Assembly, because the problem that Karen and her colleagues were about to tackle resided in the Assembly shop.

It was there that one of their core products was made up by taking component parts, made upstream by stamping and bending metal, and brazing them together into a whole assembly. This work was carried out by trained women operators, who were slow, meticulous and painstaking. Too slow. The company invested in a state-of-the-art automatic collating and brazing machine to replace the plodding women. It didn't work. Why?

The components, though fabricated to nominally exact dimensions, were too inexact, too variable. This hardly mattered to the women, who carefully hand-selected components to achieve a fit, discarding any components which failed to meet the needs of the

assembly integrity. This resulted in high scrap rates of components for inadequate quality. The new machine was blind, unable
to select and try to fit components which matched to produce a finished assembly. Presented with a random supply of component
parts it tried to assemble them willy-nilly. So what had been a
heap of rejected components was turned into a more expensive
heap of faulty assemblies by the undiscriminating machine.

Karen and her colleagues had learned and used their SPC so
well that by now it was fully internalized, no longer a novelty
approach, just another tool of the mind to be employed wherever
appropriate. Still a satisfying tool to use in the daily routines, but
no longer the exciting thing it had been in the early days. This is
how things are in that process of 'culture change' known as total
quality management. There is an initial explosion of enthusiasm
as the new technique is learned and applied; eventually the dust
settles, the new knowledge loses its shine, and the intellectual
climate lapses into its customary languor. This is so universally
true you could make philosophical postulates out of it.

Price's postulates

- Work is intrinsically boring.
- The more effectively work is done the more boring it
  becomes.
- Progressive work is long periods of boredom alleviated by
  short bursts of excitement.

These are stated as general observations, applicable to the major-
ity of our workforce – the television-set assemblers, supermarket
shelf-stackers, cardboard box-makers, bank clerks, dairymaids,
laundrymen, dentists, undertakers . . . the whole toiling mass
boring itself to death in order to stay alive. Perhaps you exempt
yourself from this collective *ennui*? Congratulate yourself that
yours is an interesting job, yours is. Is it? Then why do you spend
so much money buying tickets to expensive seminars to listen to
the insults of some overpaid guru? To *learn* something? Whatever
do you learn in such congregations that might ever be a scrap of
use to you? No. You go to these firework and razzmatazz events
for one reason only – to alleviate your boredom! And why not?

Karen and company were becoming bored again. They were

making money out of SPC, and they loved the work of doing it, but it *was* becoming a bit old-hat. Which is why the arrival of the assembly machine-that-does-not-work was such a godsend. It broke the boredom.

So they did some SPC on the components, explored the origins of excessive variation which made random assembly impossible. But their tool kit was too limited to lead them to the answer to the question 'which processing factors are causing the unacceptable variation in the components?' Big money rested on the solution; how could they work it out?

They needed another tool. So they were introduced to one, and taught how to use it. They equipped themselves with Taguchi experimentation design. They put various factors into the array – component lengths, springback, degree of lubrication – of those things they imagined might be affecting the outcome.

People have been heard to say that quality is common sense. They might be right, some of the time, but not all of the time. The assembly problem was itself the outcome of common-sense production methods hallowed by years of practice. Taguchi used *uncommon* sense to achieve quality. So they were able to bring the new machine into full commission and start making money out of it.

The accolade was awarded when a delegation of executives from a Japanese customer's UK plant paid a visit. It included some Japanese nationals. They were enthralled with the competence and involvement of the workforce. Taguchi? 'What is that?' they asked, and faxed headquarters in Tokyo to tell them they had found it.

Education. The Romans who thought the earth flat. Simple Simon and his Occam's razor. Mr Greensmith who thought that a wheel should be round. The A-team and their simple tools for turning data into information into money into honour.

Education. What is it for? How much of it do you need? How much of it do you want?

Perhaps you think education is a Good Thing, worth having for its own sake. An excellent reason for wanting it, even though it might be no more than a sovereignty of the ruling mythology – it sure as hell beats ignorance.

Education as a possession, a trophy, like the bimbo woman on the arm of a swaggering mogul who doubts his own potency? Or as an impressive string of imposing letters after your name: proclamations of intellectual prowess, credentials of worthiness, academic equivalent of the giant curving wickerwork penis-cones sported by the men of Peronnet, filled with hollow promise? Or as a graduation photograph of yourself with a new degree and a mortar-board propped on your mother's television set to torment jealous neighbours with less-accomplished offspring?

Education as a qualification for entitlement to promotion to higher responsibilities; education as bogus wisdom claiming a right to more money?

Education to make money? Years ago I was the friend of a man from whom I am now separated by more than two hundred million pounds. His. Not mine. His education consisted, he says, of two things only, taught to him by his father. One – coins are disc-shaped so that they will roll around. Two – coins are disc-shaped so that they will stack on one another. The trick? Knowing when to roll and when to stack. My education was infinitely more splendid than his; it distracted me from the humdrum work of stacking coins, so mine rolled away. Beware of education; it can be a way of staying poor.

Thomas Sheridan told us in 1796 that education holds the answer to 'evils and disorders under which this country labours'. His words seem to me to be true today. Education is the key opening the door to success, both national and personal.

So those of us who love learning, bearing in mind that love is the basis of quality, had best avail ourselves of more education, if we are not to end up as a nation of hamburger-flippers, theme-park varlets, and moronic serfs on the assembly lines of factories owned by foreigners.

There is no shortage of supply; very much the opposite. We have some of the finest educators and facilities in the world. Educational programmes are on offer from such marvellous institutions and repositories of talent as the Open University and the educational publishing establishment, with their long experience as providers of knowledge. There has never been a greater need for education and there has never been a better supply of it.

That was supposed to be a by-road about education. It is turning into a long highway in its own right; time we looped back to the main narrative which is about writing.

You can become a moderately successful writer, whether you have been chopped out of the company as it was 'down-sized' (a euphemism which makes a sacking sound like a natural phenomenon of biological inevitability such as the shedding of leaves by Autumn trees) or whether you are still clinging by your fingernails to your job. Either way you are probably scared, and therefore impotently angry.

Use your anger to help you cope with your fear. Set yourself a target income to be earned by getting your words into print. There are plenty of publications prepared to pay modest fees to help fill their page space, and modest fees mount up. If you work at it. If you still receive a salary, set out to double it by working on the side. So few of us can afford the ascetic luxury of living on one salary, so generate yourself a supplementary income in your spare time. Aim to double your income for a start. I know it can be done; I did it for years. I rarely had fewer than three careers running in triple harness. These days I'm down to two.

There is nothing to stop you, except yourself. Oh, and, of course, the envy of your colleagues. Envy is jealousy armed with a weapon and intent on inflicting damage. It is one of the most evil of the vices of the ego. But that, as they say, is what friends are for.

Your true friends are your words. They are the regiments of soldiers summoned out of your imagination to fight the good fight. Rank upon rank, obedient to your command. A disciplined multitude marching to your drum, and a horde held in reserve in the hills. An army so powerful it can bring death to tyrants and destruction to empires. This is no exaggeration. This is no artistic flight of fancy. This is not the wishful thinking of a Walter Mitty mind. If you doubt the truth and the reality of it I can direct your attention to the testimony of those who survived the battles. Or point to the graves of those who did not.

Does any of this surprise, or even alarm, you? Did you think that 'writing' was a namby-pamby activity bereft of passion? Work for nerds? A way of passing time in Pleasantville? It can be, if that is what you want it to be.

You *can* write, if you want. To be successful as a writer (whatever *that* means) you need to accept only *one* condition: you must do as the great Welsh writer Dylan Thomas directed: 'Love the words'. Because love is the basis of quality. Love the words.

If you feel inspired to write for any reason other than your love of words then I wish you well. I hope you will enjoy the praise and the money that might be yours; because I know for sure that you will have enjoyed neither your work nor that part of your life spent doing it.

Option 2: The Management Consultant

Consultant is often a fancy word for salesman or saleswoman. Except in the field of medicine, where a consultant is a highly learned doctor in a specialism, who is used as a source of knowledge and expertise by medical generalists. In this context a lot of prestige comes with the respected title 'consultant'. This has been filched by non-medical opportunists. Hawkers of plastic windows tart up their selling by adopting the title 'double-glazing *consultant*'; peddlers of insurance policies earn high commission by calling themselves 'financial *consultants*'. Anybody is free to call themselves 'consultant'.

Like that four letter word I've been telling you about, this is another word, intended to lend a spurious authority to its user, that has now become spattered with muck and threadbare from overuse. The word which is coming into fashion to supersede it is 'counsellor'. This carries a connotation of patient and caring sagacity. You can watch counsellors counselling on television programmes. The person being counselled is visible as a silhouette to avoid the embarrassment of being identified while whingeing in front of the camera about having been hideously abused and permanently cranked. The counsellor sits in the full glare of the lights, wearing an expression that passes itself off as deep interest and nodding heartfelt sympathy but is in fact nothing more than boredom and long suffering in the good old quest for cash. There is money in counselling: you can earn a living by looking caring and listening to people who will pay you to listen because for them merely being listened to is a delicious novelty. It's called 'psychiatry', when practised by qualified doctors. Lower down the professional scale they call it 'stress counselling'. I would have a go at it myself, but for the fact that you have to keep your mouth shut and your ears open, and that's not one of my strongest traits. I have too low a boredom threshold, and find it hard to resist the temptation to mock the afflicted as mercilessly as I mock myself. They couldn't stand it as I can, because I am well used to it. So I stick with consultancy, but I think I might start calling myself 'counsellor'.

A management consultant sells certainty in times of doubt. With the right organization, and access to a hype-engine of Hollywood magnitude, a consultant can be turned into a celebrity. A celebrity is somebody who is famous for being well known. Micky Mouse is a celebrity. At a certain point in the progression of this academic show business the celebrity is changed, like a metamorphosing grub, into a guru. Thereafter the messenger becomes the message; even though the original message may be one of infinite beauty and truth it is overlaid by so much glitz and glitter that the sinners who crowd around the guru's feet clamouring for salvation are too dazzled to see it. Style has eclipsed content. But it's fun; it breaks the boredom of earning your daily bread. There is wisdom to be won from the mouth of the guru, once you learn how to listen to it. You can use it to try to change organizations.

There is an amazing arrogance in the very idea of the 'management of change' by an outside consultant. Yet it happens. I have been allowed to stick my nose into a lot of companies while I was sticking my hand into their till. After a while changes happened, big changes sometimes. Somehow.

People ask me, 'What do you actually *do* in a company when you are trying to change its culture?' (Do I *try* to change *culture*?)

In all honesty, because I am mainly (but not completely) an honest man, I have to admit to them, 'To be honest with you I don't really *know* what I do. All I know is that after I've been there for a while changes begin to happen.'

This reply tells them nothing, because I don't really know what I do except talk, but sometimes they persist (I think they are planning on becoming consultants themselves and are just picking my brains – a meagre harvest) and ask again, 'But you must do *something*; what is it you do?'

Then I dig myself a trap to see if they will push me into it. I tell them, 'You might just as well ask the bull what he does when he is invited to service the needs of the cows who are his clients. He *inseminates*, with *semin*-ars. Brings new life into being. That is what I try to do – bring new life into the company.'

This statement of truth is generally greeted with a quizzical look followed by a knowing response, 'Ah, bull. *Bull*! I get it! Mushroom management. You keep them in the dark and sling bullshit at them!' And I realize they have completely and absolutely and forever missed the point. They have pushed me into the trap of their own ignorance.

I *'bring new life'*, did I say? Phew, there's arrogance for you! Time for another vignette.

Vignette: 'Is there life in the old dog . . .?'

Science is a testament to the reasoning power of the human *mind*: our marvellous world of technology is its monument. Science analyses and explains natural phenomena; that's what it is for. It takes the old and synthesizes it into new forms, enriching our quality of life. It is a voyage of exploration into our materialist world. To science everything is reducible to understandable bits and pieces, can be cut into manageable parts. In the life sciences all organisms, which are assemblages of component parts, can be described in terms of their structure – anatomy – and their function – physiology. It is all a matter of applied physics and chemistry. Even our work organizations lend themselves to scientific scrutiny; after all, a manufacturing or business company is itself a sort of hyper-organism, divisible into the structures and functions which are its components. Scientific method is a powerful paradigm of understanding. Will it ever meet any boundaries which it will be unable to breach? Such as the creation of life itself?

Scientists are already able to take a soup of simple elements, and by striking it with a bolt of electricity convert the simple material into the more complex forms of amino-acids, the 'building blocks' of protein and hence of life itself. They are by now capable of creating the glimmerings of artificial intelligence in a box of wires and microchips. What next . . .?

The dizzying prospect of what science might yet achieve sends my mind spinning into fantasy: I am spectator of a scenario in the near future . . . .

The scientific team is gathered around its apparatus. They are about to have another crack at creating life. Nothing as elementary as electrocuting a chemical goulash this time; no, something altogether more ambitious: they are about to create a dog. A dog? Why a dog? Why not? Man's best friend and all that; besides, we don't have the space to build anything bigger, like an elephant. OK, let it be a dog.

They have the *anatomy*. Sheafs of detailed engineering drawings that show the size and shape of every bone and every gristly fibre of tissue, the location of every hair follicle, the curve of every claw – everything necessary to assemble all the component parts into a unified whole. Where did they get them all from? Don't ask. When they tell you that the entire universe was created X billion years ago as a Big Bang you never ask them *what* went bang, do you? So be quiet and observe with respect as you patiently await the miracle they are about to perform.

They begin the work of assembling their build-your-own-dog kit. Always begin with the anatomy – *structure* first! Function after. They put the jigsaw of bones together, carefully lapping the articulated joints so that the assembled machine will run smoothly. Squidging the greasy loops of entrails into the visceral cavity with the casual skill of *cordon bleu* cooks stuffing sausages into a turkey. Fastidiously implanting into its assigned socket in the naked pelt every bristle and every single hair. Has anybody *counted* the hairs, *numbered* them? Yes, the computer. That's OK then. Now to syringe the lifeblood into the pipes of the circulatory system, check the pump, try the valves. That's it. Finished. Fully assembled. A handsome animal, heavy-shouldered and narrow-flanked. Coloured gleaming black with a touch of tan on the muzzle and chest and under the tail. A Rottweiler, glossy with newness.

That's got the anatomy sorted out, the structure; they move on to the physiology, the *function*. Is the bile the right shade of neon-green? Have you checked the pH of the gastric juices? What about the glycogen to sugar ratio? Are the hormone levels correct in the endocrine system? All very, very complicated: a battery of chemical tests to meet the functional specification that came with the kit. That's it. All tests completed and results approved. All work done. Anatomically and physiologically a perfect dog . . . .

Does it bite, mister?

Why doesn't it bark?

Because it's dead.

Something is missing. The scientists prod the canine cadaver in the ribs; they get no response. They clip on the electrodes and flick a few thousands volts through it; not a twitch. 'I'm sorry, Dr Frankenstein', one of the assistant scientists confesses resignedly, 'but something seems to be missing, something *vital*.'

Something is missing. They got the anatomy right. They got the physiology right. Yet the dog is dead. Being rational people, whose rationalism is able to 'explain' anything and tries to explain everything (like Corny and his mushroom theory only on a higher academic plane) but is unable to explain the nature of *mind* from which rationalism springs, they have tried to animate the inanimate, and failed. Don't they know that anything as *irrational* as life cannot ever be created by rationalism? *Only life can bring life*. Like the bull in the herd. Even Corny the village idiot comprehended *that*.

This paradigm is applicable to companies. The company, that hyper-organism, that organization which the change-agent (consultant?) sets out to change is also a thing of anatomy and physiology, of structure and function. Just like the dead dog. To bring the dog to barking life a third ingredient is needed, a *vital* spark. And so with the organization. This is what the change-agent is for: to spark off change, 'cultural' change, by inseminating the organization. This is bull work. The bull worker can be a man or a woman, because the inseminating medium is an implantation of *ideas*, and the world of ideas transcends the corporeal world of gender. Ideas are playthings of the *mind*, and anybody who hopes to change organizational culture and its behaviour must first of all *change minds*. With ideas. Time we listened to the idiot Aaron Godman again.

The idiot's tale 2: 'The very idea . . .'

I see that he who claims to be the author of this book is going about his favourite pastime again – doing nothing: leaving it to me to tell you about ideas and their potency.

I lead him to ideas. (But before we go on let us pause so that I can assure you that the things we are talking about now are in no way an irrelevant digression from the theme of the book. They are *deeply* to do with consultancy and culture change, with TQM.)

So, I bring him to ideas. First we shall reflect upon the nature of ideas; then we will sample some. First, their nature . . . .

The world of ideas is like an ocean. An ocean wider and deeper and older than any ocean imaginable.

Entry into these waters is a matter of choice: you are free to go in or to stay out.

So you stay out. You limit your contact with the ocean to nothing more than a stroll along its beach. But you are not unaware of it; neither are you immune to its influences. Without listening you hear its rhythmic soughing as it swills up the sand, followed by the soft staccato of popping and crackling while it is dribbling its retreat. The ocean is breathing. Stop, sit and really listen. Within the space of a minute your own breathing will be attuned to the ocean's rhythm. Deep, calming, restful.

You don't have to take my word for it; you can try it for yourself. You don't need to travel to the seaside to do it either; you can do it tonight, when you go to bed.

When your head hits the pillow close your eyes and envision a field of golden wheat under a blue sky. All you can see in your mind's eye is a prairie of golden grain swaying under a sky of perfect blue. Hold the picture, hold it . . . you are now breathing to the ocean's ancient rhythm, and it makes you feel good, calm, serene, relaxed.

Can you *measure* it as a scientist would find it necessary to measure it? No, there's no need to. Does it 'exist'? Well, you are experiencing it, so it *must* 'exist'. Do you still, as a materialist, persist in your denial of the possibility of non-material influences?

It's only an idea. From the Sanskrit of about 4,000 years ago, if you must know. Only an idea – pretty powerful though, powerful enough to have affected your breathing. Let us look further into the power within this ocean which is the world of ideas.

As we said before, entry to this world is optional, though its influence is all-pervading and unavoidable; even if you go no closer to it than its edge it will affect you.

You are at liberty to go as close as you want. You can paddle in its shallows, cavort playfully in its surf, or swim down into its deeps where the stronger currents are running, the groundswells which shift continents and change the shapes of worlds. The ideas are there, awaiting their time, waiting until the world is ready, waiting to be born into the light of day. Sometimes they are born prematurely, and lie ignored like a neglected foundling until they are noticed and then embraced. Like the following . . . .

Vignette: worlds in collision

Worlds in Collision is the title of a book published in the 1950s whose author, Immanuel Velikovsky, dared to propose that the dinosaur extinctions of sixty-five million years ago were the outcome of meteorite or asteroid impact upon the earth. This was an unconventional view. Upholders of the conventional wisdom of forty-odd years ago ridiculed the ideas and shunned the author.

Scientific literature today espouses catastrophe theory. The notion that the mass extinctions of species during prehistory might have been caused in the manner proposed by Velikovsky is now acceptable to orthodox science. His ideas are welcomed; they have entered the body of conventional wisdom. His name is not. They are his anonymous monument; his name goes unremarked. This is an act of plagiarism on the institutional scale.

He put forward other intellectually daring ideas: these too were ridiculed but are now assuming respectability and acceptance. His name is never mentioned.

As a famous British politician once said, 'It's a funny old world'.

If you look at a map of the earth, or at a globe representing the planet on its 23.5° tilt, you will see that the globe's surface is conventionally gridded by a series of arbitrary lines. There are the parallels of latitude, starting with zero at the equator and running through 90° to each of the poles. The meridians of longitude circle the globe at 'right angles' to the parallels of latitude, running from pole to pole in the manner of a network containing the globe. The zero meridian is drawn through Greenwich in London (because the English were the dominant maritime power when the map was drawn, so they drew it) and the meridians then extend eastward and westward at 15° intervals until they coincide 180° from Greenwich. These grid-lines are nothing more than a navigational convenience; they actually *do not* '*exist*' in reality. They are none the less powerful for that; you can use them to find your way around the world.

Now, looking at the globe roughly in the region of latitude 40° north to 60° north and longitude 15° west to 20° east, we see part of a continental land mass with an island close by it to the north-west of it. We are looking at a map of continental Europe – France, Germany, Spain . . . with Great Britain to its upper left.

Now imagine a global catastrophe. A massive asteroid hurtles out of the void and collides with planet Earth, much the same as it is supposed to have done sixty-five million years ago when it is said to have caused the extinction of the dinosaurs. This one is too late to kill the giant reptiles; instead it wipes out the whole of humankind. The planet survives, as planets do; mankind has perished. Gaia, the beautiful Blue Planet, sighs her relief.

The land mass between latitude 40° and 60° north, and 15° west to 20° east is still there. There is still a island to the northwest of it.

Is it *still* Europe – France, Germany, Spain . . .? Is the island *still* Britain?

No, *they do not exist*; now they are no more than geological formations jutting out of the sea. That is all they are. They are nameless. There is nobody left to give them names, to have ideas.

A clash of symbols

But until the asteroid strikes again and snuffs out *homo sapiens* they will retain the names we have conventionally chosen to call them by. Great Britain will exist *as an idea*. France, Germany, Spain . . . the others, will exist, as *conventional ideas*. France, Germany, Spain . . . the others will exist, as *conventional ideas*.

Nothing more, but nothing less.

These ideas, like all ideas, are *powerful*. So powerful that they even declare war on one another from time to time. Ideas. Things of the mind. Powerful phantoms by which we live and die. Ghosts fighting other ghosts. Symbols clashing.

Would you like to try a bit of symbol building and symbol clashing for yourself? Take twelve matchsticks and divide them into two groups of six.

Arrange three of the first group into a triangle, an isosceles tri-angle, and lay it on the table, apex uppermost. Use the other three to form a second triangle on top of the first, base uppermost. You have made a star shape, six-pointed.

Arrange two of the second six as a cross. Add the remaining four matches to the four ends of the cross to form four right angles in a clockwise direction. You have made a crooked cross.

What have you *done*? You have transformed useful matches into dangerous symbols. Turned trivial sticks into stupendous emblems, a Jewish Star of David and a Nazi Swastika. Splinters into words.

Mankind, you are so murderously foolhardy, such a willing slave to the tyranny of your own symbols, prepared to kill or be killed at their bidding, dying for ideas.

Ideas are not only powerful; they are able to recruit other ideas into alliance.

How is it that ideas are so powerful? Because they direct actions. They 'justify' actions. Ideas sustain the belief which guides and legitimizes behaviour.

We act as if what we believe to be true is really true.

This pronouncement should be of great interest to anybody trying to alter organizational behaviour, seeking to change corporate culture towards TQM. It is a key component of mega-change. What follows from it is:

> To change behaviour it is necessary to change belief.

Or, to put it the other way round,

> Altered belief is a prerequisite for changed behaviour.

This is a dynamic equation for change.

By way of illustrating this point let us look at a couple of examples of how it has been used, taken from mankind's appalling history of persecution and exploitation. These are horror stories, but they are of use to us.

A spoonful of sugar helps the bitterness go down

From the year 1637, when the first sugar plantation was grubbed out of Barbados's rank vegetation, and after 1834 when Britain made slavery even more profitable overnight by at last declaring it illegal, fortunes were amassed out of sugar. From its sweet bonanza great estates were purchased, titles and respect bought, splendid cities built, excise duties paid.

This was a vast industry. More than 300,000 shipping-tons engaged in it every year. Outward from booming Liverpool in Autumn laden with cloth, salt, iron utensils, muskets, gunpowder, bound for the West African coast on the first leg of the infamous Triangular Trade. Discharge the trade goods and take on board a richer cargo – slaves, as many as could be shoe-horned into the ship. Make the Middle Passage to the West Indies. Auction them off like cattle, scrub their mess out of the hold and fill it with rum and sugar for the homeward leg. Oh to be in England now that April's there. Home again, gold in your pocket, blood on your hands, and a mind brutalized beyond belief by the evil business of making money out of the misery of others. Three hundred thousand tons of cargo a year, and every ton paid for by the life of one slave. Twenty-four million human beings transported out of Africa: thirteen million died in transit, eleven million landed in chains. This guilt is too bitter for a Christian gentleman such as you to bear. Shame of such magnitude as this needs a coating of sugar before it can be swallowed.

To salve your conscience you recruit three specious ideas, which will legitimize your barbarity so that you may live in peace with yourself and your criminal wealth. They assure you these three things about the people to whom you brought misery and death . . .

1.   They are *unlike us*. They are less than human: animals who do not share our higher feelings and educated sensibilities, no better than dogs or horses ('it is obvious').
2.   *Science proves this* to be so. The blackamoor's brain is less developed than the European's, more like a monkey's ('it is observable').
3.   *God wills it*. It tells you so in Holy Writ. We deliver them from darkness ('it is ordained').

This is the Triad of Deceit, and a wonderful device it is for preparing the path of persecution, to lend a spurious legitimacy to the vicious exploitation of one group of people by another. Here is a further example of its employment taken from the archives of abuse.

It is not included in this text to titillate or to capitalize on a shocking historic event; it is here to illustrate – as an extreme example – the nature of certain styles of relationship and response to authority, and how ideas can be perverted into instruments of evil. Therefore it has a bearing on our attempts at 'culture change' in a workaday world, where the Triad of Deceit is alive and well, though in less exaggerated form. To make mention of it is not to demean the awful memory of it. It is to honour it, humbly.

Juden raus!

They were labelled '*Untermenschen*'. Long before the stinking cattle trucks crammed with their dazed cargo of Jewish 'sub-humans' were sent clanking eastward on their tragic one-way journey the track to immortality had been laid with the three lies of the diabolical trinity, the three specious ideas so powerful they could be used to attempt the annihilation of an entire race of people.

The trains were going to Poland. To a village near Rybnik where the *Wehrmacht Blitzkrieg* smashed through the frontier, a little place nobody had ever heard of, called Oswiecim, a name nobody was able to pronounce. So they had changed it – to Auschwitz, where the victims were gassed like rats with the pesticide Zyklon B and then burned to ashes. This was so monstrous a crime against humanity that even half a century afterwards no birdsong is heard there to lighten the keening of the ghosts. An act of infamy so appalling it defies comprehension. How was it *possible*?

Easy. The three ideas . . .

1. They are *unlike us*. They are less than human.
2. *Science proves it*. Measure the circumference of the Semitic cranium, divide it by the length of the Semitic nose and there you have it, the index which is your ticket to the death camp. All you need is calipers, ruler and pseudo-science.
3. *God wills it*. Mother Church, in her chaste silence, was heard to acquiesce.

The tyrant's triad of ideas made possible history's celebrated six million.

This is how the exploitation of one group of people (the power-less) is 'justified' by another group of people (the powerful). In an authoritarian culture.

What has *this* to do with TQM?

The *Lumpenproletariat* (work makes free)

An overheard conversation:

'Total quality management is about harnessing every name on the payroll, using all the talent which traditional systems of management overlook. Getting the best out of everybody.'

'What, the workforce as well?'

'Yes, the work people as well; they're on the payroll so they will be mobilized by TQM.'

'Ah, yes. Got a problem there, though.'

'Problem? What problem?'

'Well, you see, they are not numerate; they cannot handle information; they are *not like us*.' ('It is obvious.')

'How can you say that?'

'Because it's true. Research *proves* it. They have lower IQs than we do. They are not as well-educated as we are.' ('It is observed.')

'You don't really believe that, do you?'

'It's the way things are though, isn't it? Always have been ('It is ordained.')

A conversation just one short moral step away from those dreadful gates whose legend declares *'Arbeit macht frei'*.

So, I, Aaron Godman, am an ideas-monger. I swim in the deeps with your author, show him the fantastic formations in the reefs of the subconscious and the collective universal mind. This is where his ideas have their origin; surely you didn't think he was capable of finding them on his own? Better let him get a word in though; he is supposed to be the person who is plaiting this rope of language with which to hang himself.

I'll very likely be back, but who can tell?

So we are talking about the *power of ideas* in this business of making cultural change. Cultural change is manifested as *behavioural change*. How do you change behaviour?

Changing behaviour

Suppose that I am some sort of neurotic, who wishes to dominate a situation for my own secret sadistic reasons (like some 'managers'). I am holding a hand-gun, a Webley .38 service revolver with six chambers in the cylinder and every chamber loaded. As in cowboy films I order you to dance, and by way of encouragement fire one round which drills a hole in the floorboards close to your feet. You dance. I command you to keep on dancing, so you jig about like a demented marionette as the bullets splinter the planks. You don't usually behave in this way, this crazy dancing-on-the-spot. Using the authority of my weapon I have changed your behaviour. As Chairman Mao of China said, 'Power comes from the barrel of a gun'. The Chinese gerontocracy still believe it; that's how they were able to send in tanks to mangle students protesting in Tiananmen Square.

But you are counting the bangs of the gun. At six you stop, breathing heavily and angrily, and revert to your habitual behaviour of languid torpor. So I reload the revolver. 'Oh no', you groan, 'the madman's at it again' and you resume your tripping of the light fantastic. Power stemming from the gun.

Trouble is, though, I have to keep pointing the gun. Take it away and the desired behaviour stops. It's the same with culture change: behaviour and action can be changed by decree, by the imposition of higher authority. But not for long.

Many years ago I was involved in a culture-change operation in a company of about two hundred people. Exercising the authority of no less a figure than the president of the corporation, the culture shift was massive and dramatic. The company was turned from a moribund loser into a dynamic winner. We agents of change congratulated ourselves and withdrew. Within three months the outfit had regressed to what it had been before; the waves of change had rolled over it but had only altered superficialities. The bedrock of behaviour – the ideas which were the foundation of culture – had remained unchanged. We realized that we had made no real change at all.

This might be where some of the companies who are reporting failure of their TQM drives might be going wrong. To address behaviour and actions *without addressing the ideas and beliefs which underpin them* is a waste of time. Many organizations, it

seems, have wasted their time in this manner. They entered a situation at the end of a sequence, instead of at its beginnings. Tended
the *symptoms* instead of the underlying *malady*. This is a common
mistake for which there is ample historical precedent . . . .

Limeys

Scurvy is a terrible sickness which never failed to afflict sailors
making long voyages. Scurvy was the unwanted passenger who
sneaked on board after several weeks at sea, by which time fresh
provisions had been exhausted. It shows itself as a general debil-
ity: the gums bleed and teeth work loose, the skin erupts into
throbbing carbuncles, a great ache pervades the limbs. Its 'treatment' used to consist of chewing tobacco to cleanse the mouth of
its foul breath, daubing tallow or smearing tar on the boils – anything that might alleviate the agony.

It was brought on by a diet of skilly. Skilly is a culinary mess of
crumbled ship's biscuits (baked as hard as tiles for preservation's
sake), pickled pork gone rotten, and weevils boiled up in a brack-
ish water. It is lacking in certain nutrients, notably ascorbic acid –
the 'vital amine', the vitamin, C. Early voyagers didn't know this.
So they treated the condition with whatever nostrum or other
came to hand. After all, this was a serious condition: scurvy
depleted the crews and impaired the efficiency of fighting ships,
hampered exploration, handicapped imperialism, adversely
affected trading profits. They tried to cure it, and failed.

Until a lateral-thinking navigator noticed that no sooner had a
tropical landfall been made, where the ship's company was able to
forage for fresh water and strange fruits, than the scurvy cleared
itself up as if by magic. So more than two centuries before vitamin
C was identified mariners took on board citrus fruits to augment
their rations. Their health-conscious slogan could have been 'a
lime a day keeps scurvy away'. The Royal Navy made limejuice
its standard daily tonic. Which is why Americans call British
'limeys', as you already knew.

But! They were no longer trying to cure the *symptoms* of the
malaise; they were unwittingly addressing its *cause*.

By addressing *action* and *behaviour* in our efforts to introduce
TQM, for the sake of performance improvement, we are doing no

better than the sailors who treated symptoms and neglected the dietary defects which gave rise to them. Just as there was some vital element missing from the nourishment that they took in, maybe we are depriving ourselves of some vital mental element, the absence of which is causing our organizations to sicken. But what? Could some of our companies be languishing due to a *lack of love*?

Try telling *that* to Rambo, the macho-manager who lives his life (life?) according to mottoes which remind him that 'only the strong survive', 'when the going gets tough the tough get going'. He fancies himself as strong and tough, a battle-scarred survivor who knows how to get going. That's why he shouts at subordinates, to prove to them – or to his doubting narcissistic self – that he really is tough. Watch him, as I have done until I'm sick of him, as he parades his managerial machismo and pumps up his ego. What the *hell* is he doing – managing this wealth-generating business or stoking his vanity? He puts you in mind of the time you were a little boy, and used to catch frogs and with infantile indifference to their suffering inflate them by blowing into a straw inserted into their anatomy – kids can be cruel, all part of growing up. But nobody's blowing him up; he's doing it all by himself. Why, you wonder. Because he believes nobody really loves him. Because he is unable to love himself. He is a frog who needs loving if he is to turn into a prince.

Remember, I am using that little word 'love' in its unsullied and sacred definition, since it happens to be the only word we have.

Let us stay with this fellow and his organization for a while. Hostile behaviour such as his provokes hostile response, spreads hatred, surliness, discord. Bullying always has and always will.

- Bullying brings fear into the company.
- Fear is the enemy of quality
- Love is the basis of quality.

I remember having read somewhere, I think it was in that compelling book *Zen and the Art of Motorcycle Maintenance*, that a Japanese manufacturer of bicycles reckoned that 'Person putting together Japanese cycle must have peace of mind', or something like that.

Peace of mind. I can identify with that. Harmony as a prerequisite of creative endeavour. I learned this from experience when I was building my own bee-hives. A bee-hive is basically a box with a few critical dimensions. Its job is to house a colony of several thousand bees, so it must be robust and stable. So you have to cut its component parts properly to achieve accuracy and squareness. Then the parts fit snugly together. It's a job you are unable to do if you are agitated. Even though the Western Red Cedar timber you are using is a forgiving wood you can only make a satisfactory hive if you have peace of mind. Harmony! A calm silence.

Bullies can think of only one thing to do with silence – break it; with harmony – disrupt it. So how do you *change* their behaviour? Not by trying to bully them back, especially if they are higher than you are in the ranking order. How, then? You change their behaviour by changing their assumptions and beliefs. How do you do that? By altering their perceptions.

There is a change sequence. It goes:

- To change behaviour we must first change belief.
- To change belief we must first change perception.
- To change perception and belief is to change *minds* with ideas.

Change *minds*! That's a tall order, but to make change permanent it just has to be attempted. If the discord which destroys peace of mind is to be damped down, and replaced by harmony from which creativity and commitment spring, then the collective mind of the company must be addressed. How? With communication.

Communication

Many words have been spoken and written about 'communication', so we might as well sling a few more shovelfuls on to the word-heap; it is clearly a subject of some importance. *Some* importance? Of overriding importance, as a matter of fact. Communication is the anti-freeze which thaws out glacial change-resistant attitudes in companies whose cultural climate is of polar rigidity. It is the searching solvent which penetrates and erodes the stonework of organizational pyramids. It is the water of meaningfulness which trickles into every arid crevice in the company to nourish growth and quench the fires of anger. It is the cement that bonds individuals into cohesive teams. It is the currents which shape *perception* . . .

$$Perception + belief = behaviour$$

It is the equation of behavioural change.

Pretty powerful stuff, communication. Who's got it? The 'communicator'. One of the best descriptions of the nature and role of the 'communicator' is that offered by Professor P.A. McKeown of Cranfield several years ago in his John Loxham Lecture to the Institute of Quality Assurance:

> There are differences in capacity and capabilities amongst individuals and blessed is the . . . company that has someone who can be called a 'high communicator'. The high communicator is significantly different from others in the way he uses and communicates information. To be successful he must be likeable because people will not go to a man who makes it difficult to get help. The high communicator is the person to whom others go for information and who constantly distributes information. He is normally, therefore, the man who reads much; does much; talks to many people inside and outside the organization; has a great variety of sources of information, and is adept at raising the information level of his group or the entire organization's. Above all, he is a very good pattern recogniser; he does well in the RAT test, the Remote Association Test. He quickly associates and puts together relevant bits of information gained from several sources for the benefit of the . . . team.

Every organization should have one. As Professor Mckeown said, 'blessed' is the company that's got one. Or cursed. It all depends upon the point of view and the framework of assumption through which the high communicator is regarded.

Suppose you happened to find yourself working with one of these high communicators, how would you handle the situation? Let us consider a couple of scenarios.

First, not only does this person happen to be a high communicator, he happens to be one of your immediate subordinates, and you are a director of the company. (This, by the way, is yet another true incident dredged from the depths of memory.) You didn't get where you are today be being too free with information; you know how to keep secrets, you do; how to drip information out strictly on a 'need-to-know' basis. Your notions of 'need to know' have been gathered from watching too many spy films celebrating the Allied Victory of half a century ago, so you behave as if you expect your managers to be captured by the enemy and put to torture in spite of the Geneva Convention. So you tell them as little as possible, lest they betray it. In so doing you actually betray them, consign them to a condition of dependent ignorance about everything to do with their working lives except that barest minimum which you decide is as much as they 'need to know'. You also let them know that there is a lot that you know that they don't know; this makes you feel superior and partly compensates for your secret conviction of your own inferiority. Powerful stuff is communication, even it its absence.

Along comes this high communicator. How does he strike you?

Maybe you summon him to your office and tell him 'You talk too much! What you're saying at nine o'clock in the morning is what everybody else is saying by ten.'

'Thank you for the compliment,' he replies, grateful for your act of recognition of his communication skills, which are in fact the basis of *leadership* skills.

'Don't tell me *thank you*,' you rebuke him impatiently, 'That's not a compliment; it's a telling-off!' Then you complain to your co-directors and the MD that here is a man too loose-mouthed to be entrusted with any information, a man who doesn't know that his teeth are there to cage secrets. This man is a curse!

Would this be your response on encountering such a high communicator, or would you *make use* of his talents? How this would be done is too obvious to be stated.

Second, he is a high communicator, and he is your boss. He does not impart information on a niggardly 'need-to-know' basis; he dispenses it generously on a 'good-to-know' premise. In a managerial culture which for years has operated in a stifling mode of paternalistic authoritarianism, in which subordinates were treated like dependent children and 'father knows what's good for you' secrecy, *he* treats you as a responsible and trustworthy adult. How do you suppose you would feel in these circumstances? Too obvious to need spelling out, isn't it?

These, of course, are two hypothetical scenarios. (Oh no they're not.) Every organization is blessed with at least one high communicator. How does the organization respond to the presence of these gifted people? As I said before, it all depends upon the standpoint from which they are perceived.

Creative communication

'In the beginning was the Word', it says somewhere. In the beginning, *before* the Big Bang? Why not? 'Word' means 'communication'. Communication conditions perception, it initiates the change process, thus . . .

Communication ---> Perception ---> Belief ---> Behaviour

Word ---> View ---> Attitude ---> Action

> We see what we believe, and we act as if what we believe to be true is really true.

Communication then is without doubt *the* most powerful of the factors influencing change. It is a sort of 'prime mover' in the sequence communication/perception/belief/behaviour. It is also the natural territory of Professor McKeown's gifted individual, the high communicator, with whom every company deserves to be blessed. Does this mean that it is the *exclusive* territory of such gifted people; does it mean that those of us who are less gifted in this respect are doomed to spend our days in the tongue-tied uncertainty of garbled communication? Or might we be able to improve our ability to communicate, by developing our less generous endowment to its fullest potential? Is there anything we can do to get better at it?

Of course there is. Like the puny muscles of the 'seven-stone weakling' who used to appear in the body-building advertisements of the pulp magazines – the one who got sand kicked into his face by huskier fellows whenever he ventured on to the beach – we can develop our communication capability as he was invited to develop his musculature – by *exercise*. He would have followed the exercises prescribed in the guide books about 'dynamic tension' written by Charles Atlas and claiming that within seven days the weakling would develop biceps like melons, pectorals like breast-plates, and a back as sinewy as a Clydesdale stallion's. We will settle for a more modest ambition, and aim to improve our communication skills by consulting the works of Dave Francis. These are the book *Unblocking Organizational Communication*, and its companion volume *50 Activities for Unblocking Organizational Communication* which is a compendium of exercises. Furthermore, seeing that one aspect of communication is that transaction under stress known as 'negotiation' we shall also equip ourselves with the book *Beyond Negotiation* by John A. Carlisle and Robert C. Parker. (Please see Recommended reading for details of these books.) These volumes are of great value in preparing the ground for company-wide TQM by *altering the perceptions* of management.

Managerial perception shift – paradigm shift

> What the undeveloped man seeks is outside; what the advanced man seeks is himself. (Confucius)

Introspection seems not to come easily to the Western manager, though corporate navel-gazing seems to be quite a popular indulgence. Individuals brought up in our materialistic culture tend to shy away from the exploration of their inner space; perhaps they are put off by the things they glimpse lurking in the darker recesses of the mind. Oriental philosophy takes a different view:

> The human mind, partaking of Cosmic Intelligence, is an abode of the Deity, which is the Spiritual Essence. There exists no highest Deity outside the human mind. (Shinto-Dinju)

Seeing that Shintoism is a strong component of Japanese religious belief perhaps it has had an effect on their industrial performance as powerful as that which Lutheran Protestantism has had on our Western work ethic. Through harmony?

But let us remind ourselves that this body of knowledge, belief, assumption and practice that we incorporate into the portmanteau title 'total quality management' is about *change*. About adapting to it and influencing its direction. So it has to be about perception. So it has to be about introspection; about looking at who we are, where we are, what we believe and how we act. If introspection is an unfamiliar activity which does not come easily to our material-istic view of the world then there are exercises which will help us. They are structured approaches to self-examination, some of which I have found useful in helping 'seven-stone weakling' clients develop into something bigger and stronger. They are to be found in Dave Francis's *50 Activities* compendium mentioned earlier which I urge you to get hold of if you aim to change your world for the better.

How change works for real

It's all very well saying 'To change actions we must change belief; to change belief we must change perception' but . . .

Whose perception of *what*?

Management's perception of the *workforce*!

Let me give you an example, tell you how it happened in the Bedlam from which my 'victims' were 'de-layered'. It happened there as it had happened before in the organizations of many of my previous clients. There is nothing clever about it. It is *simple*. But it alters managerial perception, causes a paradigm shift. It breaks the prevailing paradigm like Humpty-Dumpty was broken – all the King's horses and all the King's men cannot put it together again. Here is how it goes . . . .

Find the strong woman; in this case study it was Karen the Outspoken. Recruit her as your second ally; the first is the boss himself (or herself, but rarely). With her teach the powerful tech-niques of statistical process control to a work team. Set the team to work on a project to do the same familiar things they have always done but to do them better. Stick a 'Before' sign in front of the project, measured in *money*. Run the project for a brief accounting period – a week, a month, but no longer. Now stick an 'After' sign at the end of the period. Measure the difference between before and after in pounds sterling. *Keep the managers out* while you are doing it. They can watch what is happening if they want to, but they must not be allowed to interfere. This is *your* show, and Karen's and the team's; not theirs. Only *one* inseminator is needed, one bull; let the other strictured bulls stand bellowing at the fence, but keep them out of the field.

Bellow they will. You are attacking and destroying their paradigm, their belief-system, their glacial and unthinking mind-set that told them that what they are now witnessing – a despised and patronized workforce showing itself capable of work hitherto confined to the exclusive realms of 'management' – *actually works*. It makes money, as well as sense.

After that you can let them into the field, those who have a strong enough self-image to accept the new order without feeling threatened by it, who are able to adapt themselves to the change. Those who are unable to do so are added to the hit-list; for them the tumbril already awaits in the car park.

Do not kid yourself that you will be making friends. If it's friends you want then get yourself a couple of dogs. Change is unpopular with some people; change-agents get blamed.

At the conclusion of the first of these exercises of talent liberation in this company a young manager asked me, a note of incredulity in his voice, 'Is this all there is to it? Is it really this simple?'

Yes, it is. To begin with. To begin with is enough for the time being. The world is not changed overnight. Like that charity organization, which invites you to 'adopt' a child in the Third World, tells you – 'Changing the world one child at a time'.

Simple. Straightforward. Nothing very ambitious to start with. Yet you know what follows insemination – gestation; this calls for a bit of patience.

Thereafter things are changed forever. As a consultant you have to pick your own projects in your client's organization; that's why they pay you so well. To change perceptions.

In your new career as a management consultant you will be a communicator and will teach communication. You will be an ideas-broker. A change-agent who alters the clients' perceptions

[handwritten: (a spreader of viruses ... an infecter.]

in order to shape their beliefs so as to affect their actions. Why? What is *your* motivation?

Will you be prompted by vanity, or greed? These spurs to personal enterprise, these well-known goads of social and material 'success' can be strong driving forces. They can carry you to achievement, to status and recognition. but no further. *Is* there anywhere 'further'? Yes, there is. We'll speak of it later; for the time being we will stay with the work of consulting to organizations, and look at its three-fold nature.

If we look upon the organization as a hyper-organism whose health is ailing, and the consultant as a 'corporate doctor', who will diagnose the ailment and recommend the appropriate medicine, there are three routes by which the patient may be addressed:

1. Structuralist. Concerned with anatomy.
2. Functionalist. Dealing with physiology.
3. Vitalist. To do with something different.

These three categories are arbitrarily chosen for the sake of analysis. Any consultant can be a practitioner of all three, though most have a personal preference for one of the three. Also, since function is often tied up with structure, to address the one is to affect the others. For the sake of convenience we'll look at them one at a time.

1.   Structuralist – the anatomist

This is the approach which tries to change the culture, and hence the effectiveness, of the organization by changing its shape. The prevailing shape of the organization is the hierarchical pyramid.

Like Don Quixote tilting at windmills because he thought they were dragons I have devoted a lot of effort to assaulting the pyramid, because I thought it was damaging to its occupants. I still think so. Ten years ago in *Right First Time* I vilified it, tried to knock it down. Now I know how Don Quixote must have felt when he saw the windmills still standing. My words were too soon. The pyramid too stable. I was on my own. The idea too unfashionable.

Fashions change: nowadays you can attend seminars to learn the importance of dismantling the hierarchy and reinventing the organization. Don Quixote is winning. Yet pyramids still stand in their thousands in our corporate landscapes, far more than in the Valley of Kings. What *is* it about pyramids . . . ?

Pyramids in upheaval

As we see, the pyramid is a very durable structure, in both its architectural and organizational manifestations. Both expressions of it are very old.

Those in Egypt have stood for 4,000 years and look as if they will endure 4,000 years more – the great pyramids, monuments to a magnificent past. Built to serve as resting places for the illustrious dead; to inter the embalmed in eternal repose, there to rest forever in gilded stillness, oblivious to external change, to moulder undisturbed until the end of time. Not too unlike how some of our organizational pyramids used to be, and how some still are.

There are those in America, the Aztec step-pyramids constructed a thousand years ago to symbolize the formal relationships of power and obligation between gods and men. Places of ritual murder, some of whose worshippers were literally required to lose heart and to die.

Very like some of today's pyramids.

Then there is the Greek version, the three-level pyramid of Plato, put forward 2,000 years ago as the ideal model of the ideal state. The pyramidal peak was occupied by a ruling caste inherited from its ruling ancestors. These were the guardians, beneficiaries of a special form of education denied to other members of the hierarchical society, disdaining trade and its talk of money. Dedicated to guarding against change, because any change can only be for the worse in this best-of-all societies. The middle tier was composed of the military, their job to ensure the safe preservation of the status quo, to supervise the residents of the pyramid's base. These were the hoi polloi, the 'oxen' and 'sheep', the hewers of wood and drawers of water. This social pyramid became the template of the English class system. It endures still.

Plato averred that the citizen exists to serve the state.

Socrates disagreed. He tipped the pyramid on to its point, apex now to the bottom, maintaining that the state exists to serve the citizen.

This argument about the freedom of the citizen, or the 'subject' in a monarchy, versus the authority of the state, still rages today. It is the stuff of political dispute and moral dialectic. A see-saw wobbling first one way in favour of the citizen, then the other in favour of the state. Central government versus local government. The company versus the employee. The collective versus the individual. It is to do with the balance of power in an ordered society. Form versus freedom. It is a *central theme* of total quality management.

The hierarchy is a command structure designed for the exercise of power, the transmission of authority, and the assurance of obedience and compliance (not necessarily 'commitment'). As a way of running large organizations, by command, by authority, then it just has to be the *only* way to make things work. How else could a military commander-in-chief deploy his vast and complex resources in pursuance of victory and conquest? His kind of enterprise calls for an organizational structure of a dozen or more levels. How else could a church exercise its spiritual authority over its 400 million believers except from the pope, Christ's vicar on Earth, through its cardinals, bishops and parish priests, a 'flattened' hierarchy if ever there was one? This organization has endured for sixteen hundred years since the first of the popes wrested power from the Gnostics by mass recruitment to form a church of overwhelming numbers, an *organized, hierarchical* church.

The hierarchy, the command structure, is the only way to exercise authority on a scale as grand as this, by demanding total obedience to doctrine and to higher authority.

But is this the way to run a company? It's the way companies are conventionally run. Try, as a change-agent, telling the person perched at the pyramid's point that you are trying to tear it down. See what sort of welcome you get.

This structuralist route to change is the hardest of the three; perhaps you'd better try a different approach.

2. Functionalist – the physiologist

Many tasks to be done to the organization are repetitive, but they *have* to be done to ensure the smooth running of the organization. So they are best formalized, incorporated into a system. Without this the rules and procedures would have to be invented afresh at the outset of every working day, would have to be *thought out* anew. This would be tiresome and senseless.

Systems are the guides to daily work. They are the essential framework within which routine tasks get done. They ensure that the right actions are taken by the right people at the right time in the right order, and for the right reasons.

Without systems there is chaos (well, there is at least *con-fusion*). All work proceeds as a process flow: systems are the canals, the conduits, the plumbing and pipework which guide the work flow in the correct direction. Systems are the essential prerequisite of efficiency.

Over the past ten years or so the systems' designers have exercised a profound and positive influence on the practice of quality management. They have produced British Standard 5750, a system of quality management, which has led to the ISO series and is now influencing worldwide the systematized approach to quality.

The strengths of BS5750 are that it provides a standardized system of quality management which is applicable to any work or business activity; its efficiency can be independently assessed, audited, and certificated; its installation provides public evidence that the company which installs it is taking quality seriously.

Today it provides its possessors with a competitive edge; tomorrow it will be a ticket without which companies are unlikely to be invited to play the business game. This does not mean that a company is unable to operate effectively and profitably *without* being certificated to BS5750. Look around you and you will see many organizations doing exactly that. But they are not doing it without systems of management; perhaps they just haven't joined the queue for a ticket yet.

There is a downside to BS5750, as there can be with anything man-made, but it is not the fault of the system itself; it is more to do with the way some people sometimes misinterpret and misuse it. This 'system of quality management' finds itself under attack because it actually does nothing to improve product or service quality; its authors never claimed it would. They wrote a system, a specification, to monitor the information flow in a business, and before anybody criticizes it they should try their hand at writing a specification – for instance one that tells you how to tie your shoe laces, and then give it to somebody who customarily wears Wellingtons and see if he can get a pair of shoes on to his feet by following the specification. It's not easy. In complaining about its alleged shortcomings – and I have done my share of that after seeing it perverted so often – you might as well complain to the plumber that your radiators are cold while overlooking the fact that you haven't lit the fire.

It has its upside as well. It is a growth industry for consultants. Although there are some excellent books available on how to implement the system there is still a demand for external advisers to help clients get it going. There is vast scope. So far about 14,000 British companies are certificated: that leaves plenty that aren't, all grist for the consultants' mills. Advertisements are appearing inviting experienced UK consultants to take their skills to America, so you could do worse than 'go west, young man'. This is not so much that phenomenon called 'a window of opportunity' in manager-ese; it's more a 'sky's the limit' chance of meaningful and lucrative employment for the victims of de-layering to make use of their work experience.

So if by natural inclination you do not fancy yourself as a *structuralist*, an anatomist who tries to change the shape of an organization by tilting at the pyramid, you could become a *functionalist*, a physiologist concerned with systems like BS5750. But be careful, bear in mind the advice of Pearl Bailey: 'What the world needs is more Love and less paperwork.' Or you could try the third route towards organizational change . . . .

Suppose an organization undergoes change. It rearranges its structure from pyramidal to another form, such as modular multicellular (as did one of my clients – a big blue chip outfit of old British lineage). It gets its *anatomy* right. It also implements the most comprehensive systems, achieves BS5750 accreditation across all its sites, getting its *physiology* right. These things it does, and nothing more. What have you got?

A dead dog?

Or a mangy cur that's only half-alive?

Would you feel confident enough to accept its leader's invitation to give a helping hand? (The boss of the blue chip I mentioned, a person eminent in his field of process technology – *process*, that's significant – invited me and a couple of others to inject some life into the company. I could see it was going to be fun so I accepted.) Would *you* accept? Yes?

Why? Because you felt flattered that a company as illustrious as this should even have heard of you, let alone want you to work with them? Wrong reason.

Why? Because they were floating in a lake of cash and offered you an up-scale fee? Wrong reason.

Two wrong reasons, try a third . . . .

Why? Because you anticipated that it might be fun to have a go? Inadequate reason, but getting warmer. *Why*, then?

Stop being impatient and I'll tell you why.

3.   Vitalist – the missionary

Because you want to change the world. Why ever you should want to do such a thing is your own business; it might be the same as the soldier at Rorke's Drift – 'because we're 'ere, lad'. It might be your way of endowing your life with its own *individual signifi-cance*, because *that* is what you are about to offer the members of your client company, did you but know it. Maybe it's nothing more and nothing less than your own 'karma', that script written for you by Kismet to be followed this time around.

Whatever it is, it had better be something a lot more powerful as a motivator than mere status-seeking and money-grubbing. As I said before, vanity and greed will carry you a long way, maybe far enough to satisfy you. But that's not far enough. You should not diminish yourself by settling for the slap on the back and the slap of money in your palm. You are bigger than that. Everybody is, but some learn it too late. Hell itself is nothing less than the truth learned too late.

You *can* change the world. Slowly. One person at a time. Or rather ten or a dozen at once, depending how many you address at one go in your inseminating sessions known in the trade as seminars. Like 'seminary', in the church. Seed-sowing, and very much *not* wild oats either.

To do this, to find the drive to do so within yourself, you will have to be *dissatisfied* with the world as it is. Your 'job satis-faction' is your dissatisfaction.

There is egoism in this. The ego – the 'self' you made for your-self as you went along – is dangerous. It always ends up wanting

[handwritten margin note: Hell is truth learned too late]

war. Yet you must use it; it is the instrument of change in this life. But you must temper and control it, with your real, inner, self. This is the self which Abraham Maslow refers to when he speaks of 'ego-transcendent altruism'. Maslow gets misunderstood. Because he produced his ladder of 'instinctual need' as a metaphor of growth towards moral maturity people tend to think of him as little more than a managerial window cleaner. Thus they miss his wisdom; that's how materialists think.

To change organizational culture you must transcend the promptings of your ego by using it to get your message across without ever letting it take charge. Never flatter yourself that you are somebody special – vanity! You are only a worker going about your work.

Your reward will be ample. Money enough, and whenever you have need of it – manna.

I might as well be brutally frank . . . .

If you have to ask the price of a Rolls-Royce motor car you cannot afford one.

If you have to ask what I am talking about you are unready. As yet.

Only *you* can know, and it cannot be faked. This is no longer a thing of the head – of the intellect – although it makes great use of intellectual concepts. It is a thing of the heart – of the spirit. Of ardour. Of anger.

Anger? Yes, that righteous indignation that flares up from deep within the belly, that gut reaction to things you find deeply offensive. That visceral response the ancient Greeks called *embrimaomai*, the sense of outrage that moves you so deeply it's enough to make you weep. The passion of affronted *love* which inspired the prophet Moses when he was a young man, the same passion as that which today inspires a few of our latter-day prophets who preach the same gospel.

Do *you* feel this fire within you? Many of our writers on management development seem to be set alight by it, though they look as if they have their flames controlled in a kind of blow-torch way. These are the writers who have discovered the true purpose – the *mission* – of personnel management, and have elected to try to change the world instead of trying to capture it in a cage of procedures and rules. You should read the things they write; buy their books. They have made their move from structuralism, dealing with anatomy, through functionalism, dealing with physiology, into the third phase of *vitalism*, to do with spirituality.

Buy their books and study them if you intend to be a consultant of this third order, a vitalist, a bull who will bring life to half-dead organizations. They have a lot to teach. Especially search for the work of Roger Harrison, in particular a pamphlet of his entitled 'Organization Culture and Quality of Service: a Strategy for Releasing Love in the Workplace' (ISBN 1 870469 00 3). I am unable to help you in this search; I can't track it down. I don't really need to because I already have one. But I suggest that you do. It will help you, whether you intend to be a consultant or not.

Back to this *embrimaomai*, this feeling of outrage, this love of what is right. What sort of things do you feel outraged about? Your answer must be something outside of you. This sounds para-doxical: how could anything outside you ignite fires of outrage within you? If your answer is that you are outraged by, say, being underpaid for what you do, forget it. This is the angry response of greed unsatisfied. If it is, shall we say, anger because somebody you fancy has rejected your advances . . . again, forget it. This is the flailing tantrums of wounded vanity.

As I stressed, in order to be free of the taint of the ego your out-rage must be detonated by an event outside yourself.

Try these. The abuse of power. The betrayal of trust. The poisoning of justice. Talent trampled on. Innocence corrupted . . . . These things happen, happen a lot, in our work organizations (as well as in our private lives, sometimes). Let us suppose that you witness some of these evils (that is what they are) being per-petrated. They are not being perpetrated against you personally; you are only a detached bystander to a display of managerial sadism. Somebody is being hurt, bullied, humiliated . . . .

Have you ever been present at one of these revolting rituals in your working life? Yes? How did you *feel*? Gratitude and relief that it was not you that was taking the beating? Or a great anger that it should be happening at all? What did you *do*? Shrink away in case your presence attracted the sadist's whip? Or did you sum-mon up that rare and most valuable commodity – courage – and open your mouth in protest, and say 'To hell with the conse-quences; I'm not going to see such things as *this* going on and say *nothing*! Who the *devil* does he think he *is* that he should treat a

fellow human being in such a cruel and wanton manner? I'll have
no more of it!'

You don't *need* to summon up the courage in these situations.
All by itself it surges from the inferno in your guts and bursts out.
To try to hold it back is to be untrue to your self. *Then* you are in
trouble. In trouble with your self. The thing that should have been
released to do its cleansing work is now locked within you, and –
paradoxically again – it turns against you. Sours into vitriolic self-
loathing, corroding your character from within.

Let it out! Lest it should kill you. And remember, the boundaries of the tyrant's misrule are *never* drawn by the tyrant. That is
your job.

This is no ordinary anger; it is an outraged compassion; this is
love in all its fury. Suppress it and it will make you afraid. When
you are afraid you will spread your fear. Fear is the enemy of
quality.

You may have gathered by now that the job of being a consultant of the third order – a vitalist inseminator – is not always easy.
It is not; not all the time: there are long periods of ease now and
again, but eventually, sooner or later, it comes. The time when you
must stand up and fight for what you believe actually arrives. Now
it is *will* versus *will*; if you are to win you had better be sure you
are on the side of the angels. Morality strengthens morale, and in
the end prevails.

I hope all this doesn't put you off becoming a consultant; you
can be a perfectly adequate practitioner without all this fire-in-
the-belly stuff. You can honestly justify your earnings by being of
great use to your clients by helping them to tidy their affairs, by
stimulating their minds. After all, in the early period of the consultancy you enjoy the power of the visiting witch-doctor. You are a
new face, a new mind, bringer of new ideas. These are all fine
things, of value to your client.

All I'm saying is that it's good to have some strong motivation
in reserve. To be the crucible of the fires of righteous indignation.
To be able to exceed your client's expectations if the need to do so
should arise. But if you happen *not* to have brought courage and
conviction with you and suddenly they are needed – then it is to
yourself that you have been untrue and to your self that you will
have to answer. This is a mistake.

You may be sure that this manufacturing and servicing nation of ours has great need of you. The evidence suggests to us that there is more discord within our companies doing more damage than there used to be. Harassment in all its forms is on the increase. People are falling sick, with a sickness of the soul if the diagnosis is deep enough, more than they ever did. Bullying, fear, belly-ache, loneliness, alienation . . . there is no shortage of patients awaiting your ministrations if you become a corporate doctor of the vitalist persuasion.

It is not easy work. But, there again, hell is an everlasting holiday.

There is another side to the coin of corporate behaviour. Many companies, from the satellite factories of the multinationals to the family firms which are the backbone of British manufacturing business, are consciously addressing these 'spiritual' or 'psychological' problems. Some of them are operating programmes specifically designed to implement Dr Deming's Eighth Point – they hope to drive out fear. In others the personnel service of stress counselling is on the increase. It has always seemed to me that to 'counsel' stress is a less effective way of dealing with it then removing its source, but maybe I'm being oversimplistic.

Karl Marx said the job of the philosopher was to explain life, but the work of the revolutionary was to change it. I would prefer the term 'reconstruct' instead of 'change'; revolutions are always disastrous for those on whose behalf they were made. By the look of it we are all becoming Marxist reconstructionists; and not before time if we are to prosper by our own efforts, as opposed to the labours of black slaves overseas and white ones at home.

Oh dear, you are probably finding all this too heavy and depressing a prospect as a way of new life in your resurrection, my dear de-layered victim. You had more than enough of it before you were chopped and would now rather try something altogether different. Fair enough. We've looked at your prospects as a writer, and as a consultant; we have yet to examine another option, that of *tycoon*, something completely different.

Righto then. Now for that 'something completely different'.

Option 3: Tycoon

I was trapped. It was a very comfortable trap, but even so I felt ensnared, was becoming restive, discontented, as young men do. How things had changed. A mere seven years (seven years? was this sense of disenchantment, the notorious 'seven-year itch' that I had heard about?) . . . a mere seven years before I had been delighted to get this job; what was going wrong? Why was a life which then had seemed to sweet now turning sour? I felt guilty about feeling ungrateful for my good fortune.

And I had been fortunate, those seven years ago, even to get the job. Pleasantly surprised to get an interview, where I met the selection committee. Such nice people, especially the personnel director. I 'imprinted' on him as devoutly as the deluded ducklings, that used to follow the Austrian ethologist Konrad Lorenz around the paddock because they mistook him for their parent, had imprinted on him. If this man is typical of this company, I thought, then I fervently wish to belong to it. How overjoyed I was when they accepted me into their organization. I had become an Organization Man.

An Organization Man is a person who puts his company and his job before *all* other considerations. Before wife, family, home; anxious to be liked by such likeable colleagues in such a caring company he will gladly subordinate everything to his job. Willingly conforming in order to win approval – mistaking it for love. Submerging individuality in the warm comfort of the collective. Dependent upon the opinions of others in order to form an opinion of himself.

It *was* a good job as well, and I was good at it, respected and liked for my ability and professionalism. So why was my complacency now being disturbed by the stirrings of self-doubt? I had *no right* to harbour such feelings of discontent. But these seeds of doubt began to grow, until they poked through the ceiling of the padded cell which was my job, as surely as buried dandelions force their way through a layer of tarmac into the light.

I was unable to suppress them any longer; I had to publicly acknowledge them. My friends noticed my unhappiness, so I was counselled. I told them that it seemed as if over the years I had voluntarily surrendered myself into the grip of a benign tyrant – my job. One who ruled not by terror, but by gentle beneficence. Their response was caring and gently beneficent. Would I like to move to another position in another location, abroad, Africa, India . . .? In other words would I like to transport my gilded cage to somewhere else? Trouble is, wherever I took it, it would take 'me' with it, and my discontent. What I was after was a new 'me', a new job, a new outfit.

'You are not thinking of *giving up* your job! Whatever will you do?' they wondered. I said I might start another one in my wife's name, because I wanted something desperately but I didn't know what it was I wanted.

Then I ran across a poem, in some reading matter other than the managerial literature and journalism that had been my staple intellectual diet for long enough. A *poem*? Reading *poetry*? Oho, *very* bad sign, is that. Poetry is for children – much too dangerous for grown-ups to read. I read:

Secret

No. It is not enough to despise the world.
It is not enough to live one's life as though
Riches and power were nothings, they are not.

But to grasp the world, to grasp and feel it grow
Great in one's grasp is likewise not enough.

The secret is to grasp it, and let go.

Wang Wei (699–761) (Translated from the Chinese by Graeme Wilson.)

The secret. A time to grasp, and a time to let go. A time to climb on to the rising wave of fortune and a time to jump off it before it crests and falls. A time to let go.

To do what? To 're-engineer' myself? To rediscover myself? To look for another job in another gilded cage with another pair of golden handcuffs? Again, it was poetry that pointed the way:

Better to reign in hell than serve in heaven. (John Milton, *Paradise Lost*.)

That's a matter of opinion, or of insight, or of poet's licence. It could be paraphrased as 'better to reign in a little hell than serve in a large heaven' (the tempting voice of the serpent?). Or 'better to be the star of your own show than a bit-player in a cast of thousands' (more serpentine seduction?). Would it be 'better' to be a big wheel in a little machine instead of a tiny cog in a gigantic machine lubricated with fatal friendliness? What was I to do?

I took the way of the poets. I let go; I resigned.

I bought a boat.

The boat

The Royal Navy had taught me a thing or two about messing about in boats, so I bought one of theirs. A twenty-one-year-old motor cutter that had spent most of its life hanging from a ship's davits and was now being pensioned off. The Admiralty Small Craft Disposal List described it as being in 'Shipwrights' Condition A1' and you can't have a better guarantee than that. Had it been a motor car it would have been advertised as a 'one careful owner, low mileage, regular servicing' job. But it wasn't a motor car; it was altogether more exciting: it was a *boat* – a *sea boat*.

What a boat! About the size of a charabanc. Clinker-built out of elm planking on oak frames, the planks and strakes overlapping each other to form the graceful sheering curves of the hull, fastened with hundreds of copper rivets. The mainframe assembly of stem-post, keel, kelson, hog, ribs, knees and transom-post held together with inch-diameter rods of solid copper peened over to keep the whole structure right and springy against the buffeting of the sea. The elm so hard with age it made pepper-fine dust as you drilled into it. The bows decked in teak to form a fo'c'sle (forecastle), the welldeck in pitchpine. Not a speck of rot anywhere; nor any holes of the teredo worm, pest of tropical waters. Somebody had *loved* this boat during its building, cared for it; their feeling for it had seeped from their finger-ends into its timbers. You *sensed* it. This was a craft of superb quality: a symmetry of sea-worthiness sculpted in wood.

Safe as well. The Navy never take unnecessary risks with the sea; they know it too well to do anything so disrespectful. They had fitted the boat with copper tanks called 'barricoes' (pronounced 'breakers') under every thwart and bench, building in buoyancy enough to support sixty souls in safety even if completely swamped. Unsinkable.

As well as grace of form it had power. A four-cylinder Dorman marine diesel, a harmony of moving metal parts housed amidships in a mahogany and brass cabinet resembling a large dog-kennel with hinged lids. At 900 rpm it turned the big phosphor-bronze screw to drive the boat at eight and a half knots – sea miles per hour – and emitted a low throbbing note as deep as a Negro spiritual. It handled like a thoroughbred, responsive to the lightest touch to its brass tiller, and the smallest turn of the wheel that controlled speed and ahead/astern mode. You could spin this boat on a sixpence, turn it in its own length, bring it to an abrupt stop in a welter of froth.

I fell deeply in love with it. And to hell with any Freudian misinterpretation of this emotion, let me assure you this was no surrogate wooden wife; this was to be my equal partner in my new business.

'Business you will be going into is it, then?' enquired a disembodied voice.

Who said that? The boat was riding quietly on its moorings forty yards from the harbour wall. I was bending over the engine, oil on my hands and sunlight on my back. I shot my head up and looked around. Nobody to be seen in the expanse of water heaving gently seaward as the tide began its ebb. Soon it would be pouring out, draining the harbour faster than an emptying bath. But not a soul to be seen. Was I hearing voices? Would it be burning bushes next?

'Do you *heah* me? There it was again! Having no eardrum in my right earhole, thanks to a 5.25 inch gun going off while I was listening to it, I hear all sounds as if they are coming from the left – monophonic. I turned, searching for the source of that cawing voice.

'I am *heah*, can't you *see*?' Then I spotted him. Or rather, his hands, clinging to the edge of the gunwale, and his head, putting me in mind of one of those Kilroy-was-here graffiti which used to adorn lavatory walls at one time. I didn't so much see his head, as his *cap*. A magnificent relic of war, a German Kriegsmarine officer's cap, high in the front with sides swooping downward into a rollicking sheer as jaunty as the bow-wave of a destroyer doing speed-trials. A cap more at home on the conning tower of a U-boat. Beneath it an urchin face, its maggoty paleness relieved only by the polished Dayglo pink of a nose with a droplet glistening on its tip. Chocolate-drop eyes as sad and sagacious as an old monkey's in solitary confinement.

'Permission to come onboard?' the face requested with grave formality. He was sitting in what appeared to be a large bottom drawer from a dresser, tarred in the interests of waterproofing with the name 'Argo' daubed in yellow on its side. Hah, this must be Jason the Argonaut looking for the Golden Fleece, I thought. Little did I realize that he had just found it.

'This is my punt,' he advised as he secured it by its tether to a cleat and swung his lankiness nimbly on to the deck. He had on a fisherman's canvas smock that presumably had been clean at some time in its remote past, but was now plastered with the dried scales of a thousand long-dead fish. They glittered in the sun as iridescently as sequins on a matador's suit of lights. Drainpipe jeans and off-white pumps worn without socks completed this seagoing scarecrow figure.

For some reason he had brought a gaff with him. An ash stave four feet long with a steel hook let into its end, a cork on its point for safety's sake. Its shaft encased in the shagreen of a bull-huss skin to provide a non-slip grip. It put me in mind of a bishop's crozier except that this was not for pulling penitents out of purgatory; it was for snatching heavy fish out of water. Gaff . . . crozier . . . the impedimentia of optimism.

'Where did you get that hat?' I asked him, in the words of the old folk-ditty about ridiculous headgear.

'Cap. Not hat,' he corrected. 'Found it. On the beach.'

He settled himself leisurely on the bench seat in the stern, negligently crossing one leg over the other and leaning back expansively in the manner of a confident business executive come to conclude a profitable deal.

'We understand you are intending to take people out fishing. On fishing-trips,' he opened the negotiations. Who's this 'we' he's on about? I wondered.

'That's the general idea,' I nodded. Angling had become the biggest and fastest-growing participant sport in the country. Anglers had run out of fresh water to fish in; they were turning to the sea. The sea is free. This represented a huge and hardly tapped market for an entrepreneur, a tyro-tycoon, such as I had decided to become. Anybody could set up a sea-angling operation. Anybody who could afford to buy a boat. It needed no licence. There was no bureaucracy to mess you about. They only restriction imposed by the law on a charter-boat operation was the limit of loading: no more than twelve fare-paying passengers allowed. That was enough to enable me to earn more money in a day than I had been paid in a week. There was nobody to extort your earnings off you either. At least, I didn't know of anybody; not yet.

'Fishing trips. On your own,' he elaborated 'Just *you* and twelve trusting passengers, on...your...own!' He shook his head, slowly, as if appalled by the endless folly of humankind, sucked his teeth, and added, '*Unwise*, very unwise, very very risky.'

'Why?'

'Well, you see, what if you are several miles out at sea, with twelve punters who don't know one end of a boat from the other, and *you* have a heart attack. How will your passengers get back? How will you get to hospital?'

I had never considered the prospect since I wasn't planning on having any cardiac or any other health problems. Perhaps I should take out key executive insurance, I thought jokingly.

'There they will be. Helpless. Miles from anywhere. In a dangerous shipping lane. They cannot see land, and even if they could they wouldn't know how to get to it. The wind starts to blow; soon it's blowing a hooligan, a full gale. Where is your *business* then? Do you *see*?' He paused, to give me time to savour this spectacle of disaster. Then he smiled reassuringly, 'What you need is *insurance*. Everybody needs insurance.'

What this impertinent ragamuffin was driving at I did not know, with his talk of insurance. I declined his offer, 'I'll risk it.'

Like all good insurance salesmen he was persistent. 'Risk it indeed,' he scoffed. 'But you *drink*, whisky and Double Diamond. We know because we've watched you in the Schooner. And you *smoke*. Men of your age who drink and smoke have heart attacks.'

I hadn't got to where I was today by giving in to salesmen's blandishments. 'I'll still risk it,' I assured him.

Unperturbed by my refusal to discuss his offer, whatever it might be, he moved smoothly into his Plan B. The one held in reserve and used only with extreme reluctance because it is of such compelling persuasiveness. 'Ah yes. Prepared to put twelve passengers at risk, but what about your *boat*? Supposing this decrepit hulk is at its moorings some dark night; you are at home miles away; there is a heavy run of melt-water coming down the river; the ebb is running fast, and the *mooring chain is parted*. It snaps, not strong enough to take the pull. *Then* where is your so-called *business*?'

I was being blackmailed. There was no other word for it. Yes there was, protection racket, extortion. If I refused to comply with whatever it was he wanted he would *cut* the mooring chain and let the boat be borne helplessly out to sea. A hundred fates might befall it. It could be run down by a ship. It could be broken on the rocks . . . 'Think about it,' he advised.

He took out an old-fashioned silver cigarette case. 'Cigarette?' he offered genially, extracted one for himself and tapped it irritatingly and unnecessarily on the back of the case before lighting it. He inhaled with the relish of a man enjoying the reward of his master plan being brought to a successful conclusion. He remained silent, allowing me time to stew in my fevered imaginings.

Languidly he blew a long slow plume of fragrant Virginia smoke into the still air, fastidiously flicked a speck of cigarette ash off the caked filth of his smock, indulged himself in a smile of triumph mixed with mockery, and asked 'Thought about it?'

I had thought about it right enough. I was going to have to buy into this protection racket. I wondered how big the Danegeld of his extortion was going to be. I acted like a man carefully weighing propositions, considering pros and cons, as if I had any choice. 'This *insurance* you mentioned. Tell me about it.'

'You recruit a crew. You set me on as your bowman. That is your insurance.'

Is *that* all he was after? A job? What a relief. I had been worrying needlessly. Every harbour has its attendant gang of youths gangling about, odd-jobbing, sculling around in dinghies, wasting their youth agreeably. I had seen others, fitter-looking lads than this skinny specimen of pimpled adolescence, hanging about in the hope of picking up a pound or two. This one was not the most promising fish in that pool of casual labour.

'Oh no,' I laughed into his face, 'If I take on a crewman it won't be you, my boy, oh dear me no, it'll be one of those others I've seen hanging on the wall, a better-made one than you.'

'You misunderstand,' he corrected me quietly and almost pityingly, 'It will be *me*. You see, *we* have decided that *I* shall be your crewman, your insurance.'

We? Of course! The mini-Mafia made up of him and his mates. The Organization. The Brotherhood. They had stitched me up.

I capitulated. They were many and I was on my own. The only thing left was to give in with grace and try to regain the initiative. Regain? He'd called all the shots so far. 'OK, then, *you* it shall be. But I shall expect you to work hard you know – no slacking, earn your wages.'

'Ah, yes, wages,' he nodded, 'I was coming to that. We will settle for the usual. That's if it's alright with you.'

The usual? What was 'the usual'? I had had in mind some small remuneration appropriate to his tender age, a bit more than pocket money but nothing extravagant.

'You know,' he explained because clearly I did not know, 'The *usual*. The three-way split.'

'What three-way split? Split of what?'

'The catch. Or in our case the ticket money. It's tradition. When the catch is landed and sold the pot is divided three ways. One third goes to the skipper – that's *you* – the next third goes to the *boat* – that's this fine vessel.' He smacked the gunwale of what he had recently described as a decrepit hulk to indicate his approval of its transformation.

'And the third third?' I queried.

'That goes to the crew.'

'But I haven't got a crew.'

'Of course you have, Boss, you've got *me*!' He had just accorded me my new title. I was 'Boss'. It looked as if my earnings would be as high as his. How nice. Surely I was not hearing aright.

'Hang on, are you telling me that you expect to be paid the same as me, and I own the boat?'

'That's why the boat gets its share, Boss. Tradition. If you want a bigger share you take it off the boat. Now do you see?'

I saw. Jason had found his Golden Fleece.

We worked out his job description. Scrub the boat. Pump out the bilges. Bring the vittles (OK, victuals) on board, and fresh water. Fuel the boat, keep the tank topped up, fill the jerrycans at the garage. Work the anchor, pick up the mooring on entering harbour. Wash the pots. Cook the meals. Heave the beam trawl if we go shrimping. Riddle the catch. Boil the shrimps. Make tea for the passengers. Dole out the bait. Rent out the hire tackle. Get it back. Stand in as locum skipper if anything incommodes me. Scrape the sea-grass and barnacles off the bottom when we careen the boat in the winter. Wash the boat. Paint the boat. Do everything.

He would earn his wages.

'By the way, lad, how old are you?'

'Sixteen . . . and a bit.'

'What's your name?'

'They call me Taff. Taff the gaff.'

Taff. Third partner in the triumvirate of boat, boy, boss. To be formed into a team, by training. Then developed into a *business*, with quality built in from the beginning.

The beginning

Business is simple. It has to do with getting money off people by legal means. Otherwise it's a racket, a scam, a criminal conspiracy. The people who legally hand their money over to you are called customers, or clients; unless you are diddling them in which case they are called fools, victims, or dupes. Customers should be happy to part with their cash, and feel satisfied with the transaction.

A customer is the person (or organization) at the other end of a transaction entered into for mutual benefit.

Why do I bother mentioning such a simple observation? To clear the air. To dispel those glib definitions like 'the customer is king', or 'the customer is God,' or 'the customer is the one who pays our wages,' or 'Rule One says the customer is always right; Rule Two says go back to Rule One.' These are slogans that hang in the mental atmosphere like mists, obscuring the simple truth, confusing our beliefs and hence affecting our behaviour.

A transaction entered into for mutual benefit. Imagine a see-saw. On the left-hand end of the plank sits the supplier, known in the European TQM model as the enabler. This is the leadership to formulate strategy, give direction to people who manage the resources entrusted to their stewardship. In our case this consisted of Taff, the boat, myself, and the sea. On the right-hand end of the plank is perched the client, looking for business 'results', as the European model has it. The customers who must be satisfied if they are to keep coming back, the shareholders expecting a reasonable return, society in general demanding ethical conduct. At the pivot of the see-saw is the process itself, to be managed efficiently to achieve the business objectives. In our case this was the boat, our process for converting inputs into outputs, clients' expectations into actualizations, aspirations into realities.

This business model holds true whether you are a charter-boat selling fishing trips or a multinational selling lavatory paper. It's just that the bigger it gets the less easy the business is to manage successfully. The key to any business success is quality. What is quality? Quality is giving the customers what they want, at a price they are happy to pay and which will yield an adequate surplus when costs have been met.

Giving the customers what they want. But what exactly do customers want? This is the first question of quality. Get the answer to this one wrong and you could find yourself frittering away an awful lot of effort to no profitable purpose.

What do customers want . . .?

'What do our customers *want*? Tell me, will you, Taff?' We were cruising a few miles offshore, on a sea as flat and grey as a bowl of orphanage gruel under a sky as pale as skimmed milk. A day of blandness, the weather apathetic with boredom, unable to think of what to do next, hoping for something to distract it from the tedium of having nothing much to amuse itself with.

We were doing trials. Taff on the tiller to familiarize himself with the boat's capabilities and idiosyncrasies, learning how to handle it. Training and education are the prerequisites of quality. Today Taff was the pupil: the boat would train him; I would instruct him. The sea would educate the pair of us.

'Taff, stop daydreaming. I asked you what do our customers want.'

'Fish!'

'Fish, you say. So why don't they just go to the fishmongers?'

'Dunno, don't ask me, Boss.'

'But I *am* asking you. *What* do our customers want?'

He pondered, as yet unaccustomed to my Socratic approach of teasing an answer already known to me in the hope of making it known to my pupil. It's a way of making yourself feel clever.

'I *know*,' he ventured, 'they want to *catch* fish. Instead of going to the fish shop.'

'What if we take 'em out and they *don't* catch any fish? Will they be dissatisfied? Shall we have to give them their money back?'

I was relaxing in the stern-sheets, sprawled on a bench by the tiller. I am an accomplished practitioner of the art of taking repose. Listening to the low gurgling rumble coming from the underwater end of the exhaust pipe, sniffing the intoxicating wafts of diesel gases bubbled through brine, watching the steaming arc of the engine cooling water spouting into the sea. At peace with the watery world.

' 'Course we don't give 'em their money back,' he sounded personally affronted by the prospect, 'fish or no fish.'

'So what do our customers *really* want, Taff? What are we *selling*?'

'Seats. Sea trips.'

'Exactly. You've got it, Taff. We are selling *experience*. We are experience-providers. We supply the unfamiliar, the things which they find novel. Like fresh air, a big sky, wide horizons, peace and quiet and a thrilling expectancy of adventure. To people cooped up all day in factories and offices. Stale air. Noise. Boredom. We sell tickets to enjoy a dream of fulfilment in the face of danger, to be enjoyed in the assurance of safety.'

'Is that so, Boss? If you say so.' My eloquent exposition of our business mission had left him both unimpressed and uninspired. I had to find a more dramatic way of driving the lesson home. No problem. I am inventive in the torment of my pupils. Time to dispense with leisurely Socratic discourse, time to *do* something.

'Taff, what is the most important service we can render to our customers?'

Instead of awaiting his answer I told him, 'Safety. Keep them *safe* at all times,' and leaping to my feet bawled 'Man overboard!' snatched a lifebelt from its bracket and dropped it over the side.

'There he goes, Taff. Drowning. Get him back. Quick!'

That certainly jolted him out of his reverie; it near-paralysed him with shock. I was timing his response, in seconds. Three gone, lifebelt bobbing in our wake forty feet astern of us, moving fifteen feet further away with every passing second. At this rate it would soon be out of sight. Better keep my eye on it so that by the time he reacts we might still stand a chance of finding it. Good job it's a lifebelt out there, and not *me* treading the water.

'Get him back, Taff!' I roared, using my 'power of command' voice.

He responded. He knew what to do; he'd seen it on the film about Jack Hawkins on the *Compass Rose*. He swung the tiller over, taking the boat into a tight turn until it was pointing more or less in the opposite direction. He scanned the sea, eagle-eyed and alert, searching. Pity he was looking in the wrong place.

'He's over there, Taff.'

He altered course towards the target, going flat out. He hit the target. Still flat out. Overshot it; now it was falling astern again.

'Missed!' he exclaimed.

'No you didn't. You've just knocked him unconscious. That's all. Better pick up the body while it's still afloat.'

He slowed right down and crept carefully up to the lifebelt so that I could bring it on board with a boat hook.

'Two minutes and forty seconds of messing about, Taff.' I shook my head in feigned disappointment. I had expected nothing better, he was not yet trained. 'Ten seconds is all it should take.'

'*Ten seconds*?' His eyes said 'liar'.

We swapped jobs. I took the tiller, gave him my watch and his instructions, and we set off again. I told him that as soon as he made his move he should keep his eye on the second hand of the timepiece while I kept an eye on the drowning passenger. He made his move, dropped the lifebelt over the side, shouted 'man overboard', and started counting the seconds.

I spun the speed-wheel into its full astern position, pulling the tiller hard over so that the boat swivelled around in its cauldron of foam until it was pointing back downtrack, went full ahead and then full astern to bring it to a stop with the lifebelt less than a yard from where he was standing. All in nine seconds.

'Nine seconds, Boss!' he shouted incredulously. 'Show me how you did it.'

Skill vs
insurance

This was the most vitally important aspect of all his training. Safety at sea. Dead customers don't come back; they also discourage others. Third-party insurance cover for up to £100,000 is no substitute for a drowned passenger and a sunken business.

Another vital business lesson was in the offing. We had answered the first question of quality: 'What does the customer want?' Now we had to ask ourselves the second question: 'Can we supply it?' Were we able to pick up twelve sea anglers at the harbour wall, bring them out to the fishing grounds, look after their needs, and get them back to the harbour again at the end of the trip?

Taff was on the tiller, I was throwing bits of bread in the air to save disappointing the small flock of seagulls which had congregated noisily from nowhere when we had attracted their curiosity by pulling something out of the sea. They would have to settle for crusts of granary loaf instead of their usual fare of fish-guts. They hung over our wake, their undersides a brilliant detergent-white against the pewter of the sky. It was darker now. There was no horizon any more, no low ridge of land visible, only an all-enveloping greyness.

'It's gonna blow, Boss.' Taff had grown up in this local microclimate; he could read the signs. The air was colder; we put our oilskins on. Then the wind arrived. Out of nowhere. The boat heeled over as a heavy gust hit the side of the cabin. Taff swung the tiller to bring us head on into the waves. Now we were rising and falling, pitching into the oncoming sea, sending spray flying over us as the boat nosed into each successive crest. The shipping forecast had promised squalls, gusting up to Force 8 – gale force. This was a squall. The weather was no longer bored. It had found its distraction. Us.

'Make for harbour, Taff my lad.'

He glanced at the sky, which seemed to be about fifty feet away, looking for a brighter patch in its leaden grey to tell him where the sun was. The sun had gone in, fed up with the wind's games. The seagulls were nowhere to be seen. There was only us: the boy, the boat and the boss. Could we do it OK?

'Which way, Boss?' No, we can't do it OK. At least, he can't. The second question of quality unanswered. Process failure! Take corrective action.

'Try steering course 210 degrees, Taff.'

In a boat at sea, like in a business in the market, it's as well if you know a couple of things: where you are, and where you would like to get to. Without either of these two items of information you are well and truly lost, and utterly bereft of direction. There is no future in it. You need a benchmark and a goal.

Taff altered course to bring the lubber-line on the compass housing over the 210° mark on its card's circumference. This card, being attached to a bar magnet and free to rotate on a pivot settles itself in a north–south direction, always aligns itself with compass north which is just a touch west of true north. The lubber-line on the rim of the compass housing marks the longitudinal axis of the boat. So if you want to steer a particular course you rotate the boat around the stability of the compass until the lubber-line coincides with the desired course. You calculate your course by knowing where you are and where you wish to get to, make a bit of an allowance for the effect of the wind and the set of the tidal current, and presto! Soon be home.

'How long before we make harbour, Boss?'

Ten miles out . . . 'An hour and a bit.'

The sea was behind us now. We were not pitching any more, just riding on a roller-coaster of an unending up and down motion as the waves passed under us. No more spray blowing over us with every wave we hit; we weren't hitting them now. They were chasing us. This can be fun, it can also be very dangerous.

'Don't let her start surfing, Taff.' Surfing is when the boat is picked up by the crest, advancing from astern, and borne along like a surf-board. You lose steering control. The water can slew your boat around on the wave-front until it is broadside-on to it, 'broached to'. Then it rolls you over; you capsize, unless you take very quick corrective action.

I sat in the cabin watching Taff and the sea through the hooked-back door. A big one was chasing after us. A steep wall of grey-green water looking like a granite escarpment on the move. About seven feet high, its face steeply tilted. It lifted our stern as it crested into cascades of foam. Foam is a mixture of air and water. Not enough water to provide buoyancy – you sink in froth – but enough to pour into your boat.

In it poured. Swilling around Taff's knees before running into the bilges. Ten or twenty gallons of it at one go. I saw fear flitting like a ghost in Taff's eyes. Drive out fear!

'You take it, Boss,' he requested in a small voice. He was being trained. By the sea.

'Bilge-pump, Taff, there's a good lad.' I took the helm. When you're riding in a following sea you keep one eye on the compass to maintain course and the other on the sea astern of you to dodge the cresters. Like any test of any skill it brings its satisfaction. Its joy, its love.

He pumped out all the water he had let in. 'What shall I do now, Boss?'

'Put the kettle on, and make us some bacon sandwiches while you're about it.'

The squall vanished, as abruptly as it had appeared. Squalls are like that, the equivalent of a sudden crisis in business. You just have to ride them out. But to do so you must have honed, and keep honing, your business skills. With training and education, so that you may profit from experience.

Taff and I dined in the directors' restaurant – the navigation table in the cabin. We had stopped the boat, cut the engine and dropped the anchor. No need to go home yet; stay and enjoy the day instead. We had answered the first and the second question of quality. Now for the third, the 'Are we doing it OK?' one. To answer this one we would actually have to do it – we would have to run the business.

The business

Running a business is simple. You identify a market need, assemble the resources required to operate the process whose product or service will satisfy that need, and get going. Simple! But never *easy*! Dame Fortune makes sure of that.

There are too many random influences at work over which you have no control but which will affect your operations. Sometimes for the better. Other times for the worse. Sometimes with trivial effects. Others with catastrophic outcomes.

Take the weather. Imagine yourself to be a trader in, say, coffee futures. You agree to buy a certain tonnage of coffee beans at the time of the next harvest in six months. You contract to buy beans at £1 per kilo. The plantations suffer a prolonged frost at a critical growth phase: the resulting harvest is disappointing. Coffee is scarce; its price goes up. What you bought at £1 per kilo you can sell for £2 per kilo. Lucky you . . . as the trader said, 'Out of this 1 per cent profit I scratch my living.'

Now to the other side of the coin. The weather is kind, harvests are heavy: there is a glut of coffee. Down goes the price, to 50 pence per kilo. You are committed to buy several tonnes of it at £1 per kilo. You would have been no worse off as a gullible 'name' at Lloyds. You lose your money, victim of pot luck, of random misfortune. To add insult to your injury you will probably be *blamed* for it as well. You were expected to control random influences. Blamed?

Try this. You are the buying-boss in a big organization. You have four suppliers of a particular service. You operate a formal vendor-rating scheme, monitoring their performance by the month and meeting them to discuss it at six-monthly intervals. This is the day you have the results to hand; they read:

Supplier	*Performance (% failure)*
Albert	9
Brian	5
Charles	4
David	6

How does your assessment go? Is it . . . congratulations Charles you've won the number one spot? As for Albert I am disappointed, you had better improve if you wish to remain a supplier. We shall review the situation in six months' time.

Six months later you have them in again to look at their half-year's performance results, which are:

Albert	8
Brian	5
Charles	8
David	3

Oh dear. You are right. Albert's got to go. Just look at his pitiful performance; he seems to have taken your warning of six months ago too lightly. Charley's performance has slipped. If he fails to improve it by the next assessment he'll be following Albert.

Now let's turn the ranking order back to front, just for the fun of it. Let us suppose that we are now looking at the results of a rating system applied to the comparative performance of schools, or hospitals, and our criterion of judgement is 'the higher the score the better'. You would clamour to enrol your gifted offspring into school A for Albert, the best chance in life and all that, and *shun* the school D for David, would you not? Here's the evidence, on which to make your 'informed choice'. If you were poorly you would crave admission to hospital A, and dread being obliged to use hospital D, don't you think? Of course, the *figures* tell you.

What do they tell you?

Nothing. Only a string of empty numbers.

These ranking tables were generated randomly with a pack of playing cards, six deals per session to represent six months, dealt to four players, A, B, C and D, who got thirteen cards apiece each deal. Aces counted as 'mistakes'.

These figures are meaningless, utterly random.

You will say I 'cheated' you. I did not. You cheated yourself, by the mere fact of ranking them in order and assuming that this procedure was more *meaningful* than a simple sequence of 1, 2, 3 and 4. It is not.

This human compulsion to measure and grade all events and outcomes is almost as overpowering as the need to 'explain' things which require no explanation. Both these attitudes drive out good sense.

This is not a trivial point; nor is this a trivial game. It is a paradigm of the profound folly of projecting meaning into data which are meaningless. It happens, a lot. It causes resources and energy to be deployed senselessly by trying to 'correct' things that are not 'wrong'. It is shadow-dancing, the unthinking pursuit of chimeras. It is like a government obsessed with producing 'league tables' in order to provide the so-called 'customers' of hospitals (newspeak for 'patients'), and schools, with the blessing of 'informed choice'. Meaningless opinions based on randomness masquerading as causation. We should not complain. We do it all the time in business and industry. We are all victims of Corny's stallion syndrome of imputing meaning into meaninglessness; of confusing association with causation. We feel safer that way; so much so that whenever the statistical methods available for testing the significance of our assumptions produce results which disagree with our prejudices, we disregard them. Such is the power of belief over reason, as we have already noticed previously in this text. This is good news for the organizational change-agent, as well as for politicians and advertising agencies: belief is infinitely malleable. You can change its shape. It is blindly power-ful, like Samson eyeless in Gaza. So, be careful what you choose to believe. Now back to business.

Business operates in a context of endless variation, a complex setting of shifting influences sometimes bordering on the chaotic. Which is why business is so interesting, so much fun.

Our sea-angling charter-boat two-man-and-a-dog business was no exception: variation, both predictable and random, had to be lived with.

The predictable variation was the tide. This variation is itself unvarying. Tides come and go to time, at regular periods, driven by the pull of the moon and to a lesser extent the sun. High water arrives when it is due and floods the harbour like a great lake. Then it duly ebbs out, draining the harbour until nothing remains except a few puddles and a trickle of river-water snaking between shifting sandbanks. Twelve and a half hours later it's back in, the harbour again a lake. At the time of full moon and new moon the tides are 'springs', high water is very high and low water is very low. At half moon the tides are 'neaps': high is now not so high and low is not so low. This is the lunar/solar cycle. In Spring and Autumn the 'equinoctial' springs are extraordinarily high and low. All periodic and utterly predictable; and all a big nuisance to anybody operating a charter-boat business out of a harbour navi-gable only during the timespan of high water plus and minus two and half hours, being at all other times too dried out to be access-ible to any floating object deeper than a duck.

In obedience to the tides' lunatic imperative we were obliged to organize our trips into two sorts. Five-hour excursions as the tide was flooding in, leaving harbour as soon as there was water deep enough to permit our escape, and returning five hours later while it was still deep enough to float us in; and seven-hour jaunts leav-ing with the ebb and staying locked out until the tide flooded the entry channel deep enough to let us through. This was the basis of our production programming. This afforded us the opportunity to work antisocial hours, or trip after trip non-stop over several tides, taking on passengers, fuel, fresh water and vittles (OK, victuals) on the run. Working our assets off, as they say, like any smart businessmen, day and night, night and day. Sounds like a song title; time for another little vignette . . . .

'Night and day, you are the one'

'What's it like, fishing at night?' one of our passengers had asked Taff, as we sat on a quicksilver sea under a brassy sky waiting for bites from fish dawdling in the summer's sunlight.

'Like it is in daylight, only it's dark,' Taff lied, 'Alright if the weather's alright, I guess.'

Thus assured, the angler consulted the eleven other passengers who constituted the angling club, and obtained a consensus to book an overnight trip a couple of weeks ahead. Weather permitting . . . .

The weather was alright on the night: calm sea, cloudless sky, fullish moon, good forecast, rising barometer reading. Promising an uneventful trip, all variables under control – tide predicted for a thousand years ahead, weather predicted for a few days ahead, all portents looking good. I should be able to earn money while taking my ease in my bunk. Nothing could go wrong. Nothing? What about the other variables – the strange ways of people and the stranger ways of fortune? What about them? Forget them; stop this unnecessary worrying. Just slip the mooring at midnight and ride the tide to riches.

The fishing party arrived promptly enough, so promptly we had nearly three hours to kill before departure. Where better to kill them than in the Schooner? Drown them like kittens. We British tend to be dedicated yet guilty drinkers; we make apologies to our chapel-bred non-conformist consciences while we lick our lips in anticipation of the first seductive taste. So we ritualize our discomfiture . . . 'Just the one, eh?' . . . 'Phew! I'm ready for this' . . . 'Tidy drop of ale is this.' Next it's 'Fancy another bevvy?' . . . 'Go on, gerrit down you, lad, do you good' . . . 'It's my round, so I'll get you another' . . . 'One for the road then?' As pint glasses, held in the correct ceremonial grip with the little finger crookedly sticking out in a gesture of delicate refinement, are solemnly raised to serious mouths.

These passengers, patently accomplished sacramental drinkers from a public-house fishing club somewhere inland, were a mixed dozen. A quartet of coalminers, gaunt grey-faced men with gravel voices and rattling chests, sucking on Woodbine cigarettes for solace. A brace of bakers, pallid jowls sagging like tired dough. A pork butcher with pinkly-shining cheeks like a shaven pig's only not quite as handsome. The publican, patron of the club, florid with occupational boozing for goodwill's sake, face resembling a shining blood-blister ready to burst and a blown-out belly to match. An off-shift crew of process workers from a petrochemical plant, their complexions yellowed to parchment by fumes, purple bags under their resigned eyes, sweating lightly with the effort of coping with biorhythms permanently dislocated by years of continuous shift working. Going fishing, to inhale the sweet unbreathed air of the summer's short night. But not yet.

By the time the fourth round was being trayed to the table nagging conscience was drunk, lying in a snoring stupor among the fag-ends and slops. Now they could enjoy themselves. Sit at ease. A happy band of hunters engaging in a bit of harmless male-bonding, teambuilding as it is called these days. Discussing strategy, exploring tactical considerations such as hook sizes, trace lengths, baits, lures, all the engrossing minutiae of anticipation known as the planning phase. The pleasant chit-chat of this steering committee was abruptly silenced by 'What the devil is *that*?' asked by somebody staring at the pub's window in disbelief.

The window was glazed with obscured glass up to shoulder height and clear panes above. Through it could be seen a well-upholstered settee slowly passing by, seemingly unsupported, as if levitating itself through the empty air.

'It's a *settee*,' said someone, 'isn't it?' We crowded to the window to get a closer look at this physical manifestation of the seeming paranormal.

'It's Sylvia's settee,' explained Taff who, being a capo in the local league of Mafiosi youth, knew about these things. 'Sylvia, and Glyn Snookerballs.'

The settee was being supported in its stately progress by its two bearers, Sylvia and Glyn. She, a daunting specimen of womanhood, stumped along on legs sturdy enough to support a full-size billiard table. Behind her, supporting the settee's trailing end, went Glyn, knees buckling.

'Why is he called Glyn Snookerballs?' one of the party innocently enquired.

'Because his name is Glyn', Taff explained, 'and he's got coloured teeth. If he had a white one like a cue ball he'd have a full snooker set. But he hasn't.'

'Ah. I see. What are they doing with the settee?' Sylvia was waddling across the road over to the harbour wall, Glyn obedient in her wake, down the steps to where a boat was waiting. They carefully lowered the settee into the boat. 'Why are they putting the settee into that boat?' Taff's interlocutor wanted to know.

'Sex,' Taff informed us.

'Sex?' echoed the nosey one as if the very notion of carnal encounter was a novel concept. '*Sex*, you say?'

'Coitus un-interruptus,' sniggered Taff, who had given these matters serious study by close perusal of certain kinds of publications which he habitually read with one hand. 'They go out to sea for it on a quiet night,' he elaborated, 'They can't do it at his house, too many nosey brothers and sisters. Can't do it at hers either because her mother's a narrow-minded old cow. So Glyn bought that boat. They put the settee in and do it in comfort out at sea. We've watched them through the Coastguard's big binoculars. Then they take the settee home again in the morning.'

Glyn left Sylvia sitting primly knees together, lips pursed, on the settee and shambled into the pub to buy the night's ration of prenuptial liquor. Like the poet Geoffrey Chaucer he knew that a drunken mouth begets a lecherous tail, and lechery was uppermost in his head.

'Goin' fishin' again Glyn?' Taff jeered at him, 'Goin' to see what you can catch on your rod? Haw, haw, haw . . .'

Glyn, though regarded as being not quite all there, but who relished recognition as much as any striving manager, put on his Jack-the-lad knowing look of half-lidded eyes, wobbling head and sophisticated sneer that he had learned at the cinema watching Robert Mitchum, and confirmed, 'You better believe it baby.' He flashed his terrifying multi-coloured grin, causing one of the crisp-eating children in the room to start to cry before burying its face in its mother's skirts.

'Don't knock the bottom out of your boat Glyn,' Taff advised. Then he explained to the rest of us that Glyn had bought, for next to nothing, a Victorian relic of a ship's lifeboat that had spent years quietly decaying on the mud of the river bank. He assured us that his advice to Glyn not to knock its bottom out was sincere, since the boat's hull consisted of little more than twenty-eight feet of wood so rotten you could poke a knife through the planking. 'It's a coffin-ship,' he concluded dramatically.

We watched the lovers leaving the harbour, the boat's one-cylinder diesel engine knocking as frantically as somebody who has awakened to find himself in a coffin with the lid screwed down, making for the setting sun. To enjoy the heady delights of drink, darkness, and each other under the twinkling constellations.

It was time for us to go as well, to sail out with the ebbing tide into the ebony sea. The spiralling turbulence from our screw glowed with ghostly pale green phosphorescence as the myriad marine micro-organisms flashed their alarm, coldly illuminating our wake. Once we came to anchor our rope and every fishing line would trail tattered pennants of this spectral radiance down the current, scaring all the fish around except maybe a few flatties grubbing a late supper on the seabed. Fishing is not always good on a summer's night. Still, the passengers hadn't come for fish, as we had already established. They had come for experience, to be enjoyed in peace and quiet.

'What's Glyn doin' now, do you reckon Boss?' Taff speculated salaciously.

'Sleeping.'

'What's Sylvia doing then?'

'Trying to wake him up.'

We motored on, steering a course by keeping the mariners' friend – the Pole Star – about forty degrees to the right of our track, riding a sleepy swell under the vaulting roof of the heavens. Silence, save for the drowsy rumblings of the diesel and the murmurings of the anglers in the floodlit fishing well, preparing their tackle. Alone, on an empty sea. Peace . . . peace . . . serene peace . . . .

Bang! The boat was brought to a sudden halt by the shock of collision. Anglers thrown forward from their seats into a tangle of tackle. Splintering of wood . . . cut the engine!

'What the devil is *that*?' One of the passengers was staring over the side in disbelief, for the second time this night.

'It's that bloody *settee* again!'

Buoyed up by the air trapped in its overstuffed upholstery the settee was bobbing heavily down our boat's side. Sylvia was clinging half-on, half-off it in a most undignified state of naked indignation.

'You careless buggers, you've rammed us,' she yelled. As if we didn't know. 'Get me off this sodding sofa before it sinks.'

'By gum, but she's a right bonny lass is that one,' one of our passengers observed appreciatively.

Her Sumo wrestler's legs were thrashing the water, driving the plankton into a panic-stricken hysteria of luminescence. She slid deeper in, flailing and hollering, glowing angel-white, haloed with the biological radiance like some ghostly creature of the deep. Taff looked on, aghast, his pubescent fantasties of female pulchritude shattered by the reality of Sylvia in the sea.

Fortunately we had on board some strong men, accustomed to handling heavy objects in tricky circumstances. Grunting with effort they heaved Sylvia's blubbery mass into the safety and embarrassment of the boat, wrapped her in an oilskin for modesty's sake and accorded her the privacy of the cabin. Glyn was found hanging on to the bent rails of the collision-dented pulpit on the bows. The settee wallowed sluggishly down current in its flotsam of shattered planking, now a minor hazard to small craft.

One hundred square miles of sea. Empty, save for ourselves and one boat a mere twenty-eight feet long, lying stopped without lights. And we had hit it. Not a glancing blow or a near miss. Oh no, right bang in the middle; our bevelled oaken steam with its brass cutting edge had cut into it as far as the keel, breaking the rotting hull in two. Could you calculate, *a priori*, the statistical probability of such an event? Neither could I; it just seemed highly unlikely, until it happened. Was this 'random misfortune'? Would they blame *me* for it?

Random? Not much of an excuse. 'Expect the unexpected', say the pundits. What is *that* supposed to mean? I did not expect, because I had no reason to expect, that in all that vast emptiness, all that unused space, Glyn's boat would choose to drift across the path of mine at the exact instant to cause collision. A couple of seconds earlier or later and we would have missed.

No excuse. Bad seamanship. Bad management of resources. Careless assumption that it would be difficult even to find just one solitary boat in all that sea, let alone ram into it. Huge oil-tankers have gutted themselves on submerged reefs for the same reason;

businessmen have foundered for the same reason – complacency. So let this be a lesson to us: never to take anything for granted, to try and avoid complacency, because complacency can lead to trouble. Come to think of it so can job satisfaction. Perhaps I was becoming too satisfied with my job of tyro-tycoon of the sea-angling trade, too complacent.

Job satisfaction and complacency are like Siamese twins, one inseparably attached to the other because they fuse together as they grow together. You can make a pseudo-mathematical equation out of it:

Job satisfaction + Complacency = Staleness

Staleness seems to be a near-universal human experience, well-attested to in folk wisdom. Like the Polish observation about marriage, which suggests that if a newly wed couple throw a coin into a box every time they make love in the first year of their marriage, and thereafter take a coin out of the box each time they do it, the box would never be emptied. Honeymoons cannot last forever. Ardour dies down, enthusiasm flags, inventiveness runs out of ideas.

Things are much the same with jobs. Enlightened companies have long known this, and countered complacency by switching managers into different jobs every few years. This rotation saves them from becoming stale after the first few energetic years of the honeymoon phase; it also has further benefits for the organization, such as the disruption of alliances which might work against the interests of the company, or the building of empires for the sake of a high subordinate head-count because that jacks up the job-points and more points means more pay.

This tendency of all things towards eventual staleness can also be observed in the world of the performing arts. For instance, thirty-odd years ago a musical group called 'Los Trios Paraguayos' burst on to the pop scene. They sang to the twanging of Paraguayan harps. Their voices were raw with the pain of living; these were hurt and hungry men. Their fingers plucked powerful melodies of haunting beauty from the harp strings; theirs was visceral music that wrenched harmonic response from

your innards. They were amateurs. They were a hit. Their sons inherited the mantle of success. They are sleek professionals, con-
summately skilled in the business of making music for money.
They are good, pleasing to listen to, but something is lacking;
something vital has been polished away by professionalism.
Something that cannot be faked.

We could incorporate this into our pseudo-equation if we wish:

Job satisfaction+Complacency+Perseverance=Professionalism

Professionalism is praised, and rightly so. It is a respected destination to which effort is directed. It is a dead end. Seemingly it has
always been so. If we look at the archeological testimony provided by the genesis of the flint axe-head we see it. An artefact
which began as a rough lump of flint skilfully knapped into a
razor's cutting edge was refined over the millennia into a polished
blade of ellipitical symmetry – with a cutting edge no sharper than
the rough forms of its predecessors. But now it had become
aesthetically pleasing to look at, a joy to behold, beyond further
improvement, at the end of its road. A perfect artefact. I have one
today in my tool shed, except that mine is forged from steel and
has a rubber-coated shock-proof haft. This is also a perfect artefact, unimprovable; and that is a good thing.

What is not a good thing is when jobs and job-holders follow
the same evolutionary path as the axe-head. The job-holder
becomes a professional, then professionalism matures (or stag-
nates) and the professional becomes 'an *expert* in the field'. In the
realms of management it might be legitimate to describe an expert
as someone who knows much but does little. A bit like the acade-
mics who observe the world of work and tell us what is happening
and how things are being done; like harem eunuchs, professional
voyeurs who know every detail of what is done but are never
called upon to do it. Or like the business school Burkes and Hares,
latterday body snatchers who study 'case studies' with the rapt
attention of early surgeons dissecting cadavers, carrion-cutters
looking for life in that which is dead. Trying to make tomorrow
like yesterday.

Time to throw in a couple of clichés:

● Nothing fails like success.

● Nothing succeeds like failure.

Let us explore these a little; see if we might tease out a bit of hidden meaning.

I used to be an avid reader of the appointments pages when I was young and hungry. More often than not I was put off by the demand 'must be able to demonstrate solid career progression'. Solid career progression? *Me*? No chance. Looking back over the short road that had been my life so far I could see too much rubble and mess. The tumbled stones of ambition gone wrong. the unfinished edifices of failed enterprise. The tangled wasteland of effort uselessly but pleasurably dissipated. Progression? Hardly. This drove me to the conclusion that faced with such impossible job-entry specifications the only person stupid enough to employ anybody as unemployable as I was would have to be myself.

I had experienced the first of these two clichés; I had been successful in a job. I had failed, by turning into a polished axe-head at the end of its evolutionary journey. Since it was now unimprovable there was only one thing to do – smash it and start all over again. So I had failed. So what? I had become a successful sea-angling boat operator instead.

But these two clichés don't run separately. They circle each other like a pair of dogs pursuing each other's tails. No sooner do you fail, than you succeed. No sooner do you succeed, than you fail. Life becomes a giddy merry-go-round. Failure and success spinning as madly as the little dancing-girl in Dickens's *Nicholas Nickleby* – 'give her a quart of gin and she spins like a top'. To switch literary references we might mention that Rudyard Kipling saw 'those two impostors, Success and Failure' as being one and the same. He was wrong: success tastes sweet; failure is bitter on the tongue. He was right in as much as they come close after one another. Perhaps this is because they are supposed to; maybe this is what life is about; possibly prolonged success might do you damage.

I suppose that the moral of these two circling clichés, if they have one, is that if you feel yourself to be a failure do not be unduly despondent because, in the words on the Persian lintel, 'This too shall pass away'. Conversely if you reckon yourself to be a success then enjoy the feeling, but briefly lest its sweetness should turn sour if you try to enjoy its taste for too long.

I was successful in my boat business, successful in the sense that I was earning a living without trying too hard. Even so I found myself once again feeling restive. Why? What was wrong with it? I must understand . . . .

Trained to be a scientist, steeped in the scientific method and weaned on Kelvin's doctrine that before you can begin to understand anything you must be able to measure it, put numbers to it (I still partially believed this partial nonsense), I decided to put numbers to my job. To render it numerical, and therefore in the spirit of Kelvin understandable, by looking at it in the light of Lawler's Expectancy Theory. Perhaps you recall my description of this view of the nature of work in my first book *Right First Time*. No? Then let me remind you.

Lawler identifies five component elements into which any job can be divided. These are:

- *Skill variety*. How varied are the demands the job makes on the qualities and capabilities of the job-holder?
- *Task identity*. Does what the job-holder is doing make any sense to the said job-holder beyond that of merely passing time to earn a crust?
- *Significance*. What is the impact on others of doing the job well or doing it badly? How much does it really matter?
- *Autonomy*. Does the job provide any opportunity for the job-holder to exercise powers of discrimination and judgement?
- *Feedback*. Does the job itself, or the organization in which it is performed, provide any guidance about the effectiveness of the way in which it is being performed?

Lawler allocates an arbitrary score of 1 through 7 to each of these components depending on how much of each of them is inherent in the job. The more of the component the higher the numerical score. The scores for five components can then be totalled to provide a measure of the complete job. To be in a job scoring 35 would clearly be an enriching experience. Remember that these scores are nothing more than the quantifying of an *opinion*, or perception, but they are none the less valuable for that. This structured approach provides a common matrix within which several jobs may be compared, or the merits of a single job assessed, such as your own, or those of your subordinates.

This Lawler grid is a useful way of guiding 'job-enrichment' initiatives, as a way of getting more work out of your team without paying them any more money. This is a legitimate application of the theory, one that I have made good use of.

It prefigures the currently fashionable nostrum known as 'employee empowerment', because Lawler's 'autonomy' element is itself a measure of empowerment; so I guess managerial fashion has propelled us backwards rather than forwards by taking one out of five elements known for twenty years and hawking it as if it were newly minted. This serves to illustrate the shallow narrow thinking of some of the nostrum-peddlers, and the comparative poverty of what they are offering.

How do you think *your* job stacks on the Lawler grid? If it totals up to anything less than about 25 you are in trouble and should think of doing something about it. How about the jobs you are expecting your underlings to do? How do they score? Anything less than 25 and you are failing as a manager; the answer is in your hands, and you can elevate your own job score whilst elevating theirs. You can enrich yourself by giving something away. (This is not another snippet of slick sophistry; it is a basic truth of life, and you had best pay some heed to it.) Giving something away will enable you to feel a success and to enjoy full job satisfaction in your 'comfort zone'. A comfort zone is a warm pond of self-adulation in which you are free to stagnate.

I was in a comfort zone in my job of sea-angling charter-boat operator. But restive, as I have already mentioned. I thought I might as well calibrate my job in terms of Lawler Expectancy Theory . . . .

Skill variety. Just as Heraclitus has it, 'You cannot step into the same river twice', no more are you able to launch into the same sea twice, or, come to that, gawp at the same sky twice: these things are constantly changing. So the skill needed to handle a motor fishing vessel varies according to changing sea and weather conditions. But the repertoire of skills is no wider than those exercised by, say, a seamstress or a surgeon, for whom stitching is stitching; or a toolmaker or a carpenter. The highest score I could allocate for this component was a 4.

Task identity. OK, we went fishing for money. We also provided a healthy recreational facility for those with the leisure, inclination, and money to pay for it. We created employment for the bait-diggers. The boat served the valuable social purpose of keeping one urchin off the street. We brought ashore a harvest of nourishing food for the boarding houses and hotels. Score another 4.

Significance. High! Get the job a little wrong and I might kill somebody; that would be bad. Get it a lot wrong and I might kill myself; that would be worse. Score 6.

Autonomy. The skipper is on his own. Whether it's an ocean liner or a fishing boat with twelve passengers command is solitary. There is nobody to turn to, because everybody on board turns to you. When you are caught twelve miles out by a howling wind and a bucking sea, and men's faces turn a sallow yellowy grey, when they whistle tunelessly or hum the tune 'for those in peril on the sea' (honestly!) you are required for swashbuckle a bit. 'Pour 'em all a mug of grog, Taff', you tell the boy, and he hands them one-eighth of a pint of 80° proof Captain Morgan let down with two-eighths of water to take the scorch out of it. Dutch courage. Don't knock it. Drink it and be damned. Autonomy? I'll say. Score 7.

Feedback. By the end of every trip you had a pretty good idea of how well things had gone, so you could say that feedback was fairly prompt. Worth a score of, shall we say 6?

Total score – 27 points out of a possible maximum of 35. Not a bad old job according to Lawler's Theory. So why was I fretting? Clearly there is more to a job, or rather to the *relationship* between a job and its job-holder, than Lawler's grid caters for. Something non-measurable maybe? Like the recurring need for self-renewal, perhaps. The secret. 'The secret is to grasp it, and let go.'

One aspect of 'variety' provided by the job of skipper is the *riches* it affords you. Somebody once defined 'riches' as 'the amount of your own personal time you are free to dispose of'. By this definition I was for all practical purposes a millionaire. All that time to spend! Once out at anchor I was free to chew the fat with the passengers, and we had some very interesting people out with us. Each with his or her own story to tell. People like the implacable Mr Purgatroyd, the Inland Revenue chieftain. The pop star Heinz (this was the 1960s) who looked as if he'd been cast in Inca gold, and his minder Eddy, who looked as if he'd seen hewn from a two-ton block of marble. A sleazy entrepreneur who wanted us to run certain items of contraband across to Ireland (no way!). A tobacco-company salesman in a pinstripe suit who came out once a month to stand like a figurehead in the pulpit gulping fresh air before handing out free cigarettes to all on board. Chairman of an electronics manufacturing company who persuaded me to install his quality management systems in my spare time. Editors and team of publishing company who bought the stories I wrote while reclining in my bunk, writing to make a change from reading. Twelve Doctors of Philosophy from a bluechip R and D laboratory who came out to get drunk. Two psychiatrists from a lunatic asylum, who continued their Freud versus Jung fight while fishing. A host of fascinating folk, from whom I learned a lot. And from whom I earned a lot. First from their fares; second from the stories I wrote about them and sold to magazines.

So *why* did I pack it all in? Well, for one thing I chanced upon yet another poem, written in the girlish hand of my eldest daughter in a school exercise book when she was ten years old . . . .

The Sea

The angry sea raced across the beach
Tossing up spray as it hit the wall
Ships were wrecked, boats were smashed
And this great sea was the cause of it all.
The wild waves rose to enormous height
Their colour blue green topped with white.

The lifeboat went out as rockets were fired
To rescue some people distressed and tired.

Then, next day, all was still,
The devouring sea had had its fill.

Angela Price

The sea had had its fill. And I guess that I had had my fill of the sea. There always comes a time to let go.

To let go. Just as you, the one who was 'let go' by the company who employed me and my axe, were set free to move on to other things. To life after death. Do you see what a *favour* I did for you?

Now you are free to be whatever you want to be. A writer? consultant? A tycoon? Or what? Now you can go for *growth*.

You can do it. Oh yes, there will be obstacles. We shall look at some of these in the next and final part of this book.

PART 4

GOING FOR GROWTH

hermit
crab and
growth

(t.v. Ray kinbaty)

'Too Big for His Boots'

Growth, growing, this is the essence of life; of course you can do it, but . . . .

The process of growth is a universal phenomenon which is interesting to observe. First, consider the *crab*.

The *hermit crab* is unable – or maybe merely disinclined, for all we know – to produce a shell of its own. Instead this soft, vulnerable shapeless creature seeks safety by occupying the empty shell of any similar marine crustacean, insinuating itself into whatever vacant carapace it comes across. Once established in its comfortable lodgings within, say, a cockle-shell, it grows. It grows bigger, taking the shape of a cockle, moulded by the cavity in which it finds itself, until it fills the available space. Its capability of growing is then curtailed by the chafing constraints of its too-snug shelter so it scuttles about the seafloor in search of a more commodious dwelling. Having found one, say a whelk-shell, it swiftly evacuates its restrictive cockle-shell and installs itself in the larger premises. Now it has room to grow, whelk-shaped this time, growing until it outgrows this shelter in its turn, and yet again is obliged to seek more ample accommodation.

This is the process of growth as experienced by a hermit crab. Second, consider the *person*.

The employable *person* (as opposed to that rare and tormented individual who by nature and nurture is utterly ungovernable and therefore unemployable by anybody except himself) is either unable – or merely disinclined – to go it alone. Being uninterested in flying solo, he finds a job. (I write 'he' not for any sexist reasons but because the double pronoun 'he/she' makes for a stumbling block in the narrative flow; no offence intended to women.) Having found one he is usually pleased to take up tenancy in it, and grow into the 'shape' demanded by his interpretation of the job description, then grow some more. Eventually the job that in the beginning seemed to offer wide scope and opportunity for self-development starts to chafe. In an effort to escape its now claustrophobic embrace he scuttles about looking for a bigger one. At this point his boss might condemn his growth aspirations by declaring him to be 'getting too big for his boots'. This is intended as an insult. It is in truth, of course, not an insult at all; it is a tribute unwittingly paid by a lesser-developed individual to a higher-developing person who just happens to occupy a lower stratum in the organizational hierarchy. This is one of the most pernicious effects of the pyramid: while proclaiming the virtues of 'self-actualization' it represses the growth of its occupants. It becomes a breeding ground of moral midgets and stunted personalities. The 'shell' of the job description, written to fit the pyramid but not the person, is inflexible, so the occupant is expected to diminish and distort himself to match the limited space it provides, and settle for being less of a person than he might be for the sake of a security its imprisonment provides. This is a form of death-in-life. All, at some time in their lives, are obliged to experience it; few to escape it.

What *is* this *growth* we are talking about? OK, so a hermit crab grows, and changes its housing as it does so. But eventually it becomes an adult crab, reaching its full size, and thereafter grows no more; it remains nothing more than a big crab. Likewise with all other non-human living things: shark and coelacanth for instance have remained thus for many millions of years, unchanging and changeless in a changing world. What is so different about human beings? We are born, we grow, we mature, we senesce, we die. Where is this 'growth' of 'self-actualization'?

It is to do with, for want of a better word, *spiritual*, or moral, growth. Whether or not you agree with René Descartes, who argued 'I think, therefore I am', and promptly claimed a monopoly of spirituality for mankind to the exclusion of the whole of the rest of creation, is neither here or there. Descartes, who was allowed by his superiors to lie abed late in the mornings to indulge his philosophizing, might have argued that 'dogs do not think, therefore they are not', which is arguably nonsensical, but what is unarguable is the fact that humankind lives a spiritual life beyond the life of the rational mind or the physical body. Maybe dogs do as well; look into a dog's eyes and decide for yourself.

I get the feeling we are treading on quicksand here. The words we are obliged to use to describe the concepts can become a turn-off. But if you have slogged through the book as far as this I must ask you to persevere a little longer; what we are saying might be of some importance to you and your future.

Just what *are* we saying? We are discussing the actualization of potential, spiritual and moral growth to fuller humanness, and developing into one of those people Maslow calls the 'altruistic autonomous self-actualizers' who have achieved a fuller maturity.

Do you remember Abraham Maslow? (His is a surname of flexible pronounceability. You can rhyme the 'low' with 'bow', as used to shoot arrows. Or with 'cow', as Americans say 'Moscow'. (Or you can pass yourself off as one of the intelligentsia as I do by giving it its *Mitteleuropa* sound 'Masloff'.) Maslovian ideas proliferated in the 1960s and early 1970s, so they are probably buried under the dust of more recent managerial fads and fashions by now, and therefore in danger of remaining unnoticed and unused. Since his words meet King Darius of Persia's specification by embodying much that is eternally true, let us exhume some of them. Let us make use of the ancestral wisdom that wiser men such as he have bequeathed to us, seeing that we are not the first men who have ever lived. There must be a useful place for a bit of *everlasting* truth in these days which, we are told, are ever-changing.

Self-actualization, the Personal Odyssey

An odyssey is an arduous journey undertaken in search of something regarded as precious. Self-actualization is a journey whose purpose is the discovery of self, or perhaps Self with a capital letter. It is not a destination; it is a trek, mainly a gradual unfolding but sometimes a Damascus-road revelation, an excursion into self-discovery, an answer to the age-old 'Who am I?' conundrum that all of us are finally obliged to solve.

Hey, I was right, we *are* treading in intellectual quicksand here; never mind, in for a penny in for a pound; let the text plod on until it sinks out of sight. Tricky territory, is all this talk of self-actualization.

'How will I know, when I meet one of these so-called self-actualizers, that I have actually *met* one?' was a question put to me by a bemused facilitator from a training board who was seeking guidance, 'How do you *recognize* them?'

People like him put such questions to me these days; they must assume that because I've grown a white beard I must have grown wise. I was obliged to disappoint him. 'What you are *not*, you cannot perceive or understand. I cannot communicate itself to you.' I quoted directly from Maslow the master himself. He remained bemused, so I added helpfully, 'I suppose it's a case of it takes one to know one. And you aren't one. Yet.' His face fell further, so out of kindness I consoled him by telling him, 'I don't know either.'

'So you're not one of them,' he concluded, 'I'm talking to the wrong person then, aren't I?'

If *you* are a self-actualizing person you will perhaps have noticed that though there are few of you around you seem to recognize each other very quickly whenever you meet. If you are not then you will have noticed, like my facilitator friend, that there are none around. Anyway, does it really matter?

It matters. 'Our people are our most vital asset,' brays the boss

in his annual report, before bragging how his down-sizing operation of laying off a lot of his staff has proved so successful that he
has awarded himself an obscene pay increase: now the company
is 'lean and mean'. How true! People *are* the organization's most
precious asset, properly used. But no outfit is better than the
synergic sum of its parts – its individual people – and is sometimes much worse when synergy is negative because of fear,
conflict, or manifest injustice. But the best organization can be no
better than its best people. The better the quality of the people in
the collective the better is its health. So the obvious and bounden
duty of the company is to employ the best people it can find, and
to develop towards their fullest potential the people it already has
on its pay-roll.

This is all cliché. It's been said a thousand times already. It is
being acted upon up and down the world of work; companies are
turning themselves into 'teaching companies', embarking on
training programmes to enhance the competences of their people.
This is a splendid thing indeed. But is competence the same as
self-actualization? Is all food jam because all jam is food?

Self-actualization embodies higher competence but goes well
beyond it. Companies whose employees have achieved higher
levels of individual actualization (let us abbreviate this into
'individuation') must clearly be healthier than those with a
less-developed workforce. As we said, many organizations are
fostering competences galore; how many are encouraging the
individuation of their members? If this higher form of personal
growth is important to the collective it is even more important to
the individual: it is *vital*. Vital in the sense of life-sustaining. Vital
in the sense that there could surely be no more worthwhile way of
spending one's days than the pursuit of personal individuation, of
moral and spiritual growth.

What a load of rubbish! (I hear you scoff). *Moral* and *spiritual*
growth indeed! Don't give *me* any of that nonsense. I'm a practical man, I am, a realist, who knows what makes the world go
round. I'm not interested in any of your airy-fairy, namby-pamby,
motherhood-and-apple-pie, Jesus-wants-me-for-a-sunbeam stuff.
I'm interested in . . .

. . . more *money*. (Why? To buy the things that advertiser's hype
tells you you are a nerd without, but forbear to tell you that once
you have bought them you'll be no more than a nerd with them?)

. . . more *power*. (Why? Power to do what? Power over whom? What are you afraid of; what deep conviction of personal inadequacy causes you to crave power for the sake of it?)

. . . more *prestige*. (Why? Have you handed your self-esteem into the custody of others without whose approval you feel yourself slighted?)

. . . more this, more that. More freedom, more beauty, more status, more . . . more . . . more of more.

Of course the needs for money, power and prestige are important. But they are to the mind what vitamins are to the body: a sufficiency is enough to maintain health. They can become addictive, and taken in heavy doses they turn poisonous. Notice that these needs are solely to do with making demands on the environment external to the person: they are 'give me' things. As such they have little if anything to do with the actualization of the self and the developing of potential. They are 'maintenance' needs, an *inflow* into the person. As such they are the opposite of actualization. To actualize the self it must be given away.

Oh dear, here we go again – another of those paradoxes that tickle my sense of humour so much I cannot help but draw your attention to them. Like some of those I have used in previous texts, such as 'Only by being weak can you be strong', 'In order to get you must give', 'In order to find yourself you must lose yourself', and so on. More metaphysics, is it? More useless smart-talk? More mystical claptrap?

No, my friend; these are the most powerful, practical and rewarding ideas it is possible to adopt. But they cannot be taken on board by those who are unready. To those who are ready they open up a joyful voyage of discovery. One of the best vehicles for generating the actualization of selves is a total quality management programme.

Another cliché! This time that discredited body of knowledge, belief and practice that goes under the umbrella heading of TQM. This is a nostrum which has just about had its day; we are in 1995 now and other approaches have begun to supersede TQM. Like the wisdoms of Maslow total quality is receding into the past, shouldered out by stronger, newer doctrines of managerial hope. It has failed us.

Well, failed four out of five of us, by all accounts. It has never failed me or my clients, so my experience tells me that my loyalty to it as a way of improvement is well justified. But mine is one small voice in all the deafening cacophony of manager-babble and organizational newspeak. TQM is out of fashion. Let me speak up for it.

It has failed, for so many; those who tried it found it wanting. Why? Because . . .

. . . TQM is a utopian ideal, a vision of the perfectability of human societies and organizations, an impracticable dream in the real world of pragmatism, conflict and compromise. This is seen as its weakness. It is in fact its true strength. TQM programmes often fail because they are implemented in a *mechanistic* manner, though the humanistic aspect of TQM is woven from those very ideas of moral growth towards higher levels of individuation which are the essence of Maslovian thinking. You could say that TQM is partly his wisdom on wheels: a vision of a better way of doing things, guided by his insights and powered by his inspirations. It provides us with a way of accomplishing greater actualization of ourselves by promoting the actualizing of others. This is an eminently worthy undertaking. A man could spend his lifetime doing little else and yet end his days rewarded by the happy assurance of having been of some value to others and true unto himself. This would be reward enough; it would have to be; he would not be disgraced by dying rich. ('He that dies rich dies disgraced' – Carnegie.)

It seems naïve in the extreme even to entertain any Utopian ideals in these days of 'greed is good' philosophy which hails money as the measure of all things. Silly to utter such notions in a society which first perverts the findings of psychology, by telling us that there are more rewarding things than money, then using this as an excuse to depress wages; and second allows some bosses, whose near-criminal incompetence has crippled the enterprises entrusted to their cynical stewardship, to vote themselves 'golden parachutes' of inflated wealth when they finally leave the wreckage their avarice has caused. On the one hand we preach the virtues of teamwork while on the other we practise the vices of dog-eat-dog individualism and to hell with the hindmost. This is our reality, because we have willed it to be so. Sleaze Rules OK.

We can change it, by a collective act of will, if we want to. This prevailing view of the nature of mankind's needs is demeaning. It

manacles us to the 'money' rung halfway up the Maslovian ladder
of instinctual need. It arrests our development and denies us the
satisfaction of our higher-order needs. Still, cash is a comfortable
cushion, I guess; more than enough for a moral pygmy.

Is money a 'bad thing', then? No, not of itself. It is neutral. It is
the lubricant which oils the machinery of business. What *is* a bad
thing is our endless preoccupation to amass more and more of it,
for its own sake. It just *has* to be the principal indicator of the
performance of a business enterprise; after all, any business enterprise is by its nature a money-machine dedicated to the pursuit of
profit. But as a goal for a man to give his life over to? As a worthwhile expenditure of our brief years? This is a riddle which each
of us is required to solve for himself.

The person who uses the Maslovian hierarchy of need as the
yardstick against which to measure his progress towards individuation and ego-transcendence is forced to choose the level to
which he aspires. Whether to settle comfortably on the money-
rung and, like Humpty Dumpty, contemplate the hollow centre of
his life, or to aim higher. Whether to bask in the light of the
approval of others, on the need-for-recognition rung, or to move
upwards, impelled by a higher brighter vision. We have choice.
We cannot avoid it.

So. To those of you who still work for salaries and to those
whose instinctual ambitions to grow into a higher state of individuation are no longer constrained by their colleagues in the
company from which they have been set free – what do you want
to do? To grow? Here are a few 'axioms' to help you. (An axiom
is defined as 'a self-evident principle, a proposition that com-
mends itself to general acceptance . . .' etc.) Though what I am
about to say is self-evidently axiomatic, as far as I can see, you
might see these statements as empty sloganizing. I can but offer
them to you in hope.

Axiom: You grow bigger only by helping others to grow bigger.

This ancient truth, of course, flies in the face of the prevailing
organizational assumption, as evinced by the prevailing organizational practice that you can grow bigger only by making those
around you smaller. This is the reductive Lilliputian approach: to
surround yourself with midgets in order to be able to congratulate

yourself on how tall you have grown. There is no love in it. Neither for self nor for those on whom dwarfism is being enforced. There is plenty of it about. Like the poisonous shade of the upas tree it's a sure way to stunt the organization as a whole.

Axiom: To help people grow you must love them.

Love. Not judge. Actions and deeds may be judged, and then either praised or condemned, but not their perpetrators. 'Hate the sin, love the sinner', as somebody once said; very likely St Paul; he said a lot. 'Do you know how to get the very best out of your people?' a successful entrepreneur once asked me, rhetorically, because he immediately added, 'I will tell you – you must *love* them. But you must love justice and honour and virtue likewise.' This was a businessman speaking, not a Sunday Christian sermonizing from a pulpit.

Axiom: To grow you must observe and obey the eternal verities – justice, honour, integrity . . . .

In the absence of a code of conduct, based on everlasting values external to the self and the organization, a man is less than an animal. Which is why, according to some, if God had not created man, man would anyway have created God. So he does. Any old god: fame, power, glory . . . all the tired old deities conjured up out of the void of the ego, the fabrication of helpers who turn out to be helpless. Without moral guidance we are lost. Sometimes it is not easy to recognize that course of decision which is 'most moral', and less easy to act upon it. It is always easy to recognize that which is 'least moral', that which is merely expedient, and easier still to rationalize our actions arising from it.

Axiom: To grow you must learn to listen to the voice of yourself . . .

. . . instead of hearing in your head the internalized voices of parents, teachers, pundits, proselytizers and the other persuaders from your personal past. Psychological research makes it terrifyingly clear that failure to do so can lead you inexorably to the dreadful gates of Auschwitz. (If you doubt this, please refer to the

Dixon,
military
incompetence

work done by Milgram, as reported by Norman F. Dixon in his
book *On the Psychology of Military Incompetence*; see Recommended reading.) Be your own man; so few of us are.

Axiom: To grow you must immerse yourself in something outside
yourself.

One way of finding yourself is to do something which obliges you
to forget yourself. Some activity which forces you to look outward. There are innumerable ways of doing this. One of my own
favourites is rough carpentry. I make things out of planks and big
nails. My latest creation is a garden seat of robust construction; I
got more fun out of making it than I do by sitting on it. The act of
building it to a design dreamed up in the imagination is nothing
less than *creative* as far as I'm concerned, and carthartic with it:
while I was doing it I was pouring myself out of myself and into
the object of my creation. OK, it may be a clumsy 'giant despair'
design of a seat but I felt better for having built it. This is because
by paying attention to *it* instead of to myself I was saving myself
from myself; paying overmuch attention to yourself can make you
sick; better to get it out. Do anything to rid yourself of yourself;
that way you'll begin to discover yourself. If you fail to rid yourself of that which is within you it will turn sour, poison you, fill
you with the venom of envy and similar negative emotions. Leave
that to your colleagues; colleagues are often adept at it.

Axiom: To grow, you must accept – love – yourself.

Forget the words of the priest who told you that you were a sinner;
he only wanted to make you feel guilty so that you could be
manipulated. That is one of the things the organized church is for,
to teach people self-abasement in order to command obedience.
Forget the strictures of the teacher who told you you were stupid
because you asked silly questions. That is what established education is for, to bend your mind to its own views, to teach you to forget how to think. You are neither sinful nor stupid; you just made a
few mistakes, that's all. Join the club. You have nothing to feel
bad about yourself for. Nor about other people. If you feel bad
about yourself you will try to disown the feeling by projecting it
onto somebody else. This is how misery spreads. So love your-

self; only then can you love another; only then can you grow and enter the estate of your real self.

Axiom: To grow you must drop your defences against sacred joy.

Sacred joy? What's that . . .? I was standing one morning at the doors of a garment factory, talking to the woman who looked after the personnel function, greeting the employees as they came in to work. Across one of the upper corners of the doorframe stretched a spider's web, sprinkled with frozen droplets of dew. They sparkled, flashed rainbow colours as the web rippled in the light breeze and slanting rays of the early sun. Its beauty held my gaze and hers.

'Isn't it incredibly beautiful?' she commented. One of the women trooping by on her way to yet another day of mind-numbing drudgery paused, and asked the personnel officer what she was looking at with such rapt attention.

'This lovely spider's web.' The woman exchanged a significant glance with her companion, an act which in the armed services would have amounted to the crime of dumb insolence. They humphed, and hurried off to their machines. Too busy to spare a moment for anything so trivial, so worthless. Had it been possible to preserve the fleeting glory of that triangle of dewy gossamer a Hollywood superstar might have paid a ransom to possess it, to drape its beauty like a bib over her boastful bosom. But it was free; and therefore without value, except to a wimpish couple of cobweb watchers with nothing better to do.

Sacred joy? Those moments of peace which pass all under-standing, rare and brief, coming unbidden; but only to a self at ease with itself.

Are any of these so-called axioms of any use to anybody? Will they *do* anything for you? Well, they will certainly lead you to no harm. They might even help you to arrive at one of the higher Maslovian hierarchy levels – autonomy. At one kind of autonomy anyway, because there are two sorts: autonomy to dominate the world, and they will not lead you to this form of mental sickness; and autonomy to love the world. To find out what this latter sort is like I suggest you get hold of Maslow's *The Farther Reaches of Human Nature* and consult pages 322 and 323 (see Recom-mended reading); they are a revelation of the extent of the possible in actualization. Thereafter you will have the advantage over my training-board facilitator friend: you will know one when you see one. You will have become one.

That will be enough of homespun axioms and self-actualization. But not of Utopianism.

The Utopian

As a personal way of passing your time Utopianism has a lot going for it. It can be used as a licence to make mischief. To tell the world that you are trying to make the world a 'better place', without adding 'for myself', is to put yourself into a near-unassailable ethical position; after all, who could criticize such a noble aspiration? From this moral high ground you can snipe at organizational misbehaviour, which is to say you can complain about whatever you happen to disagree with; you are, after all, doing it all 'for the best'. Using the philosophy's fine precepts about the perfectibility of human society as an intellectual scaffolding you can build yourself a pedestal on which to stand as the conscience of the company. Not only might you achieve some measure of improvement here and there; you can actually have a lot of fun doing it. There is a delight to be had in putting your stick into the cauldron of the company and stirring up the status quo. Trouble is, status quo has ways of fighting back.

I found myself recruited into the ranks of the Utopians quite early in my career. Before they let me loose into civilian life the Navy had me counselled by a priest, one of God's commandos kept on the payroll for such a purpose. His little chat was the services' equivalent of the headmaster telling you about the mysteries of sex the day before you left school, a preparation for the shock of leaving the protective cocoon of the institution before being expelled into the dazzling confusion of the external world. A sort of born-again experience.

'It is a wild and disorderly world out there,' he advised. How does he know, I wondered; had he ever been out there? 'You will be *on your own*, you know, just you and your god.'

Well, that's alright then; sounds a pretty formidable team when the Almighty is your ally.

'I will offer you some sound advice, to help you,' he proceeded, 'First, always strive to keep your mind, your heart, and your bowels open . . .'

I nodded. That sounded easy enough.

'. . . and your mouth shut.'

Ah . . . oh dear . . . I'd guessed there would be a catch.

'Always breathe with your diaphragm; this will calm your passions.'

Another catch, fancy telling *that* to a young man permanently slavering after women.

'Do not worship at the feet of the false gods of money, lust, or rebellion against those set in authority over you.'

The holy triad – poverty, chastity, obedience. I might manage the first of these, but not the second, and certainly not the third. I had no intention of entering a Trappist monastery.

'But above all other things', my spiritual mentor persisted, 'always *find yourself a star to steer to.*'

An aim in life, something other than money, carnality, or Marxism. Sounds OK.

'Espouse a *cause*. Select a guiding vision, something desirable yet forever unattainable.'

This was my chance to bring this rigmarole to a conclusion. 'A cause. I see. Say, like trying to make the world a better place for mankind.' That should do, I thought.

'That should do,' confirmed the padre, 'That should keep you busy for the rest of your life. Now, let us pray . . . .'

Powerful stuff, prayer. Like fulminate of mercury it has to be handled with care. I once knew a young and devout Christian woman who hated her job. For four days she prayed to God to relieve her of its tiresome burden. On the fifth day she was sacked.

Trying to change the world into a better place is a long-term undertaking, long enough to preclude any prospect of redundancy. It is a long job because it is to do with making change, change of *belief*, of conversion from one mind-set into another, of cultural change. This is work for prophets; there is an arrogant assumption of god-like power on the part of the change-agent. There has to be. This is his inspiration, motivation, gratification. This is his excuse for indulging himself in the pleasures of making mischief. There are two distinct strategies for going about it.

First, there is the way of *mass* conversion. In a religious context this is the Billy Graham style of doing things. A large congregation is assembled and word-whipped by the fervour of the preacher into a mindless hysterical clamouring for immediate salvation. It works, for a while. It gets its converts, though how long their conversion persists once the initial ecstasy has abated is anybody's guess. But it's fun for some while it lasts.

This approach has its organizational parallel in some total quality programmes. The entire company is exposed to an explosion of razzmatazz, fired up by the hot gospelling and crusading zeal of the ranting preacher, emotionally provoked into shining-eyed enthusiasm eager to clasp the new cult of perfection to its collective breast and sing the hallelujahs. How long this kind of conversion endures once the initial euphoria has evaporated is *not* anybody's guess – in four cases out of five the promised land fails to materialize out of the mirage of hyped-up hope. This is a matter of record. But, as above, it's fun for some while it lasts.

Second, there is the other strategy of conversion. This is the opposite of the mass-baptism method: this is the conversion of an organization's culture through the agency of the individual. The way of the disciple, of changing the company culture by changing one person at a time. Ten years ago, in *Right First Time*, I described how this can be done, but I'll tell you again:

> You are the change-agent. Yours is a vision of a better way of doing things in the work organization. You do not wish to waste this vision, so you use it sparingly by seeking out those individuals in the client company who are endowed with the biggest ears and mouths; in a word, the *natural communicators*. Their ears become the vessels into which you pour your message, their mouths the trumpets which will amplify and propagate it. Remember you are a Utopian whose task is to alter the cultural climate, yours is an active not a passive role. You are a rain-maker who causes climatic change, not a meteorologist who idly observes it. This is how Maslovian self-actualizers exert their altruistic autonomy – by helping others towards their own actualization. Others who will then help others . . . who will help yet more others in their turn . . . ripples spreading from the pebble of the message dropped into the receptive ear. Ripples which persist long after the pebble has sunk; a message which resounds long after the messenger has moved elsewhere to peddle his path to perfection.

Ah, the path towards perfection, do you think that this is a road that all would gladly tread? Is this not the broad avenue that any rational person would elect to follow? Rational, yes; but rational behaviour is rare, the *irrational* so often prevails. Consider the story of a young man called Mike.

The vendetta of the perverse conspirators

The job of Mike, as quality manager in a company engaged in the manufacture of high-grade packaging products, was to obtain certification to BS5750 for his organization and thereafter lead it towards a TQM culture. The first of these goals he had already achieved; the second was proving to be not quite so easy; there were obstacles in the path. Although Mike was as yet unaware of it one of the biggest of these boulders on the trail to TQM resided within himself – he was naïve. Another massive barrier, of which he was also in ignorance, lay within the heart of his boss – who was not naïve.

His boss had risen to his position of higher authority through the diligent application of sheer 'hard work'. The Prussian route for the stupid. Being untalented and barely educated, yet endowed with a strong dash of native cunning, the kind of hyperactive busy-ness which masquerades as 'work' in our culture was the only way open to him in his climb up the pyramid. He had striven slyly and ruthlessly, and now believed he had grown bigger by cutting other men down to size, whereas in fact he had merely gone higher. Somehow the higher he had climbed the more embittered he had become; his eminence had not brought him happiness. He served no master apart from his own self-interest. If this did not happen to coincide with the company's or his boss's interests, he camouflaged it to make it look as if it did. To his boss he was a cringing sycophant; to his subordinates a bawling tyrant. He was also a consummate conspirator.

The company had recently achieved the distinction of being appointed as packaging supplier to a multinational pharmaceutical house celebrated for its insistence on quality; this was an accolade to be cherished; there must be no dud deliveries to this demanding client; too much delicate negotiation had gone into the acquisition of the business to put it at risk from slipshod quality.

No need for anxiety. Mike was on the ball. He had negotiated realistic standards; he and his powerful client agreed common procedures, clarified definitions, did all the things necessary to ensure honest trading. Things went well. Week after week, delivery after delivery of output integrated smoothly into the client's manufacturing system. Records were maintained, quality continuously monitored and assured. Even though Mike's boss had gloomily predicted that it would be over-optimistic to expect zero rejections from such a fastidious customer Mike was able to report exactly that – 'zero rejections' – at each of the weekly progress meetings. This pleased Mike.

It did *not* please his boss. This is not what he had so pessimistically prophesied. Things were going too well, *unbelievably* so. This was worrying! So he took action to correct this undesirable state of affairs.

He secretly contacted his opposite number in the customer's company, a man of equivalent rank and of equal deviousness, to ask a favour. What favour? To arrange for a delivery to be rejected. Why? To put that arrogant young upstart Mike in his proper place.

So the pair of them conspired to pervert the course of honest business, colluded in an act whose only purpose was the humiliation of a junior colleague. A delivery was duly rejected; the customer claimed to have found it to be faulty. Mike's archives of the quality of output were comprehensive; he checked them. No record here to substantiate any rejection, so he went to see the offending output on the customer's premises, where inspection of the delivery against the specification proved it to be acceptable. First round to Mike.

A few weeks later the unsavoury pair of plotters struck again with another attempted rejection. Again Mike checked his records, thankful he had maintained them, and with a further visit to the customer refuted the attempted rejection. Second round to Mike.

Mike was by now becoming a little less naïve. His boss was becoming no less furious; the authoritarian character hates being thwarted, especially by those 'under' him.

'I am not happy with your management methods and information storage and retrieval systems', the boss told Mike, 'so I have asked the customer to send us an expert to have a look at what you're doing; he will report in due time.' The hatchet-man arrived, he found 'holes' in the systems, and duly reported. Third round to the boss.

The boss decided to consolidate his victory. 'I'm calling in a quality expert from Head Office to see what you're up to,' he informed Mike, who happened to know for sure that there was no such expert at Head Office or anywhere else in the corporation, but . . . . The next hatchet-man arrived. His verdict was, 'Sorry about this farce, Mike, you obviously know more than I do about quality,' and he declined to deliver the damning report so desperately demanded by the boss. Fourth round to Mike.

The boss, however, held a trump card: the annual appraisal, perverted into a phoney ceremony of assessment involving two participants, the judge and the accused. This appraisal is to do with that concept of managerial control called 'management by objectives'.

It is based upon a Taylorized reductionist view by which the art and craft of management is broken down into a cluster of tasks. It is at one remove from the true purposes of work which are twofold – serving the conversion process and meeting customers' needs – so it is detached from reality to the point of meaninglessness. The only meaning remaining in this little yearly pantomime is the playing out of its ordained script by a pair of opposing roleplayers. If it does nothing more it at least satisfies the vanity of the person playing judge. Its script starts with the easy bits: 'State the key results achieved by the job-holder.' Mike gave a couple of these: first, zero rejections for quality from their most demanding customer; second, line scrap down at less than half of 1 per cent of throughput. Then it comes to the best bit: 'State those objectives the incumbent has failed to achieve.' This was the ace up the boss's sleeve: 'During the year the incumbent completely lost the confidence of our most important customer due to inadequate quality systems,' he smirked. He had been savouring these words for weeks, waiting for the day of assessment when they were to be uttered to devastating effect. 'Therefore the job rating of the incumbent cannot be raised above 80 points.' This rating of 80 points, in an 80 to 120 range, kept Mike at the salary status of 'new man, new job', which meant no pay rise for Mike. Fifth round to the boss?

Put not thy trust in princes: Mike was naïve no longer, but neither was he angry. He realized that his boss had 'won' only by reaching for the weapon of his formal authority, and in so doing he had changed the rules of the game in order to end it. Morally Mike was the victor, and he also knew that the game would go on. Tyrants keep on tyrannizing; the boundaries of their tyranny are never drawn by them, only by the tyrannized. Mike had drawn the boundary, with the help of his *alliance*. Mike, you see, was a man of integrity, who had ages ago thrown in his lot with allies who included Truth and Justice. These stand outside the organization, aloof from petty politicking, powerful in their own right. They are to do with morale, and as Napoleon Bonaparte pointed out, victory is dependent three-quarters on moral consideration and only one-quarter on military matters.

The contest between Mike and his boss continued awhile; quality continued to be superlative and inimpeachable. So the boss changed the rules once more. He committed his final and most irrational act of all – out of sheer frustrated rage he turned his emotional sword upon himself, and died. To save his face. His passing was lamented by nobody more than by Mike, who had *loved his enemy*.

This is a true account. One small testament to the *irrationality* which affects the supposedly rational way in which we conduct our affairs. It tells us yet again the power of emotion to override reason. And what is the most powerful of the emotions? *Love*.

In the last analysis love is all that matters, because love is all there really is, which is why . . .

. . . LOVING WORKS.

Update: A Gigantic Hoax?

Life goes on while the writer sits inside his cell of self-imposed solitude, where every third day is a Thursday, wondering what is happening to the passage of time and the progress of the outside world.

In the outside world it is, of course, business as usual. While the scribbler sits in aloof detachment describing things in the abstract, at one remove from hectic involvement with reality, real people are doing real things. Innovating, creating, making changes. Especially to that form of work we call 'management'.

Management is a broad church. It has its zealots, dogmatists, sects, and dissidents. It is an arena of lively debate and novel thinking.

The most recent novel thinking is very novel indeed. A savant in the United States suggests that management has degenerated into little more than the manipulation of symbols; has become an abstract exercise in number juggling and information processing divorced from the real world of making and doing things. He may be right; though as far as I can see there is nothing 'abstract' about traffic speeding down a highway, or a glass bottle, or a pile of groceries at a supermarket check-out. These are very concrete things. OK, they can be mathematically modelled by management, and sometimes the model distracts us from the thing we are modelling and it loses its roots in reality. So he may be right.

A British thinker has ventured even deeper into blasphemy. He reckons that the very idea of management as a legitimate and valuable activity is a gigantic hoax, perpetuated by its beneficiaries – 'managers' – for reasons of self-interest. If this is the case then I have been duped into becoming a hoaxer and my life's work has been wasted. Like yours. Like that of four million more of us in the UK. Like many millions throughout the developed world. *If* this is true.

True or false, it looks as if total quality management turned out to be a hoax for four out of five of the companies who tried it.

Might we therefore ask, 'Does TQM work?'

We might as well ask if socialism works, or if the ten commandments work. Clearly they do not. After seventy years of despotic endeavour socialism collapsed. After two thousand years of spiritual exhortation professing believers still murder, rob, and rape each other, often in Christ's name. Set against this dismal record TQM's success rate of one out of five is a pretty respectable score. And if these things have not worked, what are we to do with them? Abandon them because they have let us down? Discard them and try something else? All because they have failed to 'work'.

They have not worked for the simple reason they were not supposed to work. That is not what they are for, by their very nature. They are Utopian ideals, dreams of perfection in an imperfect world, stars to guide us. Socialism is a vision of a better and more equitable society. Christianity an idealized code of personal conduct. TQM a creed which mixes both of these in the workplace. It is not the ideals which have failed us; it is we who have failed our ideals. Whenever ideals are ignored or perverted we slide into disappointment and dog-eat-dog barbarism. We need our ideals if we are to become more human.

But ideals can be dangerous. They can encourage idealists to be carried away on the strength of their conviction of their absolute rightness; they can stray beyond proper boundaries, as TQM has done. Let us remind ourselves of what TQM is for:

> Its prime purpose is to improve performance by alleviating the boredom of those whose work is intrinsically boring.

Allow me to put that another way:

> Its purpose is to harness the talents of those whose work affords for little scope for personal expression.

Now to rewrite it in a third form, that of manager-speak:

> Its purpose is to actualize potential and foster job enrichment and satisfaction.

As I said, to alleviate boredom.

Which means it is most properly offered to people whose jobs are inherently boring; and hardly necessary to those whose jobs are by their nature less boring. Some of the jobs we require people to do have dullness built into them. They originate in the sterile and dehumanized dogmas of so-called scientific management. Jobs of this lineage, so stupefyingly undemanding that they are best suited to the mentally retarded and capable of sending normal folk stupid, provide TQM with its greatest scope for making greatest impact.

In contrast, other sorts of work, in which interest and excitement are intrinsic elements – like the warm glow felt by a nurse as a grateful patient recovers from illness or injury, or the adrenaline thrill that tingles the nerve of a police officer arresting a difficult suspect – are outside the proper boundaries of TQM.

Yet TQM is to be found there, in these work organizations, where it will be of least use because it is of least need. It has been driven by its zealots willy-nilly into hospitals, police stations and other inappropriate places as if it were a universal panacea. Following the eminently valid concepts of this Utopian ideal 'managers' extend it beyond its validity. They use it to exercise spurious authority.

For example . . . a midwife, who over the years has safely delivered more than a thousand squalling infants and lovingly reassured their sweating mothers, is sent on a 'communication course'; is told to learn 'body-language', and study 'transactional analysis'. Required to recite 'vision and mission statements', as if childbirth had changed since the time of Dickens and his gin-swilling midwife Sarah Gamp, or since the Stone Age even.

Or take the case of the police officer, bruised from having exercised 'sufficient force' during an arresting encounter with a flailing maniac high on drugs, being lectured about 'customer satisfaction' and the importance of 'interpersonal skills'.

All this new-fangled 'coaching and counselling' (an American euphemism for what used to be called a bollocking session), with its patronizing assumption that wisdom is directly proportional to rank.

All being perpetrated in the name of total quality management, and all amounting to . . . what, a gigantic hoax, perpetrated by a new breed of 'managers'?

There is yet another wart on the nose of TQM – money.

Part of TQM is the 'empowerment' of a workforce because these days we know that money is not a motivator; it is a short-term satisfier unable to inspire and sustain commitment. Apparently this half-truth is held to apply to everybody except the bosses of lately privatized utilities such as gas and electricity. Their fellow directors award these men of stunning banality stunningly high money rewards; their greed makes mockery of work psychology. When challenged by committees of enquiry composed of the Great and the Good, their stock attempt to justify their pathological mix of vanity and greed is to claim they work long hours. Their typical workday begins at 0630 and ends thirteen hours later. Every hour of it stuffed with detail, with not a second left unaccounted for. No time left to them for creative contemplation or intellectual playfulness, their minds so boring they are unable to think of a better reason for pillaging the coffers than to claim long hours. Not even the wit to boldly proclaim that they, and only they, thanks to their length of experience and inborn quality, are capable of doing the jobs they do for so much money. Not even the strength of character to indignantly ask how dare they be questioned about the offence against fair play their inflated salaries inflict.

Let them keep the money while fools like us work for job satisfaction and personal fulfilment. As a bishop once said, 'You can tell what God thinks of money just by looking at the people to whom it is given.' So be grateful, endure poverty, it's character-building. Isn't it? The British Government evidently thinks it is; they have coined the slick slogan 'Low Pay is better than No Pay', to justify their decision to try and make us labour-competitive against Taiwan, whose people work for next to nothing, and the People's Republic of China, whose prisoners work for nothing at all. Stiff competition indeed.

Having recently witnessed 'the end of socialism' are we now observing the end of capitalism? 'The end' not in the sense of ceasing to be; more in the sense of journey's end, of arrival at a destination. Has it brought us back to plantation slavery's modern equivalent, product of its master–servant mentality which it never relinquished? Is capitalism able to exist only as an institution operated for the benefit of the few exploiting the many? Its unacceptable face?

This would be a sombre prospect if it were the only philosophy of work that capitalism is capable of constructing. Luckily there are chinks of bright light visible through the callous gloom. They are to do with an alternative way of ordering the social structure of our businesses; they are to do with democracy in the workplace.

Democracy in the workplace is the Utopian ideal to which TQM directs us, its ultimate destination, its hidden agenda. It is the fullest expression of employee empowerment. It has an illustrious pedigree and a long tradition . . .

David Dale (1734–1806). Scottish mill-owner, philanthropist and evangelist.

Robert Owen (1771–1850). Welsh son-in-law of David Dale. Enlightened mill-owner at New Lanark in Scotland, philanthropist, humane employer.

Robert Dale Owen (1801–77). Son and grandson of the above. American Congressman and founder of New Harmony colony in Indiana.

Prince Ito and his fifty-five fellow nobles who owned and ruled Japan until 1850 when they voluntarily relinquished power and possession to the nation, thus laying the foundation for Japanese industrialization.

Ernest Bader, founder of the Scott–Bader Commonwealth in England in the 1950s, who said something to the effect that 'that which is morally wrong cannot be politically or socially right', and built a successful worker cooperative enterprise doing as the Japanese nobles under Prince Ito had done – shedding exclusive power and possession.

There were others. They showed us that Loving Works.

Do you think that the very idea of worker democracy is nothing more than pie-in-the-sky? Impractical philosophizing incapable of working in the real world of today with its harsh economic climate? Then look to Brazil, to . . .

Ricardo Semler, of São Paulo, who has encouraged his manufacturing operation to grow and become democratic and to prosper even in times of economic depression. If you doubt that 'Loving Works' buy his book and read the truth for yourself. It will open your heart as well as your mind, show you the place to where the philosophy of total quality management will lead you. If only you will let it.

Alas, democratic management is not as easy as control by command, or management by fear. To turn the humanistic ideal into organizational practice calls for a person of exceptional talent at the top, somebody of vision, enlightenment and love as well as good business sense. Although I have met many people of high personal calibre in my journeys through Great Britain plc I have never been lucky enough to encounter anyone of Semler status, a person with the humanism to envision an ideal and the power to implement it. An entrepreneur who has reaffirmed that a social conscience and capitalism, far from being mutually exclusive, can be brought together to form a winning combination. The only British name of like calibre that comes to mind is that of Anita Roddick of Body Shop, a strong woman of the sort to whom this book is dedicated: a practical idealist who has demonstrated that righteousness can be rewarding, a worthy custodian of the ideals without which our society will degenerate, a reminder that without values nothing is worth anything. Not even money.

Let Loving Work be the service *you* render.

APPENDIX

Exercise 1

Communication:
The Yi Calendar

Objectives

- To study communication processes in problem solving.
- To develop skills in discriminating between relevant and irrelevant information.
- To develop skills in structuring information.

Preparation

This is a small group training activity conducted by groups with between four and seven members. Any number of groups can undertake the activity at the same time.

Prior to the activity, each of the thirty items of information is typed on to a separate index card.* The information needed for

___

(* *Note*: all information given on the cards is true.)

preparing sets of cards is below. One complete set of cards is required for each participating group. The cards should not be numbered, and should be shuffled before use.

Copies of Yi Calendar: Exercise Brief and Yi Calendar: Review should be available for each participant.

Time required: about one hour.

Method

The coordinator introduces the activity and hands out Yi Calendar: Exercise Brief. Each participant also receives approximately the same number of cards, each with an item of information. The cards are distributed randomly.

Participants are reminded that they may not exchange cards. When the introduction is completed the coordinator starts timing the exercise.

After the group has agreed on an answer the coordinator stops timing and checks the result. The correct answer is 'there are ten months in the Yi year'.

If several groups are conducting the activity at the same time, it may be useful to compare results. The winner is the group that correctly solved the problem in the shortest length of time.

The activity is completed by conducting a review. This is structured by distributing a copy of Yi Calendar: Review to group members and asking them to complete it privately, and then discuss the data collected.

YI CALENDAR: PRE-WORK

Instructions to typist

Type each of the thirty items below on a separate card (approximately 5 inches by 3 inches). Do not number the cards.

The investigation of the Yi calendar was carried out by Liu Yaohan and Lu Yang.

Liu Yaohan is a member of the Institute of Nationalities.

The Institute of Nationalities is part of the Chinese Academy of Sciences.

Lu Yang is Dean of Astronomy.

Lu Yang and Liu Yaohan gleaned details from 'bimos'.

A 'bimo' is a professional sorcerer of the Yi people.

Professional sorcerers kept an oral tradition until recently.

Most solar calendars divide the year into twelve months.

The Mayan Indians divided the year into eighteen months.

A Mayan month had eighteen days.

The Yi calendar is based on months.

The Yi calendar does not have the same number of months as the Gregorian or Mayan calendars.

All the Yi months are the same length.

The Yi year is virtually the same as the contemporary tropical year.

The contemporary tropical year is very similar to the Gregorian calendar.

The Gregorian calendar has approximately 365.25 days per year.

The basic unit of the Yi year is a period.

The Yi calendar is closely tied in with astronomical cycles.

In the Gregorian calendar the date of New Year is decided arbitrarily.

In the Yi calendar New Year occurs when the 'handle' of the big dipper constellation points vertically north.

The Yi calendar has five 'spare' days a year to distribute as holidays.

The Yi calendar has an extra spare day each four years (leap year).

There are three periods in a Yi month.

The earliest twelve-month calendar was invented by the ancient Egyptians.

The Mayan Indians had a calendar which ignored the phases of the moon.

The basic unit in the Yi calendar is a twelve-day period.

The Yi year is the same length as the Gregorian year.

There are fifty-six minority nationalities in China.

The seasons of the Yi year are determined by the position of the sun against a stellar background.

The Yi calendar is unlike any other so far detected by anthropologists.

YI CALENDAR: EXERCISE BRIEF

The Yi people, who number nearly five million, live in South West China in the provinces of Sichuan, Guizhou and Yunnan. They used a unique calendar until recent times. The members of your group have been given certain true information and you are required to determine the number of months in a Yi year. You may share the information you have been given orally, but may not show your cards to anyone else.

YI CALENDAR: REVIEW

Spend a few minutes privately reflecting on the activity you have just completed and answer the questions below. Then discuss the experience with other members of your group for thirty minutes.

1.   What were your initial reactions on beginning the task?

2.   How was the process of information sharing managed?

3.   What were the most useful aids to problem solving?

4.   At what point in the activity did difficulties occur?

5.   If you were asked to tackle a similar activity again, what should be done differently?

The author wishes to thank Gower for permission to make use of this exercise, taken from Dave Francis's book *50 Activities for Unblocking Organizational Communication*.

Exercise 2

Negotiation

How to play

The trainer selects two teams, of three to four people per team –
Group A and Group B.

If the trainees are not known to the trainer it is worthwhile consulting the senior trainee, who knows the others and their idiosyncrasies, so as to select a 'Rambo' type of personality to be
included in each of the teams. This can lead to a more vigorous
and illuminating exchange between the opposing teams. If the
total training group consists of more than the six or eight people
chosen to play in Group A or Group B the non-playing people can
serve as observers to the exercise.

Group A is sent outside the training room; Group B remains
inside.

The trainer tells Group B (in the room) that he will serve as
intermediary between the two groups, and will now go outside to
ask Group A whether they wish to play Red or Blue to open the
playing. He invites Group B (in the room) to contemplate its game
plan: what will be their response to whichever colour Group A
decides to play?

The trainer leaves the room and asks Group A (outside the
room) to play either Red or Blue.

He returns to the room and informs Group B of Group A's decision, and asks them to respond by playing Red or Blue.

Group B responds to Group A's play by counter-playing either Red or Blue. This completes the first round of the ten rounds and fixes the team scores according to the Rules. There are four possible scores (see Rules).

The trainer goes out of the room and tells Group A which colour Group B played, and in so doing what score was achieved for the first round.

The second round is played: Group A open by choosing Red or Blue, then choice is communicated to Group B who decide to play either Red or Blue, thus fixing the score for Round 2. This is added to the score for Round 1.

And so on, for ten rounds, with opportunities for Group A to return to the room for face-to-face discussion after Round 4 or Round 8, but only by mutual consent.

The trainer must remind the teams that the objective of the exercise is to 'End the game with the highest positive score for your team'. He must not elaborate on this; this, and only this, is the objective.

The Red/Blue exercise

Objective: End game with highest positive score for your team.

Rules:
1 There are two teams.
2 You will choose to play either **Red** or **Blue**
3 You will be scored as follows:

Group A	Group B	Score A	Score B
Red	Red	+3	+3
Red	Blue	−6	+6
Blue	Red	+6	−6
Blue	Blue	−3	−3

4 There are ten rounds.
5 You can have a conference with your opposing group after the fourth round. (However, this can only take place at the request of **both** groups.)
6 You can have another conference after the eighth round, if **both** groups choose this.
7 The ninth and tenth rounds score **double**.
   ● If both groups play **Blue**, each scores '−6'
   ● If one group plays **Blue**, the other **Red**
     Red = −12; **Blue** = +12.
   ● If both play **Red**, each scores '+6'.

Use the following scoresheet.

SCORESHEET

Move	Coloured played A	B	Score A	B
1				
2				
3				
4				

(Conference Point)				
5				
6				
7				
8				

(Conference point)				
9 (double score)				
10 (double score)				

Totals

What did I learn: About my perceptions of the other party?

About myself?

The purpose of the exercise is to learn to appreciate that it is only possible to 'win' by allowing your 'opponent' an equal 'win'.

This is a win/win transaction of conciliation, i.e. the basis of an Enhancing style of Customer/Supplier Relationship.

Acknowledgement

The author wishes to thank John Carlisle, Robert Parker and the publisher John Wiley and Sons, for their kind permission to make use of this exercise, taken from the book *Beyond Negotiation*.

Recommended reading

Carlisle, John A., and Parker, Robert C, *Beyond Negotiation*, Wiley.

Dixon, Norman F., *On the Psychology of Military Incompetence*, Futura.

Francis, Dave, *50 Activities for Unblocking Organizational Communication*, Gower, Volume 1 1987, Volume 2 1991.

Francis, Dave, *Unblocking Organizational Communication*, Gower, 1987.

Maslow, Abraham, *The Farther Reaches of Human Nature*, Penguin.

Pirsig, Robert M., *Zen and the Art of Motorcycle Maintenance*, Bodley Head/Corgi, 1974.

Price, Frank, *Right First Time*, Gower, 1984.

Semler, Ricardo, *Maverick*, Arrow, 1993.

Vanek, Jaroslav (ed.), *Self-Management*, Penguin.

Woodcock, Mike, *50 Activities for Teambuilding*, Gower, 1988.

Index